Down Home Dairyland: A Listener's Guide

By James P. Leary and Richard March

Madison, Wisconsin
2004

Developed under the auspices of Wisconsin Arts Board, University of Wisconsin–Madison, and Wisconsin Folk Museum. Originally published by University of Wisconsin-Extension, with support from the Department of Liberal Studies and the Arts, Division of Continuing Studies, University of Wisconsin.

Revised and reprinted 2004 by the Center for the Study of Upper Midwestern Cultures, College of Letters and Science, University of Wisconsin, 901 University Bay Drive, Madison, WI 53705 http://csumc.wisc.edu

Contents

Illustrations

Places are in Wisconsin unless otherwise indicated.

Preface

Folk Music in Terra Incognita

In 1976, the year of America's bicentennial, the Smithsonian Institution produced the summer-long Festival of American Folklife on the mall in our nation's capital. The festival's Regional America section was dominated by a huge map of the United States. Reproduced from Alan Lomax's classic *Folk Songs of North America* (1960), the map was shaded to indicate musical regions and festooned with place names invoked in songs. While names abounded in the East, the South, and the Far West, the Upper Midwest was terra incognita. Complete voids yawned in Iowa and the Dakotas, while the only place dotting Wisconsin was, improbably, Northfield—as if that Minnesota city had been run across the border after Jesse James's bank heist.

It is past time to fill the void, to place "Driving Saw Logs on the Plover" and "Aye Bane a Swede from Nort' Dakota" on America's folk song map. Although little noted by scholars and the general public, the Upper Midwest's folk music is as rich and complex as that found anywhere in the United States. Here is the territory with the greatest variety of Woodland Indian cultures. Here are the nation's densest enclaves of Belgians, Finns, Germans, Norwegians, South Slavs, Swedes, and Swiss. Here is the place where the world's greatest variety of polka styles flourish. Here are growing populations of African Americans come north from the Mississipi Delta, of Mexican Americans who followed the migrant workers' trail, of refugees from Southeast Asia. Their music has become the region's music, and the region's music has much to tell about the American experience.

The Region on Radio

Since its broad inception in the 1920s, radio more than any other medium has encompassed the musical pluralism of the Upper Midwest. Potentially on the air for anyone, it has given performers not only the means to reach kindred audiences across geographical space, but also the opportunity to captivate strangers across cultural space. From the late 1930s through the 1950s, for example, stations like Rice Lake's WJMC typically appealed to their entire community with eclectic musical programming that included various live ethnic hours, a rustic "barn dance" show, local church services, and an array of country, rock, pop, and classical recordings. Certainly today's AM talk radio and FM monogeneric formats have narrowed the musical range considerably. Yet even in the homogenized 1990s the region's adventurous sonic travelers can tune in Finnish dance tunes on KAXE, Ojibwa drums on WOJB, Croatian tamburitza on WJMS, Czech brass bands on WAUN, Slovenian accordions on WTKM, Hmong songs on WORT, Swiss yodels on WEKZ, and a good deal more.

Wisconsin Public Radio, this country's first public radio station, has broadcast eclectic programs, including regional music, for a long time. In the late 1970s Tom Martin-Erickson and Judy Rose began producing "Simply Folk," a program chiefly of upper midwestern musicians working within the folk revival and singer-songwriter traditions that have been a significant part of the American musical scene since the late 1950s. In 1984 Rose also produced "The Wisconsin Patchwork," thirteen half-hour programs that distilled the more than seven hundred performances recorded in the 1940s by Helene Stratman-Thomas—a

University of Wisconsin music professor acting on behalf of the Archive of Folk Song at the Library of Congress—from Wisconsin loggers, miners, farmers, Woodland Indians, and European ethnics.

The involvement with the Upper Midwest's traditional music, however, extends nearly to the beginnings of radio. Founded in 1917, Wisconsin Public Radio featured occasional performances of Irish, Norwegian, and Winnebago traditional music in the 1920s. By 1933 Grover Kingsley, "the Old Time Fiddler," held forth on a weekly noon farm program, and Saturday afternoons included a fiddlefest with such regulars as Blanchardville's Arne "Swede" Mosby and George Mattson.

Mattson, a fiddler from a Deerfield farm family, was pumping gas on Madison's Williamson Street amidst the Depression when he joined with guitarist K. W. "Wendy" Whitford, a farm kid in his late teens from Albion. For their stint on public radio, Mattson combined lively Anglo-Celtic fiddle tunes (like "Cleveland Two-Step," "Kentucky Hornpipe," and "Flop-Eared Mule") with the Norwegian lilt of "Auction pa Strømmen's"; and Whitford drew upon his family's store of such old-time songs as the sentimental "Mother's Picture on the Wall" and the Irish immigration ballad "Barney McCoy." Nearly sixty years later, on January 12, 1992, Whitford's "Barney McCoy" resounded once more over Wisconsin Public Radio-this time as part of a "Down Home Dairyland" program, "Wendy Whitford: The Soul of Wisconsin's Country Music."

Down Home Dairyland

We (folklorists Rick March and Jim Leary) launched the initial thirteen half-hour installments of "Down Home Dairyland" on Wisconsin Public Radio in 1989. Emphasizing the "traditional and ethnic music of Wisconsin and the Upper Midwest," the series drew on our collective musical experience within the region. One of us, Rick March, grew up in Chicago where he absorbed the Croatian tamburitza music of his own ethnic community and was fascinated by the blues and gospel sounds of black neighbors. The other of us, Jim Leary, was raised in northwestern Wisconsin's Rice Lake where Scandinavian dialect songs, Swiss yodels, Bohemian polkas, lumber-camp fiddling, and Ojibwa powwow drums were a part of everyday life. We met in the early 1970s while earning our Ph.D.s in folklore at Indiana University, and by the decade's end we were each doing research on the Upper Midwest's traditional music.

By the mid-1980s March was employed as the traditional and ethnic arts coordinator for the Wisconsin Arts Board, while Leary was laboring as a freelance folklorist with strong ties to the Wisconsin Folk Museum and the University of Wisconsin–Madison's Folklore Program. We were both involved with presenting traditional musicians to the general public through festivals, concerts, publications, and documentary recordings. Radio loomed as a more consistent and effective means of offering the Upper Midwest's traditional music to a broad audience.

In 1986, March began an early disc jockey version of "Down Home Dairyland" on Madison's listener-supported radio station, WORT. Meanwhile we both had been doing occasional guest segments on Wisconsin Public Radio's "Simply Folk." The current "Down Home Dairyland" emerged as our coproduction under the aegis of the Wisconsin Arts Board, the Wisconsin Folk Museum, the University of Wisconsin–Madison, and Wisconsin Public Radio. The first thirteen installments,

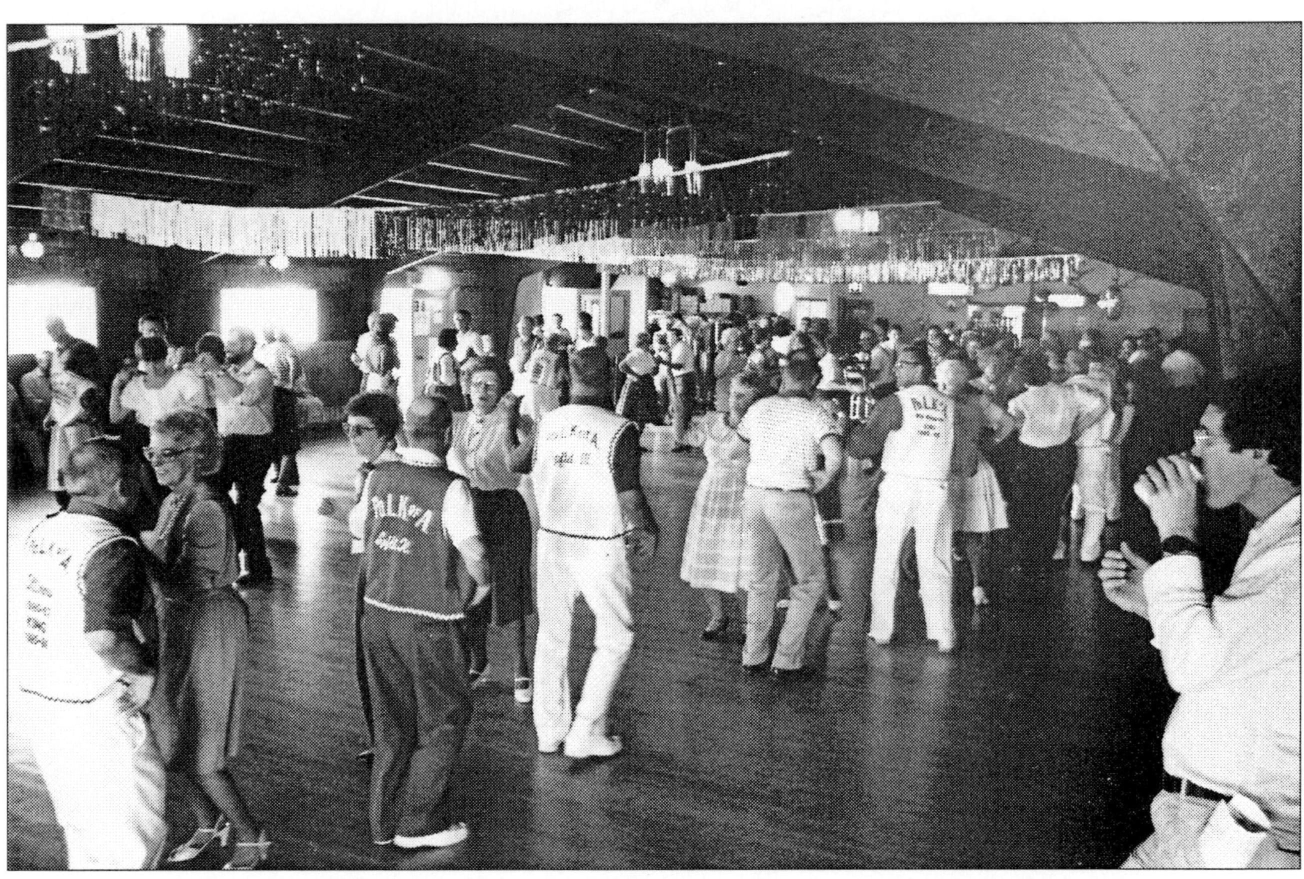

Richard March (extreme right) observing line schottische dancers at the Red Barn, Evansville, 1988 ***Photo: Jim Leary***

Jim Leary and Bill Koskela at the North Country Folk Festival, Ironwood, Mich., 1982 ***Photo: Ellen Porath***

produced in 1989, set a pattern. Each drew heavily upon regional field and archival research to combine sound recordings, interviews with the musicians, and our commentary. An additional thirteen programs were produced in 1990, followed by fourteen more in 1992.

Each set of "Down Home Dairyland" programs was conceived of as the last. Yet for every show produced, the germ of others emerged. For example, the general dearth of women performers on early commercial recordings—attributable to sociocultural constraints rather than ability—spurred us to offer "Women Polka Band Leaders." Likewise an omnibus show, "The Many Forms of Wisconsin Indian Music," suggested subsequent programs on specific tribal, generic, and pan-Indian musical practices.

As time passed, we were reaching an increasingly diverse audience, Wisconsin Public Radio was interested in additional programs, there was an abundance of fine music to draw upon, and we were having fun. Since 1992, "Down Home Dairyland" has been a regular weekly feature on Wisconsin Public Radio. With our annual "season" radically expanded from thirteen to fifty-two weeks, we modified the program's format to accommodate increased production demands. We added opening and closing musical themes, adopted a "news compatible" twenty-five-minute duration, exchanged an abundance of interview excerpts for more of our on-air commentary, broadened the regional scope from the Upper Midwest to the entire Midwest, and offered more tightly focused programs. From fall 1992 through 1995, we have produced 125 programs in the "new" twenty-five-minute format.

A Listener's Guide

This *Listener's Guide* complements the original forty half-hour versions of "Down Home Dairyland" that aired in three-month blocks during 1989, 1990, and 1992. Forty short essays and a smattering of photographs correlate with each of forty radio programs. The programs are not in their original sequence, however. While the radio series sought variety from week to week, the essays strive for continuity from page to page. Collectively, they survey traditional and ethnic music in the Upper Midwest, with a particular focus on Wisconsin. Ideally, each will be read in conjunction with listening to the corresponding radio program. Indeed the essays are not scripts, but parallel commentaries which elaborate upon important points, develop additional themes, and chart references. All place-names in the essays are in Wisconsin, unless otherwise indicated.

For those inclined to follow the trail of research, printed sources are indicated parenthetically within each essay (e.g., Densmore 1932), while interviews merit an additional "I" (e.g., Wolfe 1985 I). The musicians and titles for performances heard on each radio program are listed at the head of each essay; and performances quoted within the body of an essay are indicated with a "P" in parentheses. Full citations are given in the References, subdivided as "Interviews," "Printed Sources," and "Recorded Performances."

An appendix contains sketches of regional institutions involved with the documenting and presenting the folk cultural traditions and Wisconsin and the Upper Midwest. They include: The Center for the Study of Upper Midwestern Cultures, University of Wisconsin Folklore Program, Wisconsin Arts Board, and Mills Music Library's Wisconsin Music Archives at the UW–Madison.

Acknowledgments

Many people and institutions have contributed to the creation of "Down Home Dairyland." Some of the interviews by Jim Leary were conducted under the auspices of the Michigan Traditional Arts Program, the Minnesota Historical Society, UP North Films at Northern Michigan University, and the State Historical Society of Wisconsin. The Folklore Program at the University of Wisconsin-Madison donated supplies and the use of field recording equipment. The Wisconsin Music Archives and curator Steve Sundell made available many rare 78 rpm recordings for airplay. The Department of Liberal Studies gave funds to develop noncredit continuing education courses and produce this *Listener's Guide*. The Wisconsin Arts Board contributed Rick March's time and funds for production. The Wisconsin Folk Museum likewise gave much of Jim Leary's time and equipment, production expenses, and access to archival materials. The Folk and Traditional Arts Program of the National Endowment for the Arts and the Wisconsin Humanities Council also supported "Down Home Dairyland."

In spite of being the coproducers, we would have been lost in the studio without the sage advice and technical know-how of Tom Martin-Erickson and Judy Rose of "Simply Folk," and without the nimble talents of Wisconsin Public Radio engineers: particularly Dusty Thompto and Rick "Rocket" Kirkpatrick, but also Tom Blaine, Steve Colón, Rich Grote, Buzz Kemper, and Marv Nonn.

In addition, we relied on other researchers in the Upper Midwest who generously shared sound recordings and documentation that were otherwise inaccessible. These colleagues include Bob Andresen, Phil Bohlman, John Berquist, Matt Gallmann, Paul Gifford, Marina Herman, Anne Lederman, Michael Loukinen, Phil Martin, Phil Nusbaum, Andy Roll, Mary Agnes Starr, and Tom Vennum.

Beyond the radio programs, this *Listener's Guide*, produced by the University of Wisconsin–Extension, profited from the cheerful professional oversight of Outreach Program Manager Nancy Gaines, the able designs of Jim Renguette, and, especially, the committed editing of Linda LaMacchia. Cartoonist Mike Konopacki likewise inspired us with his ability to transform a few rough ideas into our bull with a concertina logo.

Nor would we have been able to pursue our radio obsession without the ongoing support of our spouses and children: Mary Bruce, Nikola March, and Maria March; Janet Gilmore, Isabella Leary, and Finn Leary. They good-naturedly suffered our many fieldwork forays, our sudden disappearances into respective music rooms to plan a show, our bouts of "intelepsy" as some new "Down Home Dairyland" idea struck us amidst family doings, and our habitual acquisition of recordings. They even had the commendable sense to restrain us periodically.

The greatest contribution, of course, came from the musicians themselves. They fielded questions with patience, graciousness, and eloquence. They gave copies of their studio recordings and many performed cheerfully "in the field." Without their talent and dedication, there would be no "Down Home Dairyland," no *Listener's Guide*. Indeed there would be no traditional music in the Upper Midwest.

Part 1

Native Sounds

Chapter 1

The Many Forms of Wisconsin Indian Music

Program 1 Performances
1. Badger Singers, "Flag Song." 2. Wisconsin Dells Singers, "My Friend, That Grizzly Bear Said So." 3. Meckawigabau, "Gí dagá wadan." 4. Frank Montano, Woodland flute music. 5. Long House Singers [women's ensemble], "Alligator Dance." 6. Preservation Singers, "Da ge na zaya nel." 7. Oneida Singers, "Hymn #18 (What a Friend We Have in Jesus)." 8. Robert ("Bobby Bullett") St. Germaine, "Lac du Flambeau Reservation." 9. Frank Montano, "My Spirit Friend."

Powwows and Perceptions

Visitors attending a performance at the Indian Bowl in Lac du Flambeau or the Stand Rock Ceremonial in Wisconsin Dells, or one of the dozens of annual festive powwows in the Upper Midwest, see colorfully garbed men and women dancers circling a large dance drum. Four or more performers around the drum sing as a group, simultaneously keeping a steady beat to guide the dancers' steps. The singers—both men and women—and the instrument form a unit referred to as a "drum." Most powwows feature more than one such aggregation, typically including a local "host" drum as well as visiting drums. To save the singers' voices and conserve the dancers' strength, the drums alternate in providing the music. An emcee indicates which drum should sing and the sort of song required at each phase of the powwow.

Though there are numerous types of American Indian music-gospel, the "courting" flute, fiddling, and country—it is the percussion instruments-rattles, hand drums, and especially the large dance drum—that continue to capture the popular imagination as symbols of Indian music.

At secular powwows, some Woodland Indian musicians use a commercially manufactured marching-band field drum, which rests on a blanket or mat and is played horizontally. But the preferred instrument—required for ceremonials—is a handmade wooden drum with rawhide heads, "dressed" with decorative trappings and suspended from the outward-curving poles of a traditional drum stand.

While non-Indian audiences may enjoy American Indian dance as an exotic spectacle at powwows or on stage, most non-Indians have little enthusiasm for Indian drum dance music. Ojibwa musician Joseph Ackley recounts a telling incident:

> I was painting a house in Milwaukee and I had some tapes on a boom box, powwow music, you know, to listen to while I was painting. Well, after a

> while, the lady there came out and said, "What is that terrible racket?" So I turned it down for a while. Then after a while, she was playing the organ in the house. So I looked through the window and said, "What is that terrible racket?" (Ackley 1992 I)

In fact, most non-Indians have probably not heard authentic Indian singing, but have learned instead—from Hamm's beer commercials and chanting Atlanta Braves fans—a stereotype of "Indian" music that is based on Hollywood theme music in western movies. Public radio station WOJB on the Lac Court Oreilles Ojibwa reservation near Hayward, Wisconsin, is one of the few tribe-operated stations whose listeners are mainly non-Indians. Jeff St. Germaine, host of WOJB's "Drum Song," joked, "When I come on, you can hear 'em [non-Indians] switching off all over the place!" (St. Germaine 1991 I).

The negative reaction of European-Americans to Indian music has a long pedigree. Numerous early and recent non-Indian observers express disdain for it. For example, Henry Schoolcraft, a government agent assigned to the Ojibwa territory early in the nineteenth century, married an Ojibwa and kept a journal that has been invaluable to researchers. But he still recorded this harsh opinion in 1821: "It is perhaps all we could expect from untutored savages, but there is nothing about [their music] which has ever struck me as either interesting or amusing..." (Vennum 1982). Missionaries disliked the non-Christian religious associations of ceremonial singing and dancing. The Reverend Gilfillan, who worked among the Ojibwa of northern Minnesota, echoed Schoolcraft's scorn. In an 1897 speech, he complained of Indians "whooping and dancing around the drum ... and having a veritable orgy which made night and day hideous for weeks" (ibid.).

The Big Drum

Some nonspecialists outside the Indian community have a more positive attitude to Indian music, but they base it on a romantic notion of its spirituality and antiquity. Actually, outsiders are unlikely to hear sacred ceremonial singing, since performing such songs for outsiders is forbidden. Furthermore, far from being ancient, perhaps unchanged since prehistory, the music of the Woodland and Plains tribes in the Upper Midwest is dynamic, ever changing and evolving. Even the use of the large drum is relatively recent. Drum Dance religion emerged in the later nineteenth century as the Woodland Indians' response to a catastrophe—the destruction of their former way of life by rapidly arriving Europeans. Its wider dissemination has continued into the twentieth century. While several types of small hand-held drums were known earlier, the big drum seen in powwows today spread from the west to the east as a specific and most notable component of a new religious belief and practice.

Big drums were first used in the Grass Dance, a messianic movement which may have originated with an Omaha warrior society. Though the Grass Dance spread widely among the tribes of the Great Plains, the Woodland tribes received the big drum from a different source, the visions of a legendary Sioux prophet, Tailfeather Woman. In the 1870s, Tailfeather Woman spent four days hiding from rampaging white soldiers in the lily pads of a west-central Minnesota lake. During this ordeal, the Great Spirit revealed to her the way of constructing the drum and performing the ritual songs. Tailfeather Woman taught her people the Drum Dance, believing its performance would stop the white soldiers from killing Indians and end the traditional emnity between the Sioux and the Ojibwa (ibid.).

Once a band or tribe make the drum and thoroughly assimilate the ritual, it becomes their duty to pass the drum and its ritual to another tribe or band. In

Powwow participants at Wisconsin Dells, postcard ca. 1920s ***Wisconsin Folk Museum Collection***

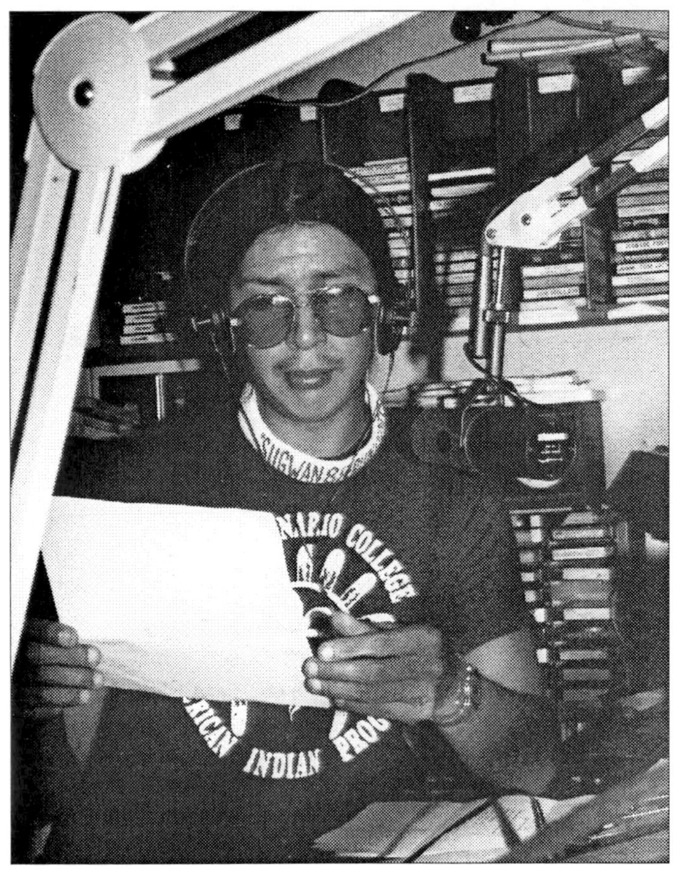

Jeff St. Germaine, host of WOJB radio's "Drum Song," Lac Court Oreilles Ojibwa reservation, 1988 ***Photo: Jim Leary***

the traditional clockwise direction, the Sioux passed the Drum Dance to the Ojibwa to their east, who in turn passed it to the Menominee, Potawatomi, and Winnebago to their south. The Sioux origin of the Drum Dance is supported by linguistic evidence. According to Ojibwa drum maker William Bineshi Baker, the Ojibwa term for the large powwow drum is *bwaanidewe'igan*, "Sioux drum." Moreover, the ritual songs exhibit Sioux musical characteristics, which differ from the musical features of older Ojibwa songs (ibid.).

The Ojibwa and Menominee regard the drum as a sacred object and treat it as a highly honored living being, a "grandfather," whose physical needs they must attend to and toward whom they must behave respectfully. They may give it a name and ritually "feed" it—by placing beside it food which they later divide among the singers—and "dress" it in decorative wrappings which they must keep in good condition. They must visit it and maintain proper decorum in its presence. When one band give the drum to another band, they bid the drum farewell and may continue to visit it in its new home.

Numerous legends recount the dire consequences of neglecting or mistreating the drum. A man who struck a drum in anger with his fist later was crippled in an auto accident. When a Menominee woman attempted to smash her husband's drum with an ax, her brother suddenly died.

Drum Dance religion, once castigated by Christian missionaries, has been enjoying a recent revival among younger Woodland Indians who are embracing a revitalization of their Indian culture in a contemporary context. Even more obvious has been the explosive growth of the secular powwows during the past two decades.

Since the powwows are intertribal and Indians often travel great distances to participate in them, they have engendered a blended "pan-Indian" musical and dance style. For example, in August 1989, when I visited Winnebago dancer/drum singer Jerry Cleveland at his Waukesha home in the Milwaukee metro area, he was preparing to depart later that day for a powwow on a Cree reserve in rural Manitoba—more than seven hundred miles away. He commented that he had designed a thinner octagonal dance drum for his group so that it would take up less room in his van and leave more space for family members to sleep on their frequent lengthy highway journeys. Moreover, he asserted that the dance style in Manitoba would be no different from the style in his local area. He expected to be a contender for the prizes offered there (Cleveland 1989 I).

Recently a contrary movement has emerged, particularly in reservation communities, to preserve tribally specific traditions. In 1992, Marvin DeFoe, the director of a youth program on the Red Cliff Ojibwa reservation, instituted a program to bring in tribal elders to teach the youth tribally specific songs, dances, and clothing design. Nowadays, at Red Cliff and elsewhere in North America, many Indian singers and dancers aspire to proficiency in both the generalized and specific traditions.

Despite a lack of non-Indian appreciation, many forms of Indian music continue to evolve in North America, with greatly varying degrees of European and/or African-American musical influence. Though Indians are surrounded by a vastly larger non-Indian population, their distinctive musics show no signs of vanishing and remain expressive forms which are unique in the Upper Midwest.

Chapter 2

Woodland Indian Fiddles and Jigs

Program 2 Performances
1. Fred Allery and Mike Keplin, "Soldier's Joy." 2. Lawrence Flett, "The Devil's Reel." 3. Dick Gravelle, "French Tune." 4. Waupoose Brothers, "Potawatomi Jig." 5. Joe Cloud, "Devil's Dream." 6. Waupoose Brothers, Fiddle tune. 7. Coleman Trudeau, "Tahquamenon River Breakdown." 8. Fred Allery and Mike Keplin, "Red River Jig." 9. Joe Cloud, "Squaw Dance." 10. Louis Webster, "Growling Old Man, Grumbling Old Woman." 11. Waupoose Brothers, "Wedding Chant."

Métis Music

The mostly male French and Anglo-Celtic immigrants who brought the fur trade to Canada and the northern United States in the 1600s also carried fiddles in their arms and dance steps in their feet. More than a few married Indians and a mixed blood, or Métis, culture emerged, blending elements of the native with the European. Beadwork—in which imported glass beads were stitched in patterns formerly executed in porcupine quills—is one such blend. Indian fiddling and step dancing is another (Lederman 1988; Mishler 1987).

Today Indian fiddlers and step dancers can be found along the American-Canadian border almost from the Atlantic to the Pacific. On the European side they are mostly French, but also Irish and Scottish. On the native side, they are Athabaskans, Crees, Menominees, Ojibwas, Odawas, and Potawatomis. Their playing combines European melodies with Indian phrasing, while their dances mingle old country jigs with the steps new world hunters have adopted in imitation of animals. Mike Page of North Dakota's Turtle Mountain Ojibwa band recalls his father telling of buffalo hunts where successful hunters, paralleling the song compositions and festive dances of Plains peoples, celebrated by making up new fiddle tunes and jigging through the night (Vrooman 1992).

From Fur Trade to Lumber Camp

Fiddling and dancing exchanges between European and Indian peoples in the Upper Midwest accelerated in the lumber camps of the nineteenth century as many Woodland peoples found work as sawyers, top loaders, and log drivers. In 1938 folklorist Alan Lomax visited the Bad River Indian reservation at Odanah, Wisconsin, where Ojibwas logged and worked in a lumber mill. There he recorded fiddler Joe Cloud, dubbing him a "Wisconsin lumberjack" in field notes and emphasizing that "the blood of Chippewa Indians is flowing in his veins" (Lomax 1938).

The bulk of this essay was condensed from J. P. Leary, 1992, "Sawdust and Devils: Indian Fiddling in the Western Great Lakes Region," in Medicine Fiddle, *ed. J. P. Leary (Bismarck: North Dakota Humanities Council). With permission.*

Born in 1885 in Hollow Lake, Wisconsin, Cloud was one of seventeen children. His father, Menogwaniosh Anakwad or George Cloud (1849-1911), was also a fiddler. Besides Anglo-Celtic classics like "Ragtime Annie" and "Devil's Dream," Joe Cloud's repertoire included that French-derived trademark of Métis fiddlers, "Red River Jig," and several "squaw dances." (This potentially pejorative term is used less frequently nowadays by Woodland Indians, although the dance persists. Usually accompanied by the big drum, it involves a dignified toe-heel circular promenade during which dancers maintain contact with the earth, in contrast to the varied movement of men's mimetic war and hunting dances.)

Alan Lomax also recorded the Rindlisbacher Group of Rice Lake, Wisconsin, in 1938. Its leader, Otto Rindlisbacher, recognized "Indian" fiddle tunes, along with those of the French, Irish, and Norwegians. Rindlisbacher played with French-Indian fiddlers like Regis Belille of the Lac Court Oreilles reservation many times, learning such "Indian" tunes as "Couderay Jig," "Couderay Reel," "Hounds in the Woods," "Indian War Whoop," and "Red Cliff Jig."

Ernest "Pea Soup" Guibord, an Ojibwa, who placed third in a Rindlisbacher-organized fiddlers contest in 1927, recalled Belille (ca. 1865–1935) as a man who made a little money picking berries, working in the woods, and playing music.

> Did you ever hear a really good fiddler play? Well, Regis had them all beat. Hands down.... Regis, he didn't read music, didn't know one note from another. But he taught himself to play in any key.... I don't know how many keys there are, but Regis played them all, from A to Z. (Guibord 1979 I)

Guibord himself was born in 1903 at Reserve, Wisconsin, on the Lac Court Oreilles reservation. His father, Joseph, was half French, half Ojibwa, and his mother was a three-quarter blood Ojibwa. His paternal grandfather, Joseph Toussaint Guibord (ca. 1840–1912) was born in Montreal. Old Toussaint traded with the Ojibwas up and down the Mississippi, traveling in a bateau, and married an Ojibwa. He was a fiddler, as were his sons Joseph and Ernest, and his grandson Ernest, otherwise called "Pea Soup" after the fondness of French Canadians for that dish. As a young man, Pea Soup worked and played the fiddle in lumber camps. He also recalled dances at four different "boweries" (covered outdoor dance halls) on the reservation. Commonly held in keeping with seasonal and national events, like New Year's Eve and the Fourth of July, these affairs combined jigging and square dancing to fiddles with such pan-Indian couple dances as the Rabbit Dance and the Forty-nine Dance performed to drumbeats: "they had 'war dances' and square dances. When they got tired of one kind of dancing, they switched" (ibid.).

The story of Everett "Butch" Waupoose exhibits a similar pattern of French-Indian ancestry, work in the woods, and syncretism between native and European traditions. Born on northeastern Wisconsin's Menominee reservation in 1938, Butch recalls that his grandfather, Wanawat,

> only had one name. And he had eight brothers. They come from that Michigan country up there, and they brought a lot of that [fiddle music] down with them. So it finally came down to us, this generation, the fourth generation. (E. Waupoose 1989 I)

Wanawat worked in nineteenth-century lumber camps with French Canadians, as did his son Dave, who married a Métis from the Frechette family. Dave

Joe Cloud and Anna Anderson with their children (L-R: Harriet, George, and Clarence), Odanah, ca. 1916. ***Courtesy Virginia Cloud Carrington***

Coleman Trudeau, Ojibwa/Ottawa/French fiddler, Macmillan, Mich., 1983
Photo: Michael Loukinen

Waupoose would leave the reservation in the winter to work as a chopper in the woods. In the spring he came home with a store of fiddle tunes. By the time Dave's son, Alex (1903–1972), began working in the woods, the Menominees had their own sawmill and logging operations. Modifying his fiddle with "Indian medicine" (deer bones and porcupine quills), Alex fiddled in Menominee camps, and for reservation square dances that sometimes included calls in the Menominee language. He also played for German neighbors at doings that included the Fourth of July, threshing parties, and the county fair.

Bob Andresen (1978) encountered the same sort of intermingling while documenting fiddlers in the early 1970s around Danbury, just across the St. Croix River from Minnesota. An unusual neutral ground where Sioux and Ojibwa intermarried rather than feuded, Burnett County was also a place where European and native peoples practiced harmony. Among them was Benjamin Connor, a fiddling homesteader of Irish-French ancestry, who had originally come to the region in 1852 to set up a fur trading post for John Jacob Astor at Fond du Lac, Minnesota. He married an Ojibwa, Odaygawmequay or "shore woman" (Winton 1976). The oldest and youngest of their nine children, William and Darius, were fine fiddlers. Darius (1873–1947) worked in the woods as a timber cruiser prior to serving as Burnett County's surveyor for thirty years. Often teaming up with Anglo fiddler Jesse Gattin and a pair of "half-breed" brothers, Gus and Alex Cadotte, Darius Connor played for numerous square dances that involved the entire community (Gattin 1973, 1974 I).

The ubiquity and legacy of Indian fiddlers in the Upper Midwest have been obscured in recent years as native peoples, quite understandably, seek to assert the distinctly Indian, and not the mixed, aspects of their cultural heritage. And yet cultural blending or syncretism is pervasive. Even the powwow, symbol of the renascence of American Indian traditions, draws upon the Euro-American structure of nineteenth-century Wild West show pageantry. When the musical story of Woodland Indian peoples is fully told, the fiddle and the step dance will take their place alongside traditional dances and the big drum.

Part 2

Anglo-Euro Fusion

Chapter 3

The Tunes of Strings and Bow

Program 3 Performances
1. Helmer Toyras, "Finnish Medley." 2. Bernard Johnson, "Cindy." 3. George Meuret, "Cripple Creek." 4. Harv Cox, "Mule's Dream." 5. George Meuret, "Barbara Polka." 6. Bernard Johnson, "Stepladder Waltz." 7. Goose Island Ramblers, "Ryerson's *[sic]* Waltz." 8. Leonard Finseth, "Randi Severson's Waltz." 9. Sarajevo, "Stara vlahina." 10. Al and the Family, "Polka."

Square Dance Messiah

In 1926 a series of Old Time Fiddlers contests swept the nation, under the sponsorship of automobile magnate Henry Ford. A cranky social philosopher, Ford not only pioneered the moving assembly line but also engaged in cultural engineering. Like other conservative and sometimes racist Wasps of his era, Henry Ford feared the "corrupting" influences of non-English-speaking "foreigners" and African Americans on life in the United States. His antidote was the promotion of old-time fiddle music and square dancing as quintessentially "American" activities.

Perhaps Ford was moved by the structural similarities of assembly-line methods, fiddle tunes, and square dances. Folklorist Louie Atterbury has argued that all three "demonstrate a distinctly American concern for process in the manipulation of a series of simple and infinitely repeatable units" (Atterbury 1979:328). Ford's dream of a narrow American folk musical range is partially realized in modern-day fiddle contests which have come to favor an increasingly uniform national fiddle style over the quirks of region. Meanwhile square dance aficionados tirelessly petition state and federal legislators to recognize their form as the offical American folk dance. Yet the southern blacks and European ethnics who labored in Ford's Detroit plants never got on the folk musical assembly line. And even those who participated in the Upper Midwest's Old Time Fiddlers contests of the 1920s were far more multicultural than their sponsor.

To be sure, a plurality of entrants were Anglo-Celtic fiddlers. Some were transplanted New England and New York State Yankees, others were upland southerners from the Ohio River Valley, and still more were Irish and Scots immigrants. The January 1926 contest sponsored by the *Milwaukee Sentinel* stressed patriotism by reserving seats for "old settlers, pioneers, and old soldiers" (Meade 1987). And the parade of contestants included a string of Irish and English names: Pat Kelly, John Mathias O'Rourke, Hugh Hickey, Walter Boyd, Curtis Allen, and M. A. Hays. Some were celebrated musicians. Thomas Croal, a Sauk Countian come to Milwaukee, won the city's contest and was still playing in 1944 when Fred Holmes observed:

OLD TIME
FIDDLERS' CONTEST

COMING TO

THE MAJESTIC THEATRE

MARCH 17th and 18th

THIRTY DOLLARS IN PRIZES

That's the inducement held out to the old time fiddlers to try their luck at the Majestic Theatre on Wednesday and Thursday, March 17 and 18. There are only two rules. One is that the contestants must be over 50 years of age and the second is that they must play by ear only. The use of music in this contest not allowed. The contest will be held both nights and competent judges will award the prizes. An entrance blank is printed below. Fill out now and mail at once. Get in on the money.

ENTRANCE BLANK

OLD TIME FIDDLERS' CONTEST

Name ....

Address ....

Phone No.......................... Age......................

Below list the titles of the three numbers to be played in the contest.

1. ....

2. ....

3. ....

Mail this blank to

Old Time Fiddlers' Contest
MAJESTIC THEATRE
Rice Lake, Wis.

Fiddlers' contest entry blank, Rice Lake, 1926 ***Wisconsin Folk Museum Collection***

Leonard Finseth, Mondovi, 1988
Photo: Jim Leary

> Scarcely is there an Irish community in the state that does not have a typical fiddler, who plays his music by ear and keeps time with the stomp of his heel. Tom Croal, who lives near Hill Point in Sauk County, is generally accorded the honor of being the last of the Irish bards living in Wisconsin. (Holmes 1944:187)

Charles Mitchell, seventy-five in 1926 and also of Sauk County, was touted as a man "who has traveled from coast-to-coast and never taken his hat off to any fiddler" (Meade 1987).

Germans, Slavs, and Scandinavians

While Croal, Mitchell, and their Anglo-Celtic cohorts charmed the crowd with such standards as "Miss McCleod's Reel" and "Fisher's Hornpipe," John Hensiak, John Imp, and Walter Rudniak, a trio of Slavic immigrants who had each been playing the fiddle for more than thirty-five years, lent variety to the program with dance tunes from the German- and Russian-held regions of Poland. The *Milwaukee Sentinel* exclaimed, "Foreign Born Can Fiddle, Too," and printed a photograph of the "Fiddling Imps," fifty-six year old John and his grandson.

Elsewhere in the region, other "foreigners" entered the fiddling fray. James Wolfe of Whitewater offered "an old German waltz" at the Janesville contest. A headline from Kenosha announced, "John Malmstrom Plays Swedish Tunes for Prize." The left-handed Malmstrom's selections reflected the cultural give-andtake common in the pluralistic Upper Midwest as he balanced an "old-fashioned Swedish polka" and a "Swedish barn dance tune" with the "Irish Washerwoman." Karl "King Tut" Schwanenberg, a German who won championships throughout Minnesota and in northwestern Wisconsin, invariably dazzled the crowd with an eclectic medley of German, southern American, and pop tunes: "Dixie," "Ach, du lieber Augustine," "Arkansas Traveler," "Where, Oh, Where Has My Little Dog Gone" (derived from the German folk song "Zum Lauterbach hab ich mein Strumpf gelorn"), and "Sweet Bunch of Daisies."

In some areas of the Upper Midwest, contestants for Ford's prizes were almost entirely Norwegian. In Fergus Falls, Minnesota, the top three performers were August Skalman, Oscar Tollefson, and Sigvald Johnson, with Earl Askeroth, Peter Peterson, Anton Stensrud, and Ole Gyldenvand putting in appearances. The St. Cloud paper proclaimed, "Norwegian Dance Tunes to Be One Feature of Old Time Fiddling Bee." In Albert Lea enthusiastic applause greeted Botolf Bridley's floral celebration of two Norwegian districts: "Lily of Sogn" and "Lily of Valders." Fiddle Ole had a solid following in Eau Claire, Wisconsin, while the Madison contest included such Norskies as Barneveld's E. Pederson, Brooklyn's Ben Gulhaug, Hollandale's Olaf Larson, and Madison's Knute Ellestad.

Contrary to Henry Ford's desire to see Wasp hegemony and a narrow strain of all-American amalgamation prevail, the Old Time Fiddlers contests of 1926 provided a forum for fiddlers of all sorts to perform in. The jigs, reels, and breakdowns of Ireland and Britain coexisted with the polkas, waltzes, and schottisches of northern and central Europe. And the most successful fiddlers—following tactics that worked best when folks of many nationalities mingled at community gatherings—mixed their repertoires and gained the endorsement of the crowd.

Although the fiddle had already begun to diminish as the dance musician's instrument of choice when the Ford contests were held in 1926, there are still many old-time fiddlers in the Upper Midwest and their tunes still speak powerfully of pioneer life. Their musical speech, however, is not monolingual American; it is the polyglot regional dialect of Anglo-Celts, French Indians, Germans, Slavs, and Scandinavians.

Chapter 4

Couderay Jig in the Buckhorn

Program 4 Performances

1. Otto Rindlisbacher, "Hounds in the Woods." 2. Thorstein Skarning, "Maj ball." 3. Otto Rindlisbacher and Karl Hoppe, "Auf dem schoenen Zurichsee." 4. Otto Rindlisbacher, "Swiss Polka." 5. Otto Rindlisbacher, "Pig Schottische." 6. Wisconsin Lumberjacks, "The Passing Away of the Lumberjack." 7. Iva Kundert Rindlisbacher, "The Pinery Boy." 8. Otto Rindlisbacher, "Halling." 9. Leonard Finseth, "Rindlisbacher's Mazurka." 10. Otto Rindlisbacher, "Couderay Jig."

Backwoodsman for All Seasons

Otto Rindlisbacher, perhaps more than anyone else, epitomized the color and ferment of regional culture in northern Wisconsin. He played Swiss tunes, toured with a Norwegian troupe, organized fiddlers' contests, and formed a lumberjack band. He made and repaired a wide array of stringed instruments. He was, by turn, a cheese maker, lumberjack, sawmill hand, cafe and tavern operator, and taxidermist. He was also an expert hunter and fisherman. Finally, he was a writer and scholar who published articles in national music magazines and assisted with the first comprehensive documentation of lumber-camp musicians.

Rindlisbacher was born in Athens, Wisconsin, in 1895. His parents were both Swiss-German immigrants who arrived first in Monroe, Wisconsin, a "port of entry" for young Swiss cheese makers come to the dairy state. The family moved to Rice Lake in 1907. Otto's mother's family were musicians in Switzerland and he began experimenting with the fiddle and the button accordion at an early age. He began with Swiss tunes, but by the time he was sixteen Rindlisbacher had acquired enough Norwegian numbers to tour with "Professor" and Mrs. Thorstein Skarning from roughly 1911 to 1921.

Skarning was one of many Scandinavian vaudeville performers who barnstormed the midwest from a Minneapolis base. He was especially well known in such Wisconsin Norwegian strongholds as Blair, Eau Claire, and Rice Lake. Handbills from the period depict an elegantly dressed "company" which put on a formal program of musical selections and skits, followed by a dance. Leonard Finseth of Mondovi recalled that Otto, "dressed up like a good Norwegian," would "carry the load" for the dances (Finseth 1988 I). By the 1920s Otto had married Iva Kundert, likewise a musician of Swiss descent, and the pair performed sporadically with Skarning throughout the decade, billed on his promotional posters as "the Rindlisbachers, Famous Swiss-Italian Alp Players."

The early 1920s also marked Otto Rindlisbacher's first recordings, on piano accordion, as he combined with violinist Karl Hoppe on four Swiss tunes for the

Helvetia label (Leary 1991b). Hoppe was a local violin teacher and bandleader who subsequently directed community bands in Chippewa Falls. The duo made their recordings in New York City and played for dances at stops along the way.

Otto Rindlisbacher's enthusiasm for Swiss and Norwegian traditional music persisted throughout his life. He was a regular performer at the Cheese Days festival in that Swissconsin stronghold, Monroe; he welcomed touring yodelers to concert dates in Rice Lake; and he composed Swiss *ländlers*—couple dances in 3/4 time—on the button accordion. He likewise made Norwegian nine-stringed *hardanger* fiddles, collected *psalmodikons*-plucked monochords—used in Scandinavian hymnody, and played an array of archaic Norwegian *halling* and springar dance tunes. In February 1929, he published "The Alphorn: The Story of a Unique Swiss Instrument Now Rarely Seen" in the music educator's magazine, the *Etude*. "The Hardanger Violin" followed in June 1938. And in 1940 and 1946, Rindlisbacher recorded Swiss and Norwegian tunes for the Library of Congress.

The Buckhorn Tavern

In the 1920s, however, Otto Rindlisbacher began drawing upon the tradition of lumber-camp fiddling encountered in his youthful logging and sawmill days. He had opened a cafe and billiard parlor, the Buckhorn, with his brothers John and Louis in 1920. Given Otto's reputation as a musician, and his custom of playing, making, and repairing instruments on site, the Buckhorn soon became a hangout for old-time musicians.

Franz Rickaby, who provides our first rich glimpse of lumber-camp folk songs, found his way to the Buckhorn in the early 1920s. Rindlisbacher informed him of the area's rich Anglo-Celtic and French-Indian fiddling, and Rickaby acknowledges Otto in *Ballads and Songs of the Shanty Boy* (1926). Nineteen twenty-six was also the year when Henry Ford inspired a national wave of old-time fiddlers' contests, and Otto Rindlisbacher sponsored two in 1926 and 1927. Not content with merely promoting such events, Rindlisbacher, who by now had taught himself to read music, set down the unnamed tunes of contestants like Freeman Ritter and William Manor in what the *Rice Lake Chronotype* termed "a booklet of peppy musical selections entitled *Twenty Original Reels*, *Jigs*, and *Hornpipes*" (Rindlisbacher 1931).

Rindlisbacher's involvement with lumber-camp music brought him eventually to the attention of Charles Brown, who directed not only the Wisconsin State Historical Society Museum but also the folklore division of the Federal Writer's Project in Wisconsin. In 1937 Sarah Gertrude Knott, director of the National Folk Festival (America's longest-running multicultural festival), asked Brown to suggest some musicians who could represent Wisconsin's northwoods. Brown immediately recommended Otto Rindlisbacher.

Rindlisbacher proposed an ambitious program to Knott in a letter on April 9, 1937. In addition to "lumberjack fiddlers and old style jiggers," he mentioned the "one-stringed 'Viking Cello' which Mrs. Rindlisbacher plays beautifully" (a derivative of the Scandinavian psalmodikon) and the narrative prowess of Paul Fournier.

> We have an expert right here on Paul Bunyan tales. In fact, he is known as Paul Bunyan: has a resort by that name ... He has formerly been active in Wisconsin Outdoor Expositions held in Chicago and has been a lumberjack and log roller. (Rindlisbacher 1937)

Promotional postcard for Otto Rindlisbacher's Buckhorn Tavern, Rice Lake, ca. 1940
Wisconsin Folk Museum Collection

Between 1937 and 1940 the Rindlisbachers' "Wisconsin Lumberjacks" performed "An Evening in the Bunkhouse"—featuring fiddle tunes on cigar-box instruments, Norwegian dance numbers, jigs, the Viking Cello, and balladry—for the National Folk Festival in Chicago and in Washington, D.C.

After 1940 the Rindlisbachers tired of the folk festival experience, although the Wisconsin Lumberjacks persisted under the leadership of Ray Calkins, an original member. Otto Rindlisbacher, however, let the world come to him. For the next thirty-five years, the Buckhorn continued to be a mecca for old-time fiddlers. Hunters, fishers, and tourists likewise flocked to the tavern as Otto's taxidermic and yarn-spinning skills rivaled his musical prowess.

The walls of the Buckhorn were festooned with stuffed animals, some of them legendary. In the 1960s the *Milwaukee Journal's* regional writer, Bill Stokes, inquired about the snow snake, the fur fish, the owl-eyed ripple skipper, and the dingbat.

> Now Otto, about some of these things on the wall? The dingbat?
>
> "Shows up mostly during the deer season. Drinks gasoline from hunters' cars and leaps in the air from hideouts and snatches bullets in midair as the hunters fire at deer." (Stokes n.d.)

The other beasts, all of them artful Rindlisbacher constructions, were described with similar sly elegance.

Otto Rindlisbacher died at eighty in 1975. The artifacts he made and acquired enrich the collections of the State Historical Society of Wisconsin and Vesterheim, the foremost Norwegian-American museum. Some of his tunes contribute to the Archive of American Folk Culture at the Library of Congress.

Chapter 5

Wendy Whitford: The Soul of Wisconsin's Country Music

Program 5 Performances
All selections except 3 and 8 are by the Goose Island Ramblers.
1. "Wendy's Schottische." 2. "Barney McCoy." 3. Robert Walker, "Milwaukee Fire." 4. "Milwaukee Fire." 5. "Brother." 6. "Reierson's Two Step." 7. "Auction pa Strømmen's." 8. Prairie Ramblers, "Shady Grove." 9. "I Worked for a Farmer." 10. "My Blue Eyes Are Gone."

Grandpa's Legacy

Kenneth Wendell "Wendy" Whitford was born on a farm in Albion, Wisconsin, February 25, 1913, the fourth of six boys. Old-time music pervades his earliest memories. His grandfather, Charles Square Smith (1849-1936), was a farmer from Albany, New York, who migrated to the Upper Midwest after the Civil War. Albion had been founded by New Yorkers in 1843, and Wendy's grandmother, an accomplished singer, belonged to one of its oldest families, the Blivins.

Soon Charles Smith was farming and fiddling for dances with his brother-in-law, Silas Blivin. Smith would take the lead part, while Silas played second fiddle and called for dancers. Charles Smith was also a fife player. As Samuel P. Bayard observed, with regard to the Middle Atlantic states:

> Fifes used to be played a great deal, and many of our traditional tunes are marches for this instrument. In rural communities of former times there were numerous fife and drum corps called "martial bands." (Bayard 1944:xiii; see also Bronner 1987:8)

When not fiddling or blowing the fife, Smith hummed and sang—often as he worked. His repertoire ranged from Stephen Foster's southern songs to comic ballads like "Barney McCoy."

Young Wendy Whitford regularly stayed with his grandparents who, in their later years, were "always singing around the house. Grandmother would sing 'My Pretty Quadroon' over the cookstove" (Whitford 1990 I). Not surprisingly, the couple's only child, Gertrude Bell Smith (b. 1880), loved old-time music. In 1894 she wrote the words of favorite songs in a notebook. Some were Victorian sentimental parlor songs like "Wait Till the Moon Falls on the Water" and "Will You Love Me When I'm Old." Others, like "The Picture That Is Turned to the Wall," concerning a family's rejection of their pregnant daughter, revealed the dark consequences of stiff-necked nineteenth-century morality. "The Burning of the Granite Mills" and "The Milwaukee Fire" were classic disaster ballads, vivid word-pictures of tragedy from an era prior to the immediacy of television. At least sixty-four people perished when Milwaukee's Newhall House burned in 1883, and the ballad circulated in Wisconsin's oral tradition for decades.

Wendy Whitford's father, also named Kenneth, played tuba in a community band. When Wendy was born, his parents had his photograph taken resting in the horn's bell. And he can still picture his mother singing to him while she rocked his cradle. From the time he could walk Wendy tagged after his grandfather. They would fish in the afternoon, have supper, and "then came the great time of the day, the twilight hour," when Grandpa Smith would get out his fiddle (ibid.). Wendy was fiddling and singing old songs before he was ten.

The Lure of the Barn Dance

Perhaps his parents dreamed he would go beyond his folk roots to become a "serious" musician. But in 1929 sixteen-year-old Whitford was injured in a car accident en route to his first piano lesson. That summer he recuperated at home. It was hot, the windows were open, and the people next door had tuned in the "National Barn Dance" over Chicago's WLS radio. The "Barn Dance," begun in 1924, was a down-home musical review that rivaled Nashville's "Grand Ole Opry" in popularity. Its performers included southern string bands, Swiss yodelers, a Little German Band, rural comedians, barbershop quartets, singing cowboys, and mountain balladeers.

Bradley Kincaid, "the Kentucky Mountain Boy," particularly inspired Whitford.

> You-all can have your orchestras, 'n jazz in minor key,
> But Brad Kincaid's Houn' Dawg Guitar's Grand Opera for me.
>
> (Evans 1969:221)

A native of eastern Kentucky, Kincaid debuted on WLS in 1928 while attending Young Men's Christian Association College in Chicago. He played an old guitar his father had gotten in trade for a foxhound. And his songs, like the old ballads "The House Carpenter" and "Sweet Kitty Wells," were ones that he had grown up with in the mountains (Wilgus 1975). Wendy Whitford wanted to play and sing like Bradley Kincaid. His mother brought a neglected guitar from the attic, strung and tuned it, and taught him his first chord. "After that I just seemed to absorb songs naturally" (Whitford 1990 I).

The Albion Town Hall was the site for musical gatherings and soon Wendy Whitford was part of the entertainment. There he met Clarence Reierson, a fiddler whose Norwegian dance tunes were as alluring and exotic to Whitford as the Kentucky Mountain Boy's venerable ballads. Dubbed "Fiddlesticks," Reierson was a Dane County farmer who led a popular four-piece band that favored Norwegian waltzes and hoppwaltzes. Wendy played with them a few times at Sons of Norway lodges and, with Reierson's coaxing, even tried to sing "Kan du glemme gamle norge." Although he lacked "the real Norwegian expression" as a vocalist, he found it as a fiddler (ibid.).

The 1930s saw Whitford performing in community halls and taverns, at fairs, in theaters, and over the radio with a wide range of regional musicians. He was part of the Lonesome Cowboys, the Muleskinners, Mickey's Ranchhands, and a number of nameless duets. In 1938, Whitford heard Vern Minor, "the Lakedge

K. Wendell "Wendy" Whitford fiddling at his home in Cottage Grove, 1979 ***Photo: Lewis Koch/Wisconsin Folk Museum Collection***

Crooner," conjure Bradley Kincaid's voice and guitar at a root beer stand in Sun Prairie. The two teamed up and were soon joined by a pair of Stoughton musicians: Alvin Hougan on bass fiddle and jug and Howard Stuvatraa on mandolin. When the group won a WLS-sponsored talent show, they needed a name and the Goose Island Ramblers were born.

The first Goose Island Ramblers lasted until 1944. The Goose Island Ramblers' second coming was in 1962. In between, Wendy Whitford performed with the Balladeers, the Montana Cowboys, and the Hoedowners. Through it all, his music remained essentially unchanged. Before he was twenty Wendy Whitford had already accumulated the repertoire that would serve him for the next sixty years. It was, moreover, a repertoire that epitomizes the musical experiences of several generations of Yankees and Yorkers who began to settle in the Upper Midwest in the mid-nineteenth century: Anglo-Celtic fife and fiddle tunes, sentimental Victorian parlor songs, ballads of love and tragedy, the mountain and cowboy songs of radio performers, and the dance tunes of Norwegian neighbors.

Chapter 6

The Goose Island Ramblers

Program 6 Performances
All selections are by the Goose Island Ramblers.
1. "Oscar's Cannonball." 2. "On the Beach at Waunakee." 3. "Swiss Yodel Waltz." 4. "Going Back to the Hills." 5. "Norwegian War Chant." 6. "Mountain Dew." 7. "Milwaukee Waltz." 8. "Break Song." 9. "Hurley Hop." 10. "Francuszka Polka."

Wendy, George, and Bruce

The Ramblers—K. Wendell Whitford, George Gilbertsen, and Bruce Bollerud—never rambled far. Their heyday, from 1962 through 1975, was inextricably linked with extended stints as the "house band" for a pair of Madison taverns: first Glen and Ann's, then Johnny's Packer Inn. Yet more than any barnstorming band, their music whirls across the cultural landscape of the Upper Midwest.

Wendy (aka "Uncle Windy") Whitford was born in 1913 in Albion, Wisconsin, and is now retired from work at Oscar Mayer's meat-packing plant in Madison. He learned to fiddle as a kid from his grandfather, Charles Square Smith. As he is fond of declaring, "my music teacher was born in 1849" (Whitford 1990 I). Whitford's mother sang old-time songs around the house, and both the rural community and nearby Stoughton abounded with traditional musicians like the Norwegian-American fiddler Clarence Reierson. The "National Barn Dance" over Chicago's WLS radio brought southern mountain and cowboy songs to Whitford in the late 1920s. He was soon strumming a guitar, donning western togs, and emulating early country or "hillbilly" stars like Bradley Kincaid. From the early 1930s through the 1950s, Whitford performed in dance halls, theaters, and over the radio with a variety of string bands, including, in the late 1930s, the original Goose Island Ramblers.

Goose Island, an English corruption of the Norwegian *godt land* (good land), had been applied by immigrant farmers to the fertile acreage surrounding a tamarack swamp near Whitford's southwestern Dane County home. *Ramblers,* meanwhile, was a popular nickname for hillbilly and cowboy bands like the noted Prairie Ramblers, who starred on WLS. Indeed it was when Whitford, Vern Minor, Howard Stuvatraa, and Alvin "Salty" Hougan needed a band name after winning a WLS talent show that the Goose Island Ramblers first emerged. When Whitford, Gilbertsen, and Bollerud joined forces in 1962, they considered calling themselves the Rumpus Ridgerunners before rambling down to Goose Island.

Taken with some changes from J. P. Leary's notes to the Goose Island Ramblers' cassette, Midwest Ramblin' *(Wisconsin Folk Museum 2001). With permission.*

"Smokey George" Gilbertsen was born in 1925 on the outskirts of Madison. An older brother had a neglected five-dollar guitar and a stack of western songbooks. Gilbertsen was picking tunes and blowing a harmonica at seven, playing for house parties at nine, and working tavern jobs for pay at fourteen. While in his teens he picked up mandolin, Hawaiian guitar, and fiddle-mastering the latter well enough to win the Wisconsin Centennial Fiddlers Contest in 1948. Like Whitford, Gilbertsen assumed a western look and entertained with such groups as the Fox River Valley Boys, the Bearcat Mountain Boys, the Badger Ramblers, the Midwesterners, the Midwest Drovers, the Rhythm Rascals, the Dakota Roundup, and the WIBA Rangers. He is a retired repairman for the city of Madison.

Bruce Bollerud, a highly regarded special education teacher in the Madison school system, was introduced on stage as "Loose Bruce the Goose, the Hollandale Wildcat, the Scourge of Iowa County." He was born in Hollandale, Wisconsin, in 1935. His Norwegian grandfather, Ben Venden, was an old-time fiddler, while his mother, Selma, chorded on the piano. Bruce would watch and listen at house parties. He acquired a bandoneon (a squeezebox resembling the German concertina) as a ten year old, but switched to piano accordion by his late teens. After forming a duo with fiddler Herman Erickson, Bollerud went on to play German and Norwegian dance music with Gilbert Prestbroten's Rhythm Rascals, Emil Simpson's Nighthawks, and bands led by current polka stalwarts Roger Bright and Verne Meisner. The late 1950s found Bollerud playing country music with Dick Sherwood. Then a rockabilly gig with the Johnson Brothers led to Glen and Ann's tavern, where the new Goose Island Ramblers soon emerged.

Norsky Polkabillies

The Ramblers' repertoire drew on the diversity of its members' midwestern backgrounds, with a strong dose of southern hillbilly music and the western cowboy sound. Wendy Whitford contributed fiddle tunes and ballads from his English forebearers, round dance melodies from Norwegian neighbors, and the western and mountain songs of radio barn dances. George Gilbertsen brought a multi-instrumentalist's penchant for fancy picking and exotic tunes (Hawaiian marches, Italian mazurkas, Russian waltzes). A natural clown, he also favored trick fiddling and novelty tunes. Bruce Bollerud offered a skein of Norwegian dialect songs, Swiss yodels, and German-Czech polka standards. And all three composed new songs in a regional vein.

Their live tavern performances were boisterous events. Bantering with the audience, punctuating tunes with bells and goose calls, donning funny hats, the Ramblers fostered a house party atmosphere and frequently invited musicians from the audience to sit in. Longtime fan Dix Bruce recalls the era:

> Smokey George, the fiddler, would ring his cow bell after most tunes, an acknowledgement of audience applause and cheers. Wendy Whitford, the guitarist and singer and sometimes fiddler, sang classic country ballads like "Soldier's Last Letter" and many that he himself had written while on the job at Oscar Mayer's packing plant. Loose Bruce Bollerud, the accordion man who also played a mean jug (Smokey George would warn the audience, "Cover your drinks, folks!"), donned a different hat for each type of song: cowboy, railroad, etc. (Bruce 1991:37)

In the late 1960s and early 1970s, their eclectic repertoire attracted both

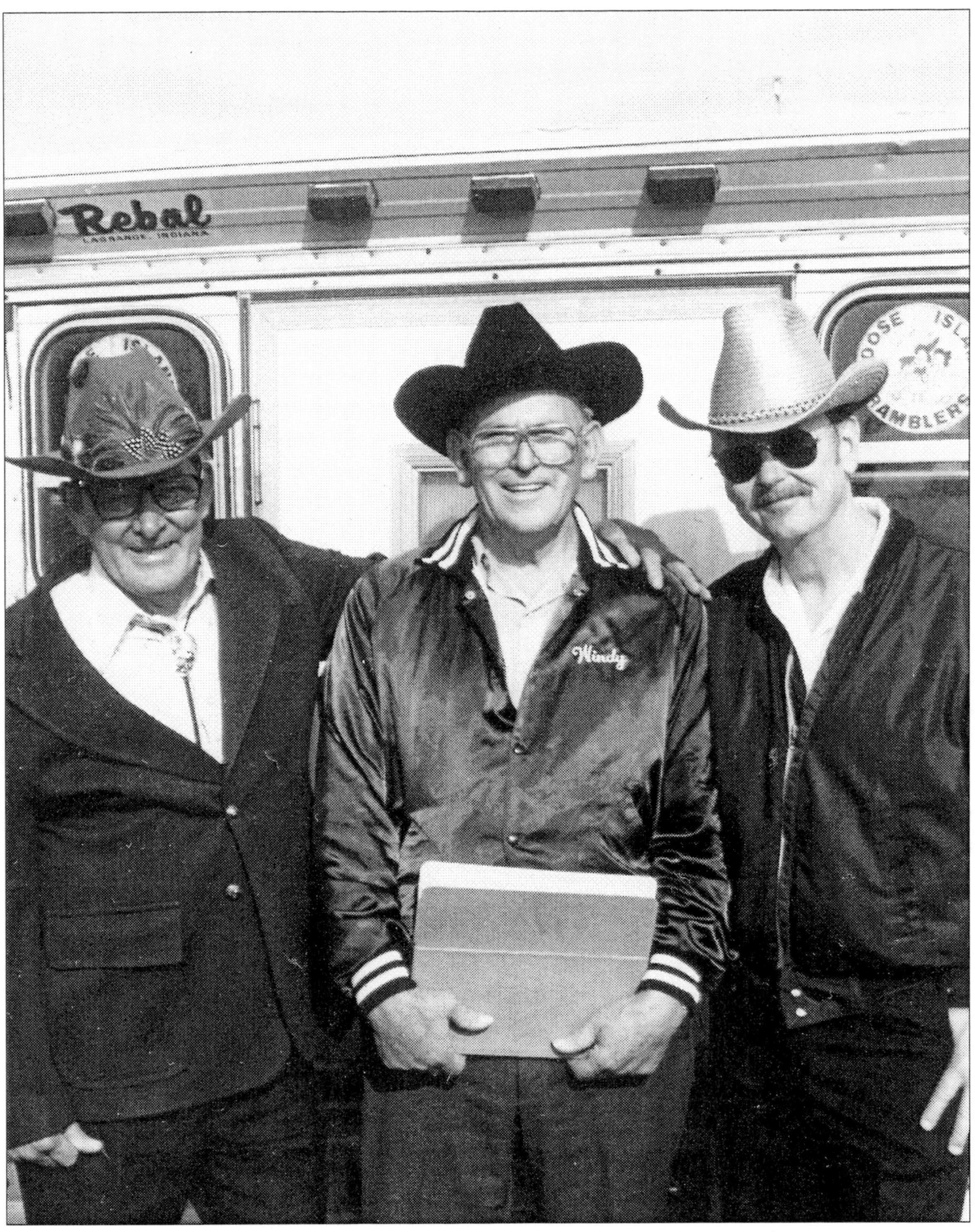

The Goose Island Ramblers—(L-R) George Gilbertsen, Wendy Whitford, and Bruce Bollerud—at a job in Mount Horeb, 1990 **Photo: Jim Leary**

Madison's ethnic working class and its college set, a remarkable achievement in an era of polarization.

Although the Ramblers disbanded in the mid-1970s, their popularity did not diminish. They were called out of retirement periodically. By the late 1980s the old recordings they had made in the 1960s were still being played on Madison area radio. The Ramblers began to play again on an occasional basis to enthusiastic throngs of old fans and newcomers who knew of them only as a legend. In 1990 *Midwest Ramblin',* a cassette, added twenty-seven new tunes to their recorded output.

Their Norsky polkabilly sound remains unique, a remarkable distillation of the Upper Midwest's foremost folk musical traditions.

Chapter 7

Wisconsin's Ethnic Country Music

Program 7 Performances
1. Ray Calkins, "The River in the Pines." 2. Leonard Finseth, "Indian War Whoop." 3. Leonard Finseth, "Swamper's Revenge on the Windfall." 4. Cousin Fuzzy, "Hillbilly Leprechaun." 5. Rodney Ristow and the Swiss Girls, "Out behind the Barn." 6. Pee Wee King, "Tennessee Polka." 7. Otto Bhhovde, "*Gamel'ost* (Old Cheese) Song. 8. Norm Dombrowski and the Happy Notes, "Great Musicians Polka." 9. Ray Rubenzer's Guys and Gals, "Yoo-Hoo Valley Waltz." 10. Andy Justmann, "Wabash Cannonball."

Lumber Camps, Schools, and House Parties

American folklorists, and country music enthusiasts generally, have long been interested in the complex relationship between southern and western traditional rural music and its commercially recorded and broadcast offshoots: hillbilly, western swing, bluegrass, rockabilly, honky tonk, and country. Meanwhile a small but significant body of writings has focused upon the rural traditions of northern musicians in the Canadian maritimes, New York State, and Minnesota (Barfuss 1983; Bronner 1987; Roberts 1978; Taft 1975). Praiseworthy inasmuch as they document the unmistakable existence of "northern country music," these studies are overwhelmingly limited to monolingual performers of Anglo-Celtic origin. Yet the multilingual progeny of European immigrants to the western Great Lakes region likewise strum guitars and don cowboy hats to play a hybrid repertoire of polkas and hoedowns on accordions and guitars.

How did European "ethnic" and Anglo-Celtic "country" music come together in America's Upper Midwest? Evidence gathered in Wisconsin shows the process at work in the late nineteenth century, especially in the lumber camps. Logging provided immigrants with winter employment and crews were often ethnically diverse. While Finnish accordion tunes or German drinking songs might resound in some bunkhouses, the ubiquitous Irish jacks, many of them veterans of Canadian camps, had the greatest impact.

Carl Gunderson, a Swede and lumber-camp cook, worked with Irishmen on the Flambeau River north of Ladysmith. Beyond vivid memories of breaking a rival cook's arm with a rolling pin, Gunderson came away with "Paul Bunyan's Ox," a version of the hyperbolic "Derby Ram," from the singing of an Irish jack (Gunderson 1973 I). Emery DeNoyer, the blind French-Canadian singer from Rhinelander, entertained loggers with a cappella ballads rendered squarely in

The bulk of this essay was condensed from J. P. Leary, "Ethnic Country Music along Superior's South Shore," John Edwards Memorial Foundation Quarterly *19, no. 72 (winter 1983):219-230 (published in 1984). With permission.*

the Irish "woods" style (Leary 1987b:21-22). Bill Hendrickson, a Finn from Herbster, learned the broadside ballad "Willie Taylor"-concerning a bold woman who follows her lover to sea-from an Irish singer, Dennis Dailey (Hendrickson 1981I). In 1914, meanwhile, Bohemian-born Jerry Novak signed on with a crew of Slavs to log on the Bad River in Ashland County. Their bosses, Yankees and Irish-Canadians, knew plenty of bawdy songs. Perhaps because he had a houseful of sisters at home, Novak retained only a "clean" version of "The Shantyboy's Alphabet."

> "A" is for axes, as all of us know,
> And "B" is for the boys who can use them also... .
>
> (Novak 1979 I)

Before entering the camps, Novak had already acquired a string of what he called "school songs" in the one-room country school he attended with Czech, Finnish, Polish, and Slovak children. Uniformly in English, these songs included patriotic anthems, popular hits of the day, rural favorites like "Put on Your Old Gray Bonnet" and "The Old Gray Mare," and blackface minstrel songs like Henry Clay Work's "In de Year ob Jubilo." A young Jenny Viitala had a similar experience amidst the homesteading Finns of Toivola, Michigan, on the shores of Lake Superior.

> After the bell rang and we sat down, the teacher read the roll call. Then we had fifteen or twenty minutes of singing. How we loved to sing! Picture fifty or more kids of every size, age, and shape singing Irish ballads and Scottish folk songs with a broad Finnish accent! (Vachon 1973:2)

Certainly these English language verses were part of an assimilationist scheme (Viitala was also punished for speaking Finnish in the schoolyard), but the songs carried their own appeal.

Beyond acquiring an Anglo-Celtic repertoire in lumber camps and schools, the Upper Midwest's European immigrants encountered dance tunes amidst the give-and-take of "doings" in the homes, halls, and outdoor boweries of rural neighborhoods and small towns. Vivian Eckholm Brevak grew up in Bayfield County, Wisconsin, amidst Swedes, Finns, Hungarians, and English Canadians. Her father, Carl, was a Swedish born fiddler with his store of old country tunes, but her most vivid musical memories centered on gatherings of "all kinds of people" in the homes of the McCutcheons, the Days, or the Cooks. In keeping with the crowd's varied composition there were "lotta square dances. Schottisches though, too, and old-time waltzes and polkas. Not modern stuff, though." Her longtime neighbor and friend, Netty Day Harvey, chimed in, "And two-steps too ... and the broom dance, and the circle two-step" (Brevak and Harvey 1981 I).

Pappy Eatmore's Barn Dance Jubilee

By the early twentieth century, the Upper Midwest's European immigrants had not only absorbed the basic elements of what would evolve into country music (Anglo-Celtic ballads, sentimental and parlor songs, blackface minstrelsy, fiddle tunes), but they had also begun to synthesize old- and new-world musical elements in events ranging from informal house parties to organized public programs.

In 1904, for example, Ashland was a bustling mill town, railhead, and port on Lake Superior where Germans, Italians, Scandinavians, and Slavs jostled with English, Scots, and Irish. Editions of the *Ashland Daily Press*

Ray Calkins playing the lumberjack's psalmodikon, the "Viking Cello," Chetek, 1988
Photo: Jim Leary

touted their musical activities, while likewise covering the appearance of such touring companies as the Great Barlow's Minstrels. When St. Agnes's Catholic Church offered a "Home Talent Minstrel Night" for one thousand onlookers, the results were predictably eclectic. Besides the obligatory "tambo and bones" blackface performers of "coon songs" and the recitation of a "Negro piece" by Hilda Bloomquist, the evening included Archie McDougall's execution of the highland fling to bagpipe accompaniment, as well as a comic "Italian and Bear Act" by John Allo and Will Garnich in which "Dago maka de beara clima the pole to the telegraph." Garnich, a Croatian, was also locally renowned for singing Irish songs, while Ms. Bloomquist was celebrated for comic renderings of Scandinavian-American dialect.

Thirty years later and thirty miles to the east, Pappy Eatmore's Barn Dance jubilee upheld the region's mixed tradition. Clearly inspired by the "National Barn Dance"—established with mostly rural southern entertainers on Chicago's radio station WLS in 1924—the Ironwood, Michigan, jubilee featured northern "polkabilly" bands, with cowboy hats and accordions, like "Curly Bradley and His Hard Cider Boys" (a Slovak, three Finns, and two Italians). While the "Boys" dispensed a mixture of hoedowns and polkas, a pair of stereotypical comics-mustachioed "Tony" the Italian workman and stalwart "Ole" the Scandinavian bumpkin—lent ethnic accents to rustic foolcry.

Nor has the ethnic-country interweaving diminished in ensuing decades. Not only have northern ethnics valued both their old-world heritage and the "new" music of Anglo-Celtic Americans, but their sociocultural experiences have closely paralleled those of the rural southerners who created country music. When Alabama's Hank Williams sang, "I left my home down on the old rural route," he was speaking to plenty in the Upper Midwest who left the land for work in industrial centers like Minneapolis, Milwaukee, Chicago, and Detroit. When Bobby Bare sang about homesick southerners on auto assembly lines in "Detroit City," he was singing to countless northerners who shared the same sentiment. Country music's "hillbilly" preoccupations with mobility, home, rural life, labor, exuberant sociability, loneliness, and religion have always been shared by the Upper Midwest's "jackpine savages."

Chapter 8

Snow Country Hillbillies: Northern Country Music

Program 8 Performances
1. Fendermen, "Muleskinner Blues." 2. Lorraine Rice, "Shoes." 3. Bobby and Lorraine Rice, "Tippy Toein'." 4. Famous Lashua, "Chocolate Ice Cream Cone." 5. Niilo Oja, "Minnesota, We Love You." 6. Robert ("Bobby Bullett") St. Germaine, "The Devil's Mouth." 7. Robert ("Bobby Bullett") St. Germaine, "Reservation Auto." 8. North Country Band, "No Count Blues."

Country's Commerical Roots

From modest beginnings as a commercial endeavor in the 1920s, country music has grown into a major branch of the entertainment industry. It is a vernacular music, rooted in the rural Anglo-Celtic and African-American musical traditions of the southern United States. When radio and phonograph records proliferated nearly simultaneously in the early twentieth century, cultural and especially musical life in rural America was transformed. No longer was it the ruralite's only option to listen to local homemade music or to wait for infrequent performances by touring troupes. Through a machine—a phonograph or a radio—one could broaden one's musical horizons. While urbanites controlled the nascent record and radio industries, they soon realized that there was a rural market for music other than the dance bands and classical orchestras of the cities.

The Okeh record company began to send out talent scouts to rural sites, set up recording equipment in a local school or warehouse, and record whatever musicians were the most popular in that area. Columbia, Victor, and others soon copied this early strategy. Okeh's scout during the early 1920s, Ralph Peer, may have been the first to present authentic southern folk musicians to the American public (Malone 1974). These locally recorded and locally marketed discs produced an unintentional benefit: the historical documentation of rural traditional music.

But the record companies quickly decided they could much more efficiently record and sell the records of a few musicians who had the potential of a more than local appeal. The careers of the earliest national country stars, Jimmie Rodgers and the Carter Family, resulted from this later marketing strategy. Rodgers and the Carters were both recorded in 1927 by talent scout Ralph Peer, by then working for Victor, in a famous recording session in Bristol, Tennessee.

Meanwhile, to compete—as they thought—with phonograph records, radio station owners also stumbled upon a way to appeal to rural listeners. Appearances by performers like Fiddlin' John Carson on Atlanta's WSB in the early 1920s produced a tremendous popular reaction. In 1923, WBAP in Fort Worth, Texas, inaugurated the era of hillbilly radio barn dances with an hour and a half program of square dance music. Within two years, WLS in Chicago began to broadcast the "Barn Dance," and WSM in Nashville started the "Grand Ole Opry."

The WLS program became the most influential country music radio show during the 1930s; NBC eventually carried a one-hour segment of it, the "National Barn Dance," coast to coast. Although eclipsed by the "Grand Ole Opry" after World War II, the "National Barn Dance" gave midwestern performers a showcase. Lula Belle and Scotty from Lebanon, Indiana, Grace Wilson from Owosso, Michigan, and the Goose Island Ramblers and Eddie Peabody from Madison, Wisconsin, were among the many Midwesterners who joined Kentuckians like the Prairie Ramblers and the Cumberland Ridge Runners in its Saturday night lineup.

Emerging by the 1950s as Music City, the center of the country music industry, Nashville brought a greater southern orientation to the music and the dominance of performers from Dixie. Nonetheless, northerners too have had influential careers in country music, most notably, Dave Dudley from Spencer, Wisconsin, and Pee Wee King from the south side of Milwaukee.

King of the Cowpolkas

Pee Wee King, born Frank Kuczynski, was from the urban Polish-American working class—a community which during his youth in the 1930s had little association with country music. His father, John Kuczynski, a skilled fiddler and concertina player, enlivened many a Polish wedding in Milwaukee with polkas and *obereks* (Corenthal 1991). While still a boy, Frank became adept at playing the piano accordion, learning not only Polish ethnic music, but Slovenian, German, and American popular music as well.

In the early 1930s Frank happened to be in an accordion shop at the moment when noted country music promoter J. L. Frank came in, looking for an accordionist for his group, the Log Cabin Boys. Frank signed on to tour with the band and soon adopted the stage name Pee Wee King. In 1935 Pee Wee married J. L. Frank's daughter and also became the leader of a new band, the Golden West Cowboys. They began to perform on the "Grand Ole Opry" in 1937, and in 1938 the band was featured in a Gene Autry film, "Gold Mine in the Sky." The Polish kid from Milwaukee settled in Louisville, Kentucky, and donned a ten-gallon hat and western wear, taking advantage of the glorification of the cowboy in the popular culture of the day.

In October 1941, to entertain American servicemen, the "Grand Ole Opry" put together the Camel Caravan, a traveling troupe of twenty performers, including Pee Wee King and his Golden West Cowboys. By late 1942 they had logged more than fifty thousand miles, putting on 175 shows in nineteen states at sixty-eight different military installations.

Through the 1940s and 1950s, the accordion remained an important instrument in the western style of country music, thanks in large part to Pee Wee's influence. He also used his musical creativity to bring elements of Wisconsin polka to country music. His Polish heritage gave Pee Wee an affinity for the ethnic melodies and the polka and waltz beats familiar from his youth. A section of the

Hello there!

It sure is nice to know that you are a regular listener to my program. Please tell your friends to listen in on WEAU at 12:00 noon, Monday thru Friday. Write when ever you can. The life of my program depends on your mail. "take care of yourself".

My Best to you,
Famous

Postcards sent out by Famous Lashua to listeners in Eau Claire, 1948 ***Wisconsin Folk Museum Collection***

melody of "Pawel walcer," a Polish concertina number, shows up in the chorus of the song "Cattle Call," which he has regularly performed with vocalist Redd Stewart.

As a songwriter Pee Wee has been even more influential than he has been as a performer. His tune "Slow Poke" was the first to gain wide popularity in the early 1950s, but the famed "Tennessee Waltz," which King and Redd Stewart coauthored in 1948, remains one of the best-known country tunes of all time and contributed to country's popular surge. Although it initially appeared as a country tune and was well received in 1948, "Tennessee Waltz" was recorded by pop singer Patti Page in 1950, strangely enough as the "B" side of a record. This version was tremendously popular; by May 1951, 4.8 million records of the song had been sold (Malone 1974).

Truck Drivin' Man

In 1952, about the time Pee Wee King's career was at its peak, Dave Dudley and his Country Caravan recorded "You Don't Care" and "Nashville Blues" on a small Milwaukee label, Pfau Records. Coming from a small town in central Wisconsin, Dudley finally made his mark in Nashville by becoming, in the mid1960s, the most visible spokesman for the truck driver as country music hero. Railroadmen had been the romantic transportation workers of early country music: the engineers got the spotlight in "Wreck of the Old 97" and "George Alley's FFV," Jimmie Rodgers was "The Singing Brakeman," and even railroad vagabonds became romantic figures in "The Hobo's Meditation" and "Waiting for a Train." As the highway took an increasing share of the nation's freight, the apotheosis of the truck driver ensued. Like the idealized cowboy, he was a traveling loner, independent, determined, brave yet kind, facing dangers daily.

Although earlier truck driving songs had been issued by singers such as Red Sovine, the Willis Brothers, and Dick Curless (perhaps the earliest was Cliff Bruner and Moon Mullican's 1939 Decca recording of "Truck Driver's Blues"), Dudley's 1966 hit, "Six Days on the Road," crossed over into pop music and set off the flood of "truck drivin'" songs which followed.

Projecting a hard-as-nails, working-class macho image, Dudley developed a virile rockabilly singing style full of Elvis Presley-like vocal slurs and guttural growls. His Mercury album, *Songs about the Working Man*, summed up the change in country music, parallel to the transformation of much of its audience, the rural populace, from farm people to blue collar workers in an industrial society.

In the 1980s, like many other country stars whose commercial success had peaked then declined in earlier decades, Dudley began performing extensively for the European, especially German, audiences who follow classic country music with a connoisseurship usually reserved for fine wines. Even in Europe he has continued performing his highway-oriented themes, but now his semi is on the autobahn; his 1990 German hit "Im Stau," meaning "stuck in a traffic jam," has English verses and a German chorus.

Part 3

Polka Heaven

Chapter 9

German-American Music in Wisconsin

Program 9 Performances
1. Fred Kaulitz, "Herr Schmidt." 2. Howie Bowe, "Little German Ball." 3. Ray Dorschner and the Rainbow Valley Dutchmen, "Putzig Polka." 4. Ray Dorschner, "Village Blacksmith Waltz." 5. Jerry Schneider, "Tante Anna." 6. Syl Groeschl, "Ve Get So Soon Oldt." 7. Heinie and His Grenadiers, "Schuhplattler." 8. Andy Justmann, "Das Kufstein Lied." 9. Harry Kosek and the Red River Boys, "By the Rivers of Babylon."

German Sundays

In 1839 Old Lutheran dissenters settled Friestadt in present-day Ozaukee County, Wisconsin, and a contingent soon established Lebanon in what was to become Dodge County. These German-speaking immigrants from Pomerania and Brandenburg were fleeing the ecclesiastical edicts of the Prussian king, William III. Throughout the nineteenth century, other ethnic Germans—whether Catholics, Protestants, or free thinkers, whether from Baltic Sea states like Mecklenburg or from alpine Bavaria, whether urban intellectuals or stolid farmers—settled Wisconsin (Rippley 1985). They dominated the state's eastern region and were so widespread elsewhere that in the 1980 Wisconsin census more than half of the state's residents claimed some German descent.

Music was integral to Wisconsin's German cultural experience from the outset. By the 1840s, Friestadt's settlers had established a band that has, with a few interruptions, persisted to the present. Not surprisingly, the Friestadt band was associated with the Trinity Lutheran Church, although it relied on the brass and reed "band" instruments of military association that had become widespread through Europe by the early nineteenth century. Besides liturgical pieces, musicians played overtures, marches, and dance tunes. They were most active in the summer, playing for church picnics, weddings, and parades. The group altered its name to the Victory Band during World War II, but reasserted its German-American identity in the mid-1960s by becoming the Friestadt Alte Kameraden (Suelflow 1954; Hilgendorf 1985 I).

Whether Lutheran or Catholic, the German penchant for balancing sacred and secular music, for combining beer with church picnics, and for going to church on Sunday morning and to the beer garden in the afternoon differed sharply from the customs of Protestant Yankee neighbors. In nineteenth-century Sheboygan, where Germans slightly outnumbered New Englanders, the latter were known to take "their pleasures moderately, and one might almost say, solemnly." Sunday amusements were anathema.

> It is small wonder that the Yankees were horrified and shocked at some of the gay and carefree customs, especially beer-drinking, dancing, card-playing, and Sunday amusements. Wherever Germans gathered together there was music, song, and general jollification. It was mainly they who patronized the saloons, beer gardens, and dance halls. They introduced dances like the waltz and polka ... which the Yankees denounced as wicked. (Buchen 1944:226.)

The efforts of Yankee politicians to close taverns were thwarted, and Sunday remains a day of social music and dance throughout Wisconsin.

Parlor Singers and Polka Bands

Bands of the sort that played for Friestadt dances were once extremely common in Wisconsin and remain in tiny but heavily German communities like Lebanon, Kiel, and Plymouth. They were, however, merely a large, public, and formalized manifestation of a bent toward social music that found more frequent outlet in small, private, informal gatherings. Rose Schuster Taylor's reminiscences of the 1870s mention numerous musical occasions in rural Dane County. The family sang German songs at bedtime; they sang and played on the porch during summer evenings; and weddings demanded music both at the event and during a charivari that preceded it. Rose's siblings hummed through combs, while her father, Peter Schuster, played the flute and what is mentioned simply as a horn. Instrumental variety was lent to frequent house parties with their neighbors and cousins, the Tiedemans, as three brothers played accordion, fiddle, and Jew's harp.

The Schuster-Tiedeman repertoire was decidedly German and included alpine yodeling. But Peter Schuster, who had worked in New York State as a young man, sang boatman's songs from the Erie Canal, and the family also favored "Negro songs," doubtless acquired from some touring blackface minstrel troupe. Their dances similarly favored such old-world round dances as the waltz, the schottische, the polka, and the galop, but they were not averse to the quadrille and the Virginia reel (Taylor 1944-46).

Comic dialect songs, with their similar juxtaposition of several cultural systems, were another indication of an evolving German-American identity. Songs like Whoopee John's "Elsie Shuetzenheim," Howie Bowe's "Little German Ball," and Syl Groeschl's "Ve Get So Soon Oldt (und Ve Get So Late Schmart)"—performed by second-, third-, and fourth-generation German Americans—have their roots in the "Dutchified" English of immigrants. While clearly enjoyed by German Americans for the gentle fun they poke at the customs and foibles of newcomers, these songs were also accessible to native speakers of English-indeed some may have been composed for "stage Dutch" theatrical performers.

Helene Stratman-Thomas recorded several such dialect songs from non-Germans during fieldwork in Wisconsin in the 1940s (Bohlman 1979:374-379). In "Oh Yah, Ain't Dat Been Fine," a German courting couple, "Katryn" and "Scharlie," discuss their future.

> Now when we get married won't we put on style?
> We'll chump on a streetcar and ride all the while.
> We've got plenty of sauerkraut always on hand,
> And live chust as good as der king of der land.
>
> (Peters 1977:148)

The noted German formula song "Schnitzelbank" (Shaving bench) depicted on a postcard from a Milwaukee restaurant, 1950s
Wisconsin Folk Museum Collection

The Jolly Alpine Boys at the Golden Zither restaurant, Milwaukee, 1964
Wisconsin Folk Museum Collection

Both Anglo-Americans and German Americans might chuckle at the fractured English and the talismanic invocation of sauerkraut. Both might appreciate the ability to embrace technological advances while retaining inherited traditions. Both might applaud the democratic every-citizen-a-king sentiments.

Polka bands are the most visible bearers of German-American musical tradition in the late twentieth century. In the 1930s, "Heinie and His Grenadiers" became the first Wisconsin German band to garner a regional following. Led by Jack Bundy, who took on the persona and dialect of "Heinie," the Grenadiers were fitted out in quasi-military band uniforms and played tight arrangements of old German folk tunes. Not surprisingly, World War II made the existence of overtly German bands with militaristic names and garb temporarily unacceptable (Leary 1991b).

Since the days of Heinie and His Grenadiers, the German identity of Wisconsin polka bands has been alternately obscured and emphasized. Some bands with overtly German instrumentation—trumpets, tuba, an accordion or concertina—have nonetheless stressed English vocals and an "American" polka sound. Bernard Robert Feil of heavily German Dodge County, for example, became "Bernie Roberts" and led one such band from the mid-1940s through the 1960s. Roberts's innovations are sustained today by the Don Peachey Orchestra (March 1991).

Fellow Dodge Countian Andy Justmann, however, has carried on parts of the overtly German repertoire with which he was raised. His polka band entertains dancers with fine German vocals and has even led tours to the European *heimat.* Syl Groeschl and Jerry Schneider, dwellers in Wisconsin's Deutschland on the eastern shores of Lake Winnebago, have made German music their trademark. Their adherence to tradition has won them national and international recognition. In 1991 Groeschl was profiled as part of the "Old Traditions/New Sounds" series syndicated on public radio stations. In May 1992, Schneider's band was brought to the Kennedy Center in Washington, D.C., to play at a fete for German unification.

Chapter 10

Ach ja!: The Syl Groeschl Story

Program 10 Performances
All selections are by Syl Groeschl.
1. "Jolly Coppersmith." 2. "Hooter Waltz." 3. "Two-Step Medley." 4. "One Beer for One." 5. "Alexander's Ragtime Band." 6. "We Left Our Wives at Home." 7. "Brass 'n' Sax Polka." 8. "Immer noch ein Tropfen." 9. "Ve Get So Soon Oldt." 10. "Herman, Take Me Home."

The Holy Land

The eastern shore of Lake Winnebago in east central Wisconsin is one of the most picturesque areas of the state. It is part of what local folks call the "land between the lakes," a square chunk of land about fifty miles on a side between lakes Winnebago and Michigan. The rolling hills are dotted with small dairy farms, each farmstead a cluster of buildings dominated by a big red barn flanked by tall silos looming like the towers of a fortified medieval fiefdom. This is real dairy country. One of the four counties in the area, Calumet, is notable for having a greater population of dairy cattle (31,700) than humans (30,867).

Some of the pastures and hay and corn fields run practically up to the shore of the glistening waters of Winnebago, a shallow but expansive lake nearly thirty miles long and ten miles wide, the largest natural lake within the boundaries of a single state. On February's ice, local spearfishers jig their hand-carved wooden fish decoys known as teasers to lure to their barbed tines the mighty lake sturgeon, a ponderous and dinosauric fish sometimes as large as the fisher.

It is hilly country. The northern tip of the Kettle Moraine, a thirty-mile-long battleship-shaped section of unglaciated land, extends into the southern portion of the land between the lakes. In hilly spots, wooded acreage still abounds, and from some of the highest hills majestic churches survey the landscape, giving rise to another nickname for the area: the Holy Land. Towns bearing the names St. John, St. Anna, Jericho, Calvary, Mt. Calvary, St. Nazianz, St. Cloud, and Eden testify to the strong, mostly conservative Catholic religious tradition of the Austrian, Czech, and southern German immigrants who settled in the area in the middle of the nineteenth century.

While the Slavic-speaking Czechs have had a linguistic impact on the northeastern section of the land between the lakes, settlers in the rest of the area mostly spoke southern German peasant dialects, and they continued to do so—in rural households—until the 1940s. Syl Groeschl, who reckons his Calumet County family has been providing old-time music to the area's residents ever since his great-grandfather Johann Groeschl immigrated in 1839, talked about the language situation during his childhood in the 1930s:

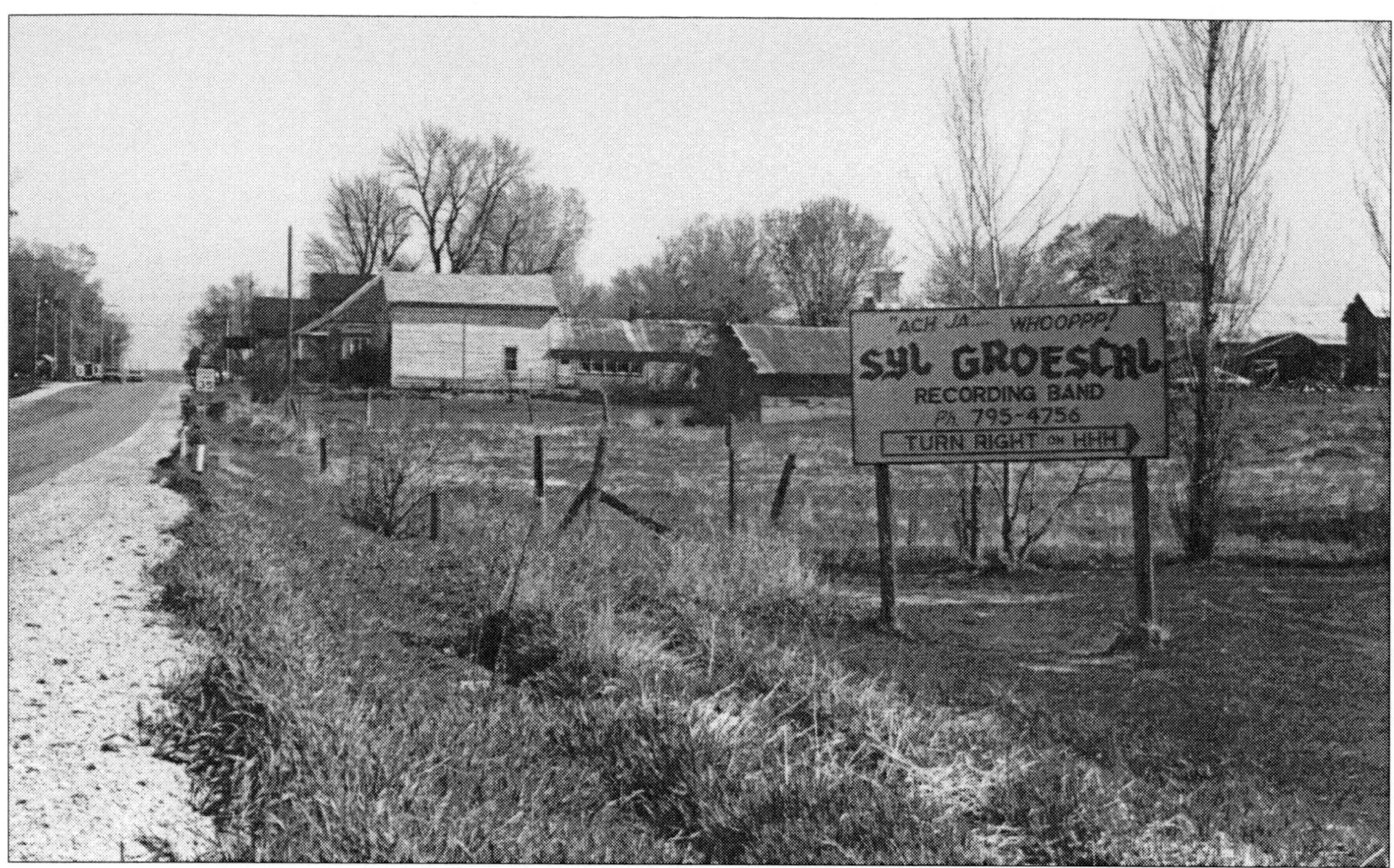

Promotional billboard on the outskirts of Calumetville, 1985 ***Photo: Jim Leary***

> My first language was German. That's just the way it was in our house.... My whole family talked German. My grandparents could hardly talk English, a very little bit of English. And it was very broken. When I started school, Catholic parochial school ... I couldn't even talk English. Very little bit, I could. All of us kids, when we were playing outside in the playground, we'd talk German. To heck with English! ... (S. Groeschl 1990 I)

This strong persistence of the German language, for nearly a century, into the fourth generation in America, is typical of the area. For many decades the rural German-speaking communities have been naturally cohesive, and only recently have they made deliberate efforts to revitalize their ethnic traditions. In short, their German-American identity came naturally but nowadays they have to work a little harder at it. The musical style and repertoire of the currently prominent old-time bands from the area, Syl Groeschl's and Jerry Schneider's, reflect the cultural influences and changes within this tight community over the past 150 years. When it comes to choosing tunes, Syl Groeschl's band is not overtly revivalistic. Syl reckons that his band still plays about five or six German folk songs passed down from his great-grandfather including such German chestnuts as "Du, du liegst mir im Herzen" and the polka, waltz, and schottische tunes his dancing audience demands. Yet he has no problem with playing old-time American popular tunes like "Old Gray Bonnet" or "Golden Slippers," country tunes like "Your Cheatin' Heart," and even an occasional recent hit song such as "All the Girls I've Loved Before." But on stage he invokes his German identity by sporting a well-worn pair of lederhosen and a rumpled *jäger* hat. When he sings in German it is with an unpretentious vocal style and in his native dialect. He sprinkles his performances with the German exclamation *ach ja!* but also with an imitation of Woody Woodpecker's laugh.

Jerry Schneider's band, comprising somewhat younger musicians, can be a bit more overtly German in their tune choices, more likely to include newer German favorites like "Das Kufstein Lied." They feature the powerful baritone vocals of bass horn player Bill Halbach, who sings in literary German with carefully correct diction. The Chilton-based band even gave a German language title to their most recent album, "Etwas schoen von Chilton" (Something pretty from Chilton). But on the album jacket they invoke not only their Germanness by displaying beer steins and inlaid button accordions, but also their local identity by posing right under a monstrous Lake Winnebago sturgeon mounted on the wall.

Merrymaking Catholics

Unlike the Bible Belt of the southern United States, where strong fundamentalist religious beliefs have been something of an impediment to secular music and dance traditions, in Wisconsin's Holy Land conservative Catholicism neither restricts secular merrymaking nor prohibits alcohol. In a thoughtful, evocative interview with ethnomusicologist Becky Miller in 1990, Valeria Groeschl, who played piano and sang in her father's band for over eleven years, recalled life in the family band and the two sides of her bandleader/tavern keeper/farmer father, Tony Groeschl:

> He knew I was really dependable and he knew, in case they had a little more fun than they should have through the night, they had a driver.... For a while there we had all of us playing. My brother Sylvester, who runs the band now, he played sax and clarinet, and my brother Tony played the trumpet and Leon played the drums. My dad was playing the concertina, bass violin ... it was a hectic life. You have to love music to do this. To do this for money, we were only getting seven dollar a night. That's all I got paid.... It was very hard on my mother when her whole family was in the orchestra. Very hard ... well, she saw her whole family leave in one car. And one accident could have wiped out the whole family.... You know we never had much time with our father. He was never home much. That we missed. Because when he was home, there was work to be done, then it was time to get ready and go play again.... I really don't know, I think it was just because he was brought up with music. His dad played the concertina.... I don't know if he started [the band] because he just loved music or ... figuring it would have a supplemental income. My dad was a great one for parties.... House was filled, two rooms, but they always had room for people. And he'd play his concertina and things, oh sure.... Kind man, strict. Religious. Even when he had the taverns. If there was nobody in there ... he had this chair and he sat next to the refrigerator, and he had his rosary. He prayed the rosary. He'd pray for his family always, so everybody would be ok. He was really a mixture.... And always church. You wouldn't dare miss church. We always had to pray before meals and things. He was very religious and very strict, like a lot of men are. But he was kind. But it was just that he was never home enough. It was very hard on my mother, very hard. She still talks about it. Because she really cared for Dad and it hurt her that she didn't have the time to spend with him. But that's the way it was. (V. Groeschl 1990 I)

Chapter 11

Music before Milking: The Very Musical Brueggen Family

Program 11 Performances
1. Brian and the Mississippi Valley Dutchmen, "At the Mill Polka." 2. Herman's Jolly Dutchmen, "Gary's Polka." 3. Ridgeland Dutchmen, "While You're Away." 4. Ridgeland Dutchmen, "Jolly Coppersmith." 5. Brian and the Mississippi Valley Dutchmen, "Cherry Polka." 6. Brian and the Mississippi Valley Dutchmen, Excerpts from "Pine Hollow Schottische," "Reh braune Augen," and "Koster's Waltz." 7. Gary and the Ridgeland Dutchmen, "Seven Beers with the Wrong Woman." 8. Gary and the Ridgeland Dutchmen with the Polka Mass Trio, "Christ Is Knocking."

Ridgeland Dutchmen

The young concertina virtuoso Brian Brueggen was born in the 1960s on a dairy farm outside the village of Cashton in western Wisconsin. Cashton is east of the bustling river town of La Crosse, in one of the most scenic areas of the state. As one approaches the Mississippi River, Wisconsin's green rolling hills become steeper and sharper in a pattern of ridges. Limestone outcroppings are frequent, and magnificent vistas culminate in the panorama of the mighty Mississippi itself, the wide channel, islands choked with trees, and luxurious wetlands along the shores. Many of its inhabitants refer to the area as the Ridgeland, and places like Middle Ridge, Ridgeville, and St. Mary's Ridge—location of the pioneer Brueggen homestead—are named for the area's notable topographic feature.

The connection of his concertina music to this land is evident in the names of the bands in which Brian has played: he started professional play with his father and paternal uncles in the Ridgeland Dutchmen and now leads Brian and the Mississippi Valley Dutchmen. Brian has also named some of his original dance tunes for local sites: "Pine Hollow Schottische" and "Brush Creek Laendler."

While Brian's music may be intimately linked to the land and local community of his birthplace, his "Dutchman" sound is also a widely known style of vernacular music played throughout the Upper Midwest. The most famed practitioners of this genre in the past, "Whoopee John" Wilfahrt and Harold Loefflemacher with his Six Fat Dutchmen, established a foothold in the midwestern mass media and entertainment business from their home base in New Ulm, Minnesota. From the 1920s—when radio and phonograph records emerged—through the 1950s, these and other leaders of Dutchman bands were striving for widespread commercial success like that eventually achieved by Nashville's "country" music.

Since the Ridgeland is only about two hundred miles east of New Ulm, the Brueggens and their neighbors heard the famed Dutchman bands via Twin Cities and La Crosse radio stations, or live when the Minnesota bands crossed the Mississippi to play for dances in places like La Crosse's Concordia Ballroom. Besides being attracted by its style, these German-American farmers liked Dutchman music for another reason: to them, it represented a modern apotheosis of German-American traditional music. Even the name Dutchman expresses both ethnicity and an American identity, since it is an anglicized form deriving from *Deutsch,* meaning "German."

If these were not reasons enough for the Ridgeland to accept the Dutchman sound, then there was Sylvester Liebl. A concertina player born in the town of Wanda, Minnesota, just thirty miles from New Ulm and steeped in the local style, Syl relocated with his family to Mormon Coulee (near La Crosse) in 1934 when he was only seventeen. Syl was already a veteran dance band musician; since age twelve he had headed a small family combo, Liebl's Concertina Orchestra. Once in Wisconsin, he renamed the band the Jolly Germans, and during World War II he changed it to the Jolly Swiss Boys to avoid anti-German sentiments.

At first glance, the bespectacled Syl seemed introverted, but when he strapped on the concertina and played a dance tune, his instinctive musicianship conveyed freedom and a raucous abandon. So innate was his musical gift that his bands never needed written music, and no one even needed to count the beat; the band members simultaneously plunged into a tune. It was as natural as breathing (Jim Kirchstein, personal communication, 1991).

Syl Liebl may have started the first true Dutchman band in the Ridgeland but others soon followed. The spell of the Dutchman style must have influenced Brian's accordion-playing and drum-beating grandfather, Herman Brueggen, who changed the name of his group from Herman's Accordion Orchestra to Herman's Jolly Dutchmen.

Brian readily admits Syl Liebl's strong influence upon his playing. Indeed, Syl's infectious and improvisatory style has inspired several younger concertinists, including Fountain City's Karl Hartwich, originally from Orion, Illinois, whose Country Dutchmen band is one of the most popular in the northern Mississippi Valley, and Brian's younger cousin, Gary Brueggen, another teenaged concertina prodigy. Since Gary's emergence as an accomplished lead concertinist in the latter half of the 1980s, Brian's paternal uncles Willard and Harry have been able to revitalize the Ridgeland Dutchmen, their old band which had endured a setback when Brian and his father Phil departed to form their own group. Syl Liebl Sr. retired from active music making in 1984, but Syl Liebl Jr. of Coon Valley has kept the family's musical tradition going with his own band, the New Jolly Swiss Boys, fronted by Kevin Liss of Stevens Point, yet another young Liebl-influenced concertina standout.

With four first-rate Dutchman bands in the area, the Ridgeland is a hotbed of this German-American midwestern music. But the Ridgeland's population is not homogeneous in terms of ethnicity or religion. Among its hillside farmers, besides the numerous German Catholics, there are many Norwegian Lutherans, some Irish, a big Czech settlement around Hillsboro, and Wasps. Each ethnic group has added its own particular influence to Ridgeland culture and traditional

Brothers Henry Brueggen, clarinet, Bill Brueggen, fiddle, and Herman Brueggen, button accordion, Cashton, 1920s ***Wisconsin Folk Museum Collection***

Brian Brueggen of the Mississippi Valley Dutchmen playing concertina at the Red Barn Polka Fetival, Evansville, 1988 ***Photo: Jim Leary***

music. In addition to a core repertoire of German music, the Brueggen Dutchman bands typically play a lot of perky Scandinavian schottisches, plenty of melodious Czech polkas and waltzes, some Irish chestnuts, country music fox-trots, and perhaps a few oompah versions of Anglo hoedown fiddle tunes.

Polka Masses

Though Dutchman is a secular tradition, the strong Catholic religious orientation of the St. Mary's Ridge community, the home place of the Brueggens, has also influenced the local music. The religious tradition is so strong in St. Mary's Ridge that the brief local history prepared for America's bicentennial practically equates St. Mary's parish with the community. According to the *Monroe County Pictorial History* (1976), the hardy group of German immigrants who settled on St. Mary's Ridge in 1855, while residing in log cabins and struggling to clear agricultural land on the steep slopes, also found the energy to walk the forty miles to church in La Crosse. In 1856 they built a small log church in their own community which was served by a missionary priest from La Crosse. A few years later, they finally received a stationary priest, S. Florentint.

The community was exclusively German until 1862 when four Irish families moved to the Ridge. More than a century later, the same families still predominate as does the vitality of their religious practice. Gary's Ridgeland Dutchmen combine the area's musical and religious heritages as active purveyors of the polka mass, a relatively recent innovation. Since its purported inception in the 1970s in Eveleth, Minnesota, by a Slovenian priest, Fr. Frank Perkovich, polka masses have been celebrated across the Midwest at parish festivals and polka fests in a variety of ethnic polka styles.

In response to many requests that their band provide a polka mass, Gary's mother, Dorothy Brueggen, compiled the songs for a mass. In some cases she penned religious lyrics to standard polka tunes. For example, Dorothy transformed the polka favorite by Chicago's Lil' Wally, "Johnny's Knocking," from the Polish folk song "Puka Jasiu," into a sacred song, "Christ Is Knocking." In other instances she borrowed items from the Perkovich polka mass, setting "We Offer Bread and Wine" to the tune of the Slovenian "Psi zalajaju" (Barking dog polka) and "At This Sacrifice" to the tune of Fred Rose's "Blue Eyes Crying in the Rain" (which no doubt entered the Perkovich mass via the Serbian and Croatian tamburitza version, "Suze liju plave oči"). The harmonizing voices of her nieces Donna Elsen, Carol Brueggen, and Kathy Wacker became the Polka Mass Trio, who perform the mass to the accompaniment of the Ridgeland Dutchmen.

A polka mass is often celebrated on Sunday mornings at midwestern polka festivals where old-time music and dancing enthusiasts from several states congregate. The music of the Brueggen family bands is firmly rooted in the folk culture of the local Ridgeland community. At the same time they are not isolated but participate in and have helped shape the broader vernacular traditions of the Upper Midwest.

Chapter 12

The Minnesota Dutchmen

Program 12 Performances
1. "Whoopee John" Wilfahrt, "Country Road Schottische." 2. Six Fat Dutchmen, "Bohemian Polka." 3. Ivan Kahle, "Blacksmith Waltz." 4. Elmer Scheid, "Hoolerie Waltz." 5. Erwin Suess and the Hoolerie Dutchmen, "Stillwater Landler." 6. Ernie Coopman and the Stagemen, "Cuckoo Waltz." 7. Deutschmeisters, "Du, du liegst mir im Herzen." 8. Whoopee Norm Edlebeck and His Dairyland Dutchmen, "More Beer Polka."

Goosetown

In the late 1860s German speakers from southwestern Bohemia along the Bavarian border began settling in rural Brown County, Minnesota, south and west of New Ulm, some eventually—by the 1880s—occupying New Ulm's *gansviertel* or Goosetown district. Coming as they did from a region noted for squeezebox players and brass bands, it was hardly surprising that these German Bohemians included such veteran musicians as Joseph Hofmeister and John Lindmeier, who soon organized bands to play for community dances, weddings, and even funeral processions (Rippley 1985).

Among their listeners was John Anthony Wilfahrt, "Whoopee John" (1893-1961). Born on a farm southwest of New Ulm, Wilfahrt was inspired by local brass bands and at age twelve taught himself to play concertina. By 1909 he was entertaining at weddings with his brother, Eddie, on clarinet, and a cousin, Edward Kretsch, on cornet. By the 1920s, with a bigger band, Wilfahrt was making records, broadcasting over the radio, and barnstorming to dance jobs every night of the week (Lornell 1985[1989]; Rippley 1992).

Initially combining the concertina/accordion sound of informal house parties with the brass and reed boom of village bands, Wilfahrt later added the piano and drums of popular American dance combos. His repertoire—grounded in German and Czech polkas, waltzes, schottisches, and ländlers—gradually extended to Scandinavian tunes and American pop. Besides producing an eclectic regional sound, Wilfahrt also charmed audiences by donning a peaked alpine hat and *lederhosen,* tossing his concertina in the air, and punctuating performances with whooping yodels.

This essay is based on an essay that first appeared in "Minnesota Polka: Polka Music, American Music," by James P. Leary, a booklet accompanying the recording entitled Minnesota Polka: Dance Music from Four Traditions, *both copyright 1990 by the Minnesota Historical Society. With permission.*

Wilfahrt's professional success eased the way for other southern Minnesota bands, which spread the German-Bohemian sound throughout the Upper Midwest. Vaguely termed old-time, Whoopee John music, the New Ulm or Minnesota sound, this music also became known as oompah and Dutchman, chiefly through the efforts of Harold Loeffelmacher (1905-1988). Loeffelmacher grew up in New Ulm, where he played tuba with the 205th Infantry Band before forming a dance band in 1932. The group was called the Broadway Band, then the Continental Band, but such urban, cosmopolitan tags did not move rural, regional audiences, and it was not until Loeffelmacher tried Six Fat Dutchmen that his career accelerated. Scores of subsequent bands have incorporated "Dutchmen"—a Yankee rendering of *Deutsch* (German)—into their names (Leary and March 1991).

Loeffelmacher's exuberant tuba playing likewise extended the work of earlier stalwarts like John "Boom Boom" Bauer. No longer just a stately "bottom," a source of solid if sedate rhythm, the tuba began to romp, to improvise, to take an occasional solo, to "oompah."

From the late 1920s through the 1950s, the bands of Wilfahrt and Loeffelmacher established a genre and spread it through the Upper Midwest via weekly radio broadcasts, scores of phonograph records, and dance jobs in rural ballrooms nearly every night of the week. Their music became one of America's great regional styles, played not only by those of German heritage but by members of every other ethnic group in the Upper Midwest.

Concertina Oompah

The Dutchman sound they pioneered did not, however, remain static. Indeed most groups playing in the 1990s look to a second generation of innovators that includes Elmer Scheid in its forefront. Scheid played concertina with the Babe Wagner Band before starting his own group in the late 1940s. He introduced the oft-imitated "hoolerie" sound, a concertina/clarinet combination played in high registers, appropriate to the ländlers of Bavaria and Austria, and onomatopoeically named for *das hoolerie und das foolerie* of alpine festivals. Whereas Wilfahrt and Loeffelmacher generally favored a "full" and "blended" sound with trumpets and saxophones dominating throughout a tune, Scheid leaned toward distinct solos, especially on his chosen instrument, the concertina. Bandleader Ernie Coopman remembers that Scheid "didn't play anything so terrible fancy, but you don't have to.... He played it so pretty and clean. Boy! And that was what I wanted to do" (Coopman 1990 I).

Ever since Scheid, the concertina player has been the central figure in Minnesota's German polka bands. Indeed, in the past several decades "concertina oompah"—concertina, tuba, and drums—has come to be regarded as the genre's essential sound. Wilfahrt and Loeffelmacher led bands of up to a dozen players, those of Scheid's generation numbered seven or eight, but by the 1980s economic factors often limited bands to five, four, even three players. As band sizes have shrunk, the concertina player not only has had to carry the melodic load but also has provided the harmonic fill of absent brass and reeds.

Sylvester Liebl showed the way. Now retired from his Jolly Swiss Boys (a name that replaced Jolly Germans during World War II), Liebl was born in the New Ulm area but moved to west-central Wisconsin in the 1930s. By the 1960s he—and other players like Jerry Schuft and Johnny Gag—began to shift from Scheid's sustained notes and flowing style to "just really working over the keyboard" with

"Whoopee John" Wilfahrt, in Bavarian garb, leading his band on live radio, Minneapolis, late 1930s ***Wisconsin Folk Museum Collection***

sixteenth notes, triplets, and trills or "warbles" created by rapid finger movement on two notes. Musician Ivan Kahle remembers Liebl's concertina:

> That music just kind of fell out of it. He was playing once at the Gibbon Polka Festival, even Elmer Scheid was watching him play. Syl said, "Get your fanny out on the floor, this is a dance not a show." (Kahle 1990 I)

Today Liebl's youthful disciples—Karl (Hartwich) and the Country Dutchmen, Brian (Brueggen) and the Mississippi Valley Dutchmen, Gary (Brueggen) and the Ridgeland Dutchmen, and Kevin Liss of the New Jolly Swiss Boys—dazzle their followers by embellishing tunes with chromatic runs. They are the Dutch men and women of the future.

Chapter 13

Humorous Scandinavian Dialect Songs

Program 13 Performances
1. Goose Island Ramblers, "Paul pa haugen." 2. Goose Island Ramblers, "Ole Olson the Hobo from Norway." 3. Ragnar Hasselgren, "Swedes in North Dakota." 4. Slim Jim and the Vagabond Kid, "Nikolina." 5. Goose Island Ramblers, "Mrs. Johnson, Turn Me Loose." 6. Bruce Bollerud, "No Norwegians in Dickeyville." 7. Vivian Brevak, "Swedish Waltz."

Peasant Comedians

When John Forsell, the celebrated Swedish opera singer, visited Chicago round 1910, he found a nearly empty concert hall. Perplexed and indigant, Forsell demanded, "Where are the other 200,000 Swedes who are supposed to live in this city?" He was told, "They have gone to hear Glada Kalle." The rotund Kalle, a native of the rural Swedish province Dalarna, was a *bondkomiker,* or peasant comedian, who played the button accordion (Ericson 1978).

In the Scandinavian halls of Chicago, Rockford on the Illinois/Wisconsin border, and Minneapolis, rustic comic entertainers consistently outdrew urbane classical performers in the late nineteenth and early twentieth centuries. Wry songs concerning the misadventures of ethnic newcomers to America were their stock-intrade. Initially offered in some backwoods old-country dialect, these songs were increasingly rendered in the "yah shure" fractured English of Scandinavian Americans.

The most noted Scandinavian comic singer was Hjalmer Peterson (1886-1960). Born in Munkfors, Värmland, Sweden, Peterson emigrated to Minneapolis in 1906. He toiled briefly as a bricklayer before discovering his life's work as the bondkomiker "Olle i Skratthult" (Ole from Laughtersville).

> In his costume of squeaky boots, overcoat, long scarf, peasant cap with a big flower, and a blacked-out tooth under a straw-colored wig, Olle would recite poems in Värmland dialect, tell jokes, and sing comic songs. (Harvey and Hulan 1982)

Through the 1920s, Skratthult toured Swedish America with a company numbering as many as twenty. Besides Olle's obligatory comic antics, the program might include Leona Carlson, "the Swedish Nightingale," and Olga Lindgren, who, clad in folk costume, performed not only Swedish traditional songs and dances but also sentimental compositions like "Barndomshemmet" (My childhood home) that expressed the immigrant's longing for the old country. The

Skratthult troupe likewise offered humorous skits and full-length plays, the most ambitious of which, *Värmlänningarna* (The people from Värmland), was in six acts. Following the evening's formal program, chairs were cleared from the hall and Skratthult's orchestra played for a dance (Harvey 1983).

Olle i Skratthult's fame as the leader of a touring company was greatly assisted by his success as a recording artist. Between 1914 and 1929 Skratthult made roughly seventy recordings for Columbia and Victor (Spottswood 1990:2715-2718). His "Nikolina," a comic song about a father's opposition to his daughter's romance, was an enormous hit. Skratthult recorded it three times and it reportedly sold an unheard of one hundred thousand copies in a narrow ethnic market (Gronow 1977:13).

Unlike the Swedes, the Upper Midwest's Norwegians were found more frequently in rural than in urban environs. They could claim some barnstorming musical and theatrical troupes, like that led by Thorstein Skarning, but none to rival the fame of Skratthult. Skratthult's "Nikolina" was, nonetheless, absorbed by a pair of Norwegian-American brothers who added a dialect-inflected English translation to their rendition of the Scandinavian hit.

Singing Scandihoovians

Ernest and Clarence Iverson (born in 1903 and 1905) grew up in North Dakota and northern Minnesota. Their mother died in 1910 and they were raised with the help of an immigrant housekeeper, Molly Ruud, who taught the boys to play guitar and sing Norwegian songs. By the early 1920s Ernest had left home to work in the Dakotas' wheat harvest, travel with a carnival troupe, run a garage, and operate heavy equipment in the Texas oil fields. While in Texas, Iverson's lanky frame earned him the nickname Slim Jim. In Texas, he was also badly injured. Unable to do any heavy work, Iverson turned to music (Pine 1980).

By the early 1930s, after five years as a radio entertainer in Iowa, Nebraska, and South Dakota, Slim Jim found a home in Minneapolis where he was joined by brother Clarence, the erstwhile "Vagabond Kid," who had begun his radio career in Fargo, North Dakota, in 1929. From the mid-1930s through the 1940s, Slim Jim and the Vagabond Kid were among the most popular entertainers in the Twin Cities' expansive listening area. Their repertoire embraced cowboy songs, hymns, sentimental recitations, polkas, Molly Ruud's old country favorites, and, besides "Nikolina," a generous dose of such comic Norsky dialect songs as "Johnson's Wedding," its sequel "Name It after Me," "When I Pumped the Organ for Tina," "Scandinavian Hot Shot," "The Vistling Drifting Snow," "I Ban a Swede from Nort Dakota," and "Ay Don't Give a Hoot." The latter pair of songs tap larger reservoirs of Scandinavian dialect tradition.

Circulating in oral tradition at least as early as 1900, the variously titled "Swede from North Dakota" shares plot elements, themes, and a stereotypical itinerant Scandinavian working man with a probably earlier song, "Ole Olson the Hobo from Norway." Bruce Bollerud of the Goose Island Ramblers learned his version in the 1930s from Roy Anderson and Bert Vinje, Norwegian immigrant hired men on the Bollerud farm in Hollandale, Wisconsin. But the song of wandering Ole has been attributed to Norwegian loggers in Wisconsin as early as 1877, and it was certainly widely known by the 1890s (Folstad 1987:34-35; Rickaby 1926: 220-221).

Dialect performers in western garb, (L-R) the Vagabond Kid and Slim Jim, postcard, 1930s
Wisconsin Folk Museum Collection

While comic Scandinavian dialect songs probably first emerged in oral tradition, they were eventually penned by professional songwriters. In the early twentieth century, tunesmiths in New York City's Tin Pan Alley sought hits by writing songs in contrived versions of African-American, Irish, Yiddish, and other dialects. "Holy Yumpin' Yiminy," produced in 1918 by the team of Grossman, Morton, and Vincent, was one such composition. In it Hilda, the stereotypical Swedish maid, boasts about her equally typecast beau, "Yohnny Yohnsson."

> Now if you look at Yohnny's picture
> You might think he's slow,
> But he seems to know
> 'Bout cows and everything...
> Oh! Holy Yumpin' Yiminy,
> How my Yohnny can love!

(Harvey 1981 P)

"Ay Don't Give a Hoot," which has been sung for the past half century by nearly everyone who has dabbled in Scandinavian dialect songs, was likewise widely popularized by an urban pseudo-Scandinavian, Harry Stewart. In the guise of "Yogi Yorgeson," Stewart made numerous dialect records in the late 1940s for Capitol Records. One of them, "Ay Yust Go Nuts at Christmas," sold a million copies in 1948 (Gronow 1982:25).

"Ay Yust Go Nuts" and other Yorgeson Yuletide sendups continue to be heard at Christmastime on upper midwestern radio stations. Indeed they share the airwaves with more recent compositions like Red Stangland's "O Lutefisk" and the Minnesota Scandinavian Ensemble's "I'll Be Home for Lefse." The persistence of such performances on radio and their association with regional notions of Christmas suggest that Scandinavian dialect songs will continue to be part of musical life in the Upper Midwest for quite some time.

Chapter 14

Ole in Dairyland: Scandiavian Ethnic Humor

Program 14 Performances

1. Jimmy Jenson, "I Left My Heart in Minneapolis." 2. Stan Boreson, "Chickens in a Sack." 3. E. C. "Red" Stangland, "Telling Jokes to Scandinavians." 4. Edwin Pearson, "Comparative Banking." 5. E. C. "Red" Stangland, "The Escaped Kangaroo." 6. Charles Widden, "Lutfisk." 7. Red Stangland and Uncle Torvald, "O Lutefisk." 8. John Berquist, "Hilda, O Hilda." 9. Oljanna Venden Cunneen, "Ole Meets Lena" and "Ole Goes to Church." 10. Olson Sisters, "The Ladies' Aid." 11. Anonymous, "Money for the Church." 12. John Berquist, "Three Uncles." 13. Stan Boreson, "The Yanitor's Tale." 14. Arnold Johnson, "Ay Don't Give a Hoot."

O Lutefisk

Of all the European ethnic groups that settled in the Upper Midwest, Scandinavians figure the most prominently in regional humor. Gift shops, hardware stores, and restaurants in such Norwegian and Swedish communities as Stoughton, Mount Horeb, Westby, Osseo, and Grantsburg, Wisconsin; Spring Grove, Minneapolis, Chisago City, and Duluth, Minnesota; and Decorah, Iowa, all carry jokebooks, buttons, bumper stickers, and novelties stressing Scandinavian jocularity and foolishness. And on local streets, folks have told each other funny ethnic stories for well over a century.

The earliest Scandinavian-American humor derived from the confusion of immigrant tongues with English. Einar Haugen, the Norwegian-American linguist, commented on the presence of "many good-natured stories ... about the use of English in Norwegian contexts" (Haugen 1969:66-67). Some offered an "exaggerated mixture," as in the case of a man from Waterloo Ridge, Iowa,

> who used English and Norwegian words side by side, e.g. "Dæ sprang en hårrå-ræbbit åver råden-trækken-væien; så bynte filleponien kikkespænne-slå" (A *hårrå*-rabbit ran across the road-track-*væi*; then the good-for-nothing pony began to kick-*spenne-slå)*.

While largely impenetrable to monolingual English speakers, such babel delighted immigrant Norwegians.

The bilingual pun figured more commonly in humorous anecdotes, however, since a fair number of Norwegian words with one set of meanings coincided with English words signifying things quite different. The Norwegian use of *barn* for child resulted in such comic misunderstandings as "in America they paint all the 'children' red." The English "grease," meanwhile, is homophonic with the Norwegian *gris,* or pig. When a Yankee farmer told the Norsky hired man to grease the wagon, he came back with a pig in his arms.

While bilingual puns are less common today, a humorous regard for lutefisk flourishes among Nordic and Anglo-Americans alike. In the nineteenth century dried cod was standard winter fare for immigrants, who soaked the board-stiff fillets in a brine including lye, then rinsed and boiled them to enjoy with *grot* (a cream pudding) and *lefse* (a pliant potato-bread resembling the tortilla). Possessing a strong odor and a gelatinous texture, lutefisk inspires powerful emotions among the immigrants' descendants. Some reject it outright as that dreadful-smelling stuff Uncle Ole used to eat, while others consider its annual consumption as an ethnic badge of courage. As Red Stangland put it in a recent song:

> O lutefisk, now I suppose
> I'll eat you as I hold my nose.
>
> (Stangland 1979:48)

The comic aspects of lutfisk were well established by the early twentieth century when Charles Lindholm authored and produced *The Man from Minnesota,* starring himself as "Charlie Lutfisk," for the Upper Midwest's vaudeville stage. Meanwhile the Swedish singer and dialect comedian Charles Widden recorded a string of codfish jokes as "Lutfisk (The yule fish)" on the Victor label in 1922. The fish's properties even entered into the Wisconsin legislature's debates in 1982. Opponents of a bill requiring businesses to alert workers to the presence of hazardous substances in the workplace remarked facetiously that churches "would have to comply with the law in order to hold their traditional fall lutefisk dinners, since the prepared fish contains lye" (M. Miller 1991). A pair of Norwegian-American legislators introduced an amendment, which narrowly passed, making it plain that the term "toxic substance does not mean lutefisk." Wags in the general public responded with buttons and bumper stickers mimicking the National Rifle Association: "Legalize Lutefisk" and "When Lutefisk Is Outlawed, Only Outlaws Will Have Lutefisk." At the decade's end, others parodied first lady Nancy Reagan's anti-drug sloganeering: "Lutefisk. Just say no."

Ole and Lena

While gags regarding lutefisk are one hallmark of Scandinavian-American humor, the characters Ole and Lena are another. The youthful Norwegian and Swedish "newcomers" who arrived in the Upper Midwest in the final decades of the nineteenth century found work chiefly as laborers. Men toiled in the woods, on Great Lakes vessels, and on farms; women served typically as "maids" and "hired girls." Their foibles and misadventures spawned corresponding humorous narrative.

Circulating first in oral tradition, they eventually found their way into jokebooks like George T. Springer's *Yumpin' Yiminy: Scandinavian Dialect Selections.*

Yump, Ole, Yump

In Escanaba, Michigan, they tell the story of Ole and Yon who agreed to meet at the dock to take the ferry to the Eagle's picnic at Maywood. As the time of departure drew near, Yon became uneasy at the failure of Ole to appear and board the ferry. The gangplank was pulled in and the ferry was slowly leaving when Ole, all out of breath, approached the edge of the dock. Yon,

A typical Norwegian-American lumberjack. Engraving by Norman Borchardt
Reprinted from Bercovici 1925

> excited and anxious that Ole get aboard, cried out: "Yump, Ole, yump. Ay tank ju can mak et in two yumps."
>
> (Springer 1932:32)

While Ole the lumberjack and hired man has been the predominant male figure in Scandinavian jokes for more than a century, his female counterpart in early collections like Springer's is more often Tillie the maid. Lena's position as Ole's consort has grown, however, over the past few decades, at least partly through the efforts of Eider Clifford ("Red") Stangland.

Red Stangland, born in 1923 in Hetland, South Dakota, was a radio station operator when he launched the Norse Press in 1973 with the publication of *Norwegian Jokes* (Stangland 1979; Wood 1990). *Uff da jokes, Son of Norwegian Jokes,* and *Grandson of Norwegian Jokes* followed, as did five volumes of *Ole and Lena Jokes.* Like Charlie Lutefisk, Charles Widden, George T. Springer, and many others, Stangland is the latest, but probably not the last, of a long line of Scandinavian-American dialect comedians who have entertained Upper Midwesterners through a succession of performances, recordings, and publications.

Chapter 15

Finnish-American Music in Superiorland

Program 15 Performances
1. Hugo Maki, "Itin Tiltu." 2. Viola Turpeinen and John Rosendahl, "Viulu polkka." 3. Leo Kauppi, "Villi ruusu." 4. Walt Johnson, "Villi ruusu." 5. Hiski Salomaa, "Lannen lokkari." 6. Oulu Hotshots, "Sakki jarven polkka." 7. Oulu Hotshots, "Maailman Matti." 8. Bobby Aro, "Highway Number 7." 9. Oulu Hotshots, "Raatikko."

The Finnish-American Homeland

From the 1880s through the first two decades of the twentieth century, more than three hundred thousand Finns emigrated to the United States, where jobs could be found chiefly in mills, mines, factories, fisheries, and lumber camps. Roughly half were drawn to the Lake Superior region, settling in the western half of Michigan's Upper Peninsula, across Wisconsin's northern counties, and throughout northern Minnesota. When they could buy land, many scratched out an existence on small farms.

These settlers and their offspring, like other newcomers to America, continued their old-country musical traditions. Hymns and social dance music were performed in homes, but institutions that fostered music were thriving by the 1920s. Suomi Synod Lutheran churches, allied with Finland's state church, established choirs, while members of the charismatic Finnish Apostolic Lutheran Church composed new hymns and adapted American gospel songs. Temperance societies and socialists built halls where musical plays and social dances were common. Cooperative stores sold musical instruments and, eventually, phonographs and Finnish-American recordings. Meanwhile ethnic newspapers advertised and reported on musical events.

The Girl Played like a Heavenly Bell

Finnish-American social dance musicians and singers took particular advantage of this institutional infrastructure. Foremost among them was Viola Turpeinen, who dominated Finnish-American musical life from the mid-1920s until her death in 1958, and whose legacy persists. Viola Irene Turpeinen was born November 15, 1909, in Champion, Michigan, west of Ishpeming, the eldest of Walter and Signe Wiitala Turpeinen's four daughters. Like many men of his generation, Walter Turpeinen was a miner, who followed his occupation to Iron River, Michigan, shortly after Viola's birth.

Portions of this essay are drawn from J. P. Leary, 1990, "The Legacy of Viola Turpeinen," Finnish Americana *8:6-11. With permission.*

Both Walter and Signe played the *kaks rivinen,* or two-row button accordion, an instrument popularized in Finland in the late nineteenth century. Viola soon learned to push-pull a melody and by her early teens she had graduated to the more expensive, versatile, and prestigious piano accordion. She was soon entertaining locally at both the Finnish Labor Hall and the Italians' Bruno Hall. In 1925 sixteen-year-old Viola attracted the attention of John Rosendahl, a musician and concert promoter. With her father traveling along as chaperon, she set off for the Duluth/Superior area on the first of many tours.

By 1927 Turpeinen and Rosendahl shifted their base of operations to New York City. As an eastern port, New York was America's closest link to Finland, a place from which to embark on tours and a conduit for news from the old country. The city's Finnish-American population supported several halls where Turpeinen and Rosendahl found regular employment as part of a company of entertainers offering plays, concerts, and dances. New York was also home to large record companies like Columbia and Victor, which began actively recording ethnic-American musicians in the late 1920s.

In January 1928, Viola Turpeinen and John Rosendahl recorded six numbers for Victor: three waltzes, two polkas, and a schottische, with Viola on accordion and John trading off on violin and banjo. The first record from that session, "Emma valssi" backed with "Kauhavan polkka," was released in May 1928 and reissued two years later. "Kauhavan polkka" is among the pair's most memorable collaborations: a searing, typically fast-paced Finnish polka, with accordion and violin interweaving relentlessly as if to push one another to the border between deft articulation and abandon; the kind of tune that reminds one that fiddlers of legend acquire their powers from the devil, and that accordionists sometimes work their instruments until the bellows pull apart. Over the next three years, Turpeinen and Rosendahl recorded four duets for Columbia and nine for Victor, while Viola cut five accordion solos for Victor.

Viola Turpeinen continued to record until the early 1950s with a number of different musicians, including her eventual husband William Syrjala of Cloquet, Minnesota, and Sylvia Polso of the Ironwood/Hurley area. Although she never again lived in the Upper Midwest, later moving from New York City to Lake Worth, Florida, Turpeinen returned on annual tours. Newspaper accounts, like this one written in Sault Sainte Marie, Michigan, in 1931, describe the sort of program that was typical of that era's ethnic-American vaudeville circuit.

> Following a musical number by Miss Turpeinen and Miss Polso on the accordions, and Mr. Rosendahl on the violin, slides of Finland were shown. A scene showing the harvest time in Finland seemed very similar to pictures of the Canadian West during harvest time, and showed the similarity of the methods used in both countries. Mr. Rosendahl explained each scene, in Finnish, as it appeared on the screen.
>
> Miss Turpeinen and Miss Polso both gave solos on the accordion, which drew hearty applause from the audience, which demanded encores. Miss Turpeinen, who is well known here through former appearances, is one of the Victor record artists and has made many popular records.
>
> Mr. Rosendahl, on the violin, played an old folk song, and gave a very humorous speech. Another solo by Miss Turpeinen which was very well

Reino Maki playing the button accordion, Washburn, 1979 **Photo: Matthew Gallmann**

> received concluded the first part of the program.
>
> After the intermission, during which coffee was served by the ladies, dancing was enjoyed until midnight, the music being furnished by the three visitors. (Polso n.d.)

It was the dancing "until midnight" that lives on in the memories of those who were there and in the imagination of more than a few who were not. Indeed reminiscent sessions on Turpeinen have become a part of the annual gathering of Finnish Americans, Finn Fest.

Viola Turpeinen was a "local girl" who left the Upper Midwest for New York City, was lauded in newspaper advertisements as a "Victor Recording Artist," and was acclaimed on musical tours to Finland. Yet she always returned to the region of her youth. In the late twentieth century, upper midwestern Finns Oren Tikkanen and Al Reko continue to perform Antti Syrjaniemi's 1928 celebration of a Turpeinen dance.

> Seldom have people danced the polka at such speed;
> Seldom have people stepped more rapidly.
> When grandmas asked grandpas for a break,
> They say they were already wet with sweat.
> And the girl played like a heavenly bell,
> Hittan tila tila hittantaa.
> And farmers danced like mowers making hay in the fields.
> Hittan tila tila hittantaa.
>
> (Reko and Tikkanen P; Syrjaniemi 1928 P)

Al Reko and dozens of Finnish-American accordionists still hear the "heavenly bell" of Turpeinen's accordion and their hands ring out her tunes.

The Oulu Hotshots of Bayfield County, Wisconsin, carry on Viola Turpeinen's musical legacy as well as any. Named for the northernmost province of Finland, Oulu was once the most densely settled agricultural community in Wisconsin (Kolehmainen and Hill 1951:53). By the 1920s, Oulu's Finnish settlers had raised a crop of accordion players and built several Finnish halls. Walter and Ailie Johnson, who first saw Turpeinen play in Oulu in 1925, began entertaining at local dances in the 1930s (Johnson 1988 I).

When they began slowing down in the 1970s, the Oulu Hotshots—Bill Kangas and Glen and LeRoy Lahti—were coming into their own. Although the accordion-playing Lahti brothers were born after Viola Turpeinen's death, their father, Rodney, encouraged them to play her music. He has never forgotten Turpeinen's summer visits to northern Wisconsin. "It was like heaven going to her dances" (Lahti 1988 I).

Chapter 16

Green Fields of Wisconsin: Irish Music in the Badger State

Program 16 Performances

1. Paddy O'Brien, "The Lament for Eoin Rhua." 2. J.W. Green, "Skibbereen." 3. Patrick Bonner, "The Maid of Kildare." 4. Charles Bannen, "Pat Malone." 5. Tommy McDermott, "The Walsh Dancers" and "Tom's Polka." 6. Boxty, "Hammy Hamilton's Jigs." 7. Tom Dahill, "The Newry Highwayman." 8. Liz and Kevin Carroll, "Hare's Paw" and "Castle Kelly."

Rebel Songs and Sentiment

When my dad, Warren Leary, was a boy in Rice Lake, Wisconsin, in the 1920s, he would often crank the Victrola for his Irish grandmother. She would listen to John McCormack sing "Mother Macree" in his unmatched tenor voice and tears would stream down her cheeks. My mother, Patricia Berigan Leary, delighted each St. Patrick's Day as her grandfather, John Berigan, sang a nineteenth-century ballad, "The Wearing of the Green," likewise popularized by McCormack.

Born in Athlone, Ireland, and trained in Italy in the bel canto tradition, McCormack dazzled American audiences during concert tours between 1909 and 1912. His numerous recordings on Victor's classical Red Seal label included the still popular "When Irish Eyes Are Smiling" and "Danny Boy" (Moloney 1982).

When I was a kid in the 1950s, the old John McCormack 78s had long since been worn out, lost, or broken. It was the Irish-American pop crooner Morton Downey who enchanted me with "It's the Same Old Shillelagh," "Galway Bay," and even "Who Put the Overalls in Mrs. Murphy's Chowder." These songs of rambunctious foolery, of rebellion, of sentimental longing immediately captured my ethnic imagination.

But apart from the voices spun in studios, I wondered about the music of my region's Irish immigrants. And so I paid attention when our old Irish neighbor, George Russell, talked of Irish singers in the lumber camps and of Red Donnelly, the Irish fiddler who enlivened Barron County barn dances at the turn of the century. There were others who told much the same story.

Shanty and Stage

The Irish immigrants who came to the Upper Midwest as miners, laborers, farmers, and loggers in the nineteenth century brought a rich tradition of singing and fiddling. One of the earliest accounts, although set down much later, is the reminiscence of Catherine Woodlawn, fictionalized by Carol Ryrie Brink in her classic children's novel *Caddie Woodlawn* (1935). It concerns life along northwestern Wisconsin's Red Cedar River in the 1860s.

Robert Ireton, the Woodlawn's Irish hired man, is presented by Brink as a hardworking fellow who was always ready with a song. His repertoire was mostly comic and included classics like "Leather Britches"—in which Paddy Haggerty feeds some gluttonous roisterers with a "leather burgoo"—as well as a set of verses that are still sung to the tune of "The Irish Washerwoman."

> Say, Ike, did ye ever go into an Irishman's shanty?
> Sure, it's there where the whiskey is plenty.
> With his pipe in his gob, is Paddy so gay,
> No king in his palace so happy as he.
> There's a three-legged stool and a table to match,
> And the door of the shanty it hooks with a latch.
> There's a pig in the sty and a cow in the stable,
> And, sure, they are fed of the scraps from the table.

This song's portrait of the happy-go-lucky shanty Irishman with his whiskey, his pipe, and his pig in the parlor was extremely common in nineteenth-century America when Irish immigrants left their famine-stricken homeland. Indeed "stage Irish" performers—outfitted with red wigs, green suits, whiskey jugs, and a blackthorn cudgel—held forth as tent show and vaudeville "Paddies" until the early twentieth century.

The songs associated with them were sung far more widely and for a longer period. While a few Irish regarded them as slander-set-in-verse, most considered stage Irish songs as simply a bit of exaggerated fun—certainly not to be mistaken for vicious stereotypes that cast the Irish as superstitious and bestial slaves of popery. In the 1920s when Franz Rickaby traveled northern Wisconsin in search of lumber-camp ballads, he encountered comic Irish singers and declared, "the hegemony in song belongs to the Irish" (Rickaby 1926:xxv). In the 1940s when Helene Stratman-Thomas sought folk songs throughout Wisconsin, she was rewarded with "Miss Fogarty's Christmas Cake," "Pat Malone," and a half dozen other humorous gems chronicling feasting, tippling, music, pugnacity, and shenanigans (Peters 1977). In the 1970s when Philip Bohlman recorded Charles Bannen, an octogenarian Crawford County dairy farmer, he found that Miss Fogarty's inedible confection and Pat Malone's whiskey-drenched insurance scam were still the stuff of songs (Bohlman 1980).

Rosin the Bow

Besides singing, Charles Bannen played the pump organ, sometimes chording for such fiddlers as old Dean Powers. Irish fiddlers, like Irish singers, commanded audiences in the homes, boweries, and lumber camps of the nineteenth century. Patrick Bonner (1882–1973) is perhaps the most eminent of the Upper Midwest's Irish fiddlers. A descendant of County Donegal immigrants, Bonner lived on Beaver Island in northern Lake Michigan where he played for dances from his early teens until his mid-seventies.

There were many Irish fiddlers on the island when Bonner was young. He learned tunes from them, but a fair number came from the "mouth music" or "lilting" of

Larry Drea tending bar at his tavern, Loretto, 1991 ***Photo: Jim Leary***

"an old lady," Kathleen O'Donnell McCauley, who knew "them old Irish reels." Field recordings of Bonner, made between 1938 and 1952, captured eighty-five tunes, including such Irish numbers as "Blackthorn Stick," "Boys of Arranmore," "Connaught Man's Rambles," "Flanigan's Ball," "Green Fields of America," "The Maid of Kildare," "Paddy's Going Away," and "Rocky Road to Dublin" (Hendrix 1988).

Tom Croal was Wisconsin's most noted Irish fiddler. Croal's parents, John and Catherine, immigrated from Ireland to the rural Hill Point area of Sauk County in 1856. Thomas, the third of eight children, was probably born in the 1860s and was certainly in his eighties in 1944, when journalist Fred Holmes called him "The Last of the Irish Bards." A railroad worker and labor organizer, Croal spent time in St. Louis and Milwaukee, winning an old-time fiddlers' contest in the beer city in 1926 *(Milwaukee Sentinel,* January 23, 1926).

He was best known and is still remembered in rural Sauk County, however. I listened to accounts of Croal's St. Patrick's Day fiddling at Drea's Tavern in Loretto in 1991, just as, a decade earlier, Phil Martin learned from locals like Jim Fargen that Croal played for events throughout the area:

> I remember once they were building a house, and they had a big dirt pile from digging out the basement, and Tom climbed up on it and started fiddling from the top, and the yard was packed with people. They couldn't dance because it was so crowded. But Tom put on quite a concert for them. He was a talented musician, not one of these rough fiddlers. He played all the old songs, and sang the verses. (Martin ca. 1980)

When Croal died, the tunes and songs went with him.

The performance of Irish music dwindled with the passing of the immigrants' children. From the 1940s until the 1980s, with the exception of a few elderly athome exponents like Charles Bannen, Irish music was confined to phonograph records. But it was not forgotten. The recent revival of traditional Irish music in Ireland and throughout Irish America has coaxed a modest resurgence in the Upper Midwest. St. Paul, Milwaukee, Madison, and Chicago currently boast Irish music "scenes," with active bands, "Irish bars," and annual festivals.

No longer an integral part of everyday home and community life, Irish music has become an overt means of celebrating Irish ethnicity, especially on St. Patrick's Day. Meanwhile the beauty of the music has attracted many non-Irish enthusiasts. The small but dedicated numbers of young players and singers suggest that Irish music in the Upper Midwest may enter its third century.

Chapter 17

From Mazo Pust to Cesky Den: Czech and Slovak Music in Wisconsin

Program 17 Performances
1. Yuba Bohemian Band, "Wedding Tune." 2. She and He Haugh Band, "City of Yuba Polka." 3. Joe and John Tomesh, "Louka zelena." 4. Vera Dvorak Schultz, "Ivanek naš." 5. Jerry Novak, "Sli panenki." 6. Moquah Slovak Singers, "Bodaj by vas." 7. Albert Wachuta, "Koline, Koline." 8. Straight Eight Bohemian Band, Chorus (Charles Pelnar, John Pelnar, Bill Slatky, Louis Kasal), "Svestkova alej." 9. Straight Eight Bohemian Band, "V zahrade." 10. Mayme Doser and Mrs. Frank Stevens, "Kdyr jsem šel čestičkou surkou." 11. Victor Kuchera and Dolly Petruzalek, "Do lestička na cekanou." 12. Phillips Czech Singers, "Cočovička."

Ceska America

Czech immigrants settled Wisconsin in the 1860s, establishing homesteads along the lower Wisconsin River and, subsequently, on the western shore of Lake Michigan in the Manitowoc vicinity. The early twentieth century saw a second wave of Czech Americans—Pennsylvania miners, Chicago factory hands, Cedar Rapids packing house workers, Nebraska sandhill farmers—seek logged-off land in such northern Wisconsin communities as Haugen, Moquah, and Phillips. Sometimes called Bohemians, after the German name for the western province of present-day Czech Republic, Wisconsin's Czechs were joined by smaller numbers of Slovaks, some of whom found their way to northern Wisconsin, though more came to Milwaukee's industrial valley.

The Czechs of the greater Manitowoc area have contributed a remarkable number of dance bands to the Upper Midwest's musical mix (see the related essay in chapter 18, "The Manitowoc Bohemian Sound"). Although such bands—led by Romy Gosz, Joe Karman, Rudy Plocar, and others—created Wisconsin's Bohemian polka sound in ballrooms and on radio, less renowned but still significant musicians and singers carried on the ethnic traditions that have led to a proliferation of late-twentieth-century Czech and Slovak festivals throughout rural Wisconsin.

The Czechs who settled within reach of the lower Wisconsin River extended old-world sociability through house parties, community bands, and the celebration of life cycle and seasonal events. As a young farm boy, Prairie du Chien's Albert Wachuta (b. 1875) learned songs "mostly from my mother, but some from other people too because in them days there was a lot of Bohemian singing" (Leary 1987b:48). When Helene Stratman-Thomas recorded Wachuta, Mayme Doser, and Mrs. Frank Stevens in 1941, they were still singing, but they lamented the loss of many old-timers.

Brass Bands and Burnt Cork

Stratman-Thomas also found a Bohemian brass band in Yuba, Richland County, in 1946. It had been organized in 1868 by Martin Rott Sr., a Czech immigrant. Besides his own bass horn, the band included Martin's brothers, Wencil and Frank, on clarinet and baritone horn, as well as Frank Novy Sr. on violin, Mathew Picha on cornet, and Michael Dedrick and Wencil Pilner on clarinets. Eventually peopled by many more Rotts, a large contingent of Staneks, and others, the Yuba Bohemian Band persisted until at least 1954 (Levy 1987). The band provided solemn marches for funeral processions, but specialized in playing for weekend dances, weddings, Fourth of July celebrations, and that two-day pre-Lenten gala, *maso pust*.

Literally translated "without meat," Maso Pust is the Czech equivalent of Mardi Gras. As a young boy, Martin Rott's great-grandson Raymond Liska (b. 1913) celebrated Maso Pust much in the manner of his ancestor. When farmers finished their chores on the Monday prior to Ash Wednesday, they changed into costumes and took their teams to Robert Novy's Yuba Opera House. Just before midnight the maskers would parade around so that judges could pick the best costumes. Those with cows returned the next night after barn chores; those without might celebrate all day. House-to-house visiting was common as well, with crowds feasting on pastries, sweet-and-sour cabbage, and pork. At midnight Tuesday, however, the music would cease and revelers would blacken one another's faces with burnt cork in parodic anticipation of the ashen crosses priests would make on foreheads in the morning, Ash Wednesday (Liska 1991 I; Barden 1982).

The old way of celebrating Maso Pust went into decline with Robert Novy's death in 1956, although the celebration has been carried on in turn by his son-in-law and daughter (Adolph and Marcella Novy Levy), and by their son-in-law and daughter (David Moen and Darlene Levy Moen). The Yuba Opera House is known nowadays as the D&D Pub. Burnt corks at midnight are abandoned, the dance has shifted from weekdays to the weekend prior to Lent, the numbers in costume have diminished, and the band comes from out of town (Kallio 1987). Maso Pust persists, but it is much transformed and is no longer the focal point for Czech ethnicity in the community.

In 1983, the Richland County Czechs of Yuba and nearby Hillsboro initiated *cesky den* (Czech day). Held on a Saturday in mid-June, Cesky Den is typical of festivals that emerged out of the ethnic revival coinciding with America's bicentennial. Unlike Maso Pust, which in its heyday was an event by and for locals, Cesky Den is widely advertised so as to attract a substantial crowd of outsiders-some of them Czech, most of them not. Part generic community festival, the event has involved performances by the high school swing choir, the building of a "100-foot banana split" by the Fire Department Auxiliary, arts and crafts, and a king and queen contest. Its chief focus, however, is on aspects of Czech culture. Local participants wear Czech costumes and prepare Czech food. They also sing, dance, and play music, thereby reenacting the old-world traditions sustained by Prairie du Chien's Czechs and by Yuba's Martin Rott and Robert Novy.

Joe and John Tomesh playing a Czech tune while their brothers and sisters—(L-R) Tony Tomesh, Lilian Dvorak, Dorothy Schwab, Albert Tomesh—look on, Haugen, 1990 ***Photo: Jim Leary***

The 1986 event included three musical elements that harken to the events favored by earlier generations. They are also elements that have become standard in festivals inspired by the ethnic revival: (1) an open microphone for musicians, (2) a performance by costumed singers and dancers, and (3) a dance/concert with a band that emphasizes an old-world repertoire.

More specifically, Hillsboro's Czech Music jamboree, with its open microphone and three-song limit, echoed the informal give-and-take of the old-time house party. Old-timers who had kept up their skills on the accordion or concertina played Czech dance tunes, while an occasional youngster sang a song learned from grandma or from a class in Czech heritage. The more formal presentations of the Hillsboro and Yuba Czech Singers—with their ethnic garb, songbooks, and squeezebox accompaniment—recalled both the musical programs of Czech fraternal halls and the costumed Maso Pust gala. Finally the She and He Haugh Band—a full brass and reed band consisting mostly of high school band veterans—invoked the old Yuba Bohemian Band with its conscious articulation of an "authentic" old-world sound.

Czech and Slovak Americans, their neighbors, and thousands of tourists can share such musical evocations of ethnicity by attending the Hillsboro festival each summer, or by traveling to Haugen, Moquah, and Phillips, where similar festivals occur. Although clearly modern departures from the more localized and private traditions of immigrants and their offspring, these regionally promoted public events nonetheless refer to the ethnic musical past while displaying its present.

Chapter 18

The Manitowoc Bohemian Sound

Program 18 Performances
1. Romy Gosz, "Ja mam kocoura (Tomcat polka)." 2. Tuba Dan and the Polkalanders, "Narrow Path." 3. Jerome Wojta (1988 I), "Svestkova alej." 4. Romy Gosz, "Svestkova alej." 5. Lawrence Duchow, "Red Raven Polka." 6. Sax Steiner, "Flying Dutchman." 7. Jerome Wojta and the Two Creeks Farmhands, "Tinker Polka." 8. Larry Hlinak, "Squeekers Polka." 9. Harold Schultz, "Louka zelena."

Bands, Parks, and Parades

Jerome Wojta's little band is called the Two Creeks Farmhands. If he were of another nationality, or from another region, one might expect him to be a fiddler, a banjo player, perhaps a guitarist, but this Czech-American farmer is from Manitowoc County, and the instrument he plays in his rural dance combo is the trumpet. Wojta emulates the style of local legend Romy Gosz. He has vivid memories of country dances where everyone was there "from the grandchild to the grandpa and grandma," where dancers swirled to the piercing trumpet and biting reedy clarinet like "big waves on the sea" (Wojta 1988 I)

Of all the musical traditions that the Czechs of east central Wisconsin brought with them from their homeland, they have nurtured none more lovingly than their brass and woodwind dance bands. Band music was all the rage in central Europe in the second half of the nineteenth century, when numerous Czech immigrants settled on farms in Manitowoc and Kewaunee counties. Like their many German-American neighbors, the Czechs, following central European custom, put considerable effort into forming local town bands to march in parades and perform afternoon concerts in park gazebos.

Town bands were requisites of civilized life; even crossroads hamlets in farming communities like Pilsen in Kewaunee County and Yuba, farther west in Richland County, had them. Czech composer Frantisek Kmoch, internationally celebrated as the Czechoslovak March King, inspired Czech Americans with his marches, waltzes, and patriotic anthems (Leary 1987a).

The early Czech brass bands typically had six or seven pieces. A pair of clarinets and one or two trumpets played melody parts, the brass and reeds taking turns as the lead voice. A pair of peckhorns (alto or baritone horns with an upright bell) played the rhythm on the weak beats, and a tuba played the steady downbeat and the bottom anchor.

The most influential band, the Pilsen Brass Band from Pilsen, started in 1910. Joe Altman was the leader and trumpet player, and Wencil Janda and George Sladky were the clarinetists, Janda playing the high-pitched E♭ clarinet. Three players were responsible for the oompah rhythm: Mike Suess and Mike Nejedlo on alto and baritone peckhorns and Frank Schleis on tuba (Janda 1976). Traveling by horse and buggy and by sleigh in heavy winter snows, the Pilsen band was extremely popular, and not only with the Czechs. The local Germans, Belgians, and Poles loved the music as well. According to one report, they were known to play as many as sixty dates in a row before having a night off! The music of very few town bands has been recorded. Fortunately, some examples of the Pilsen band's music have survived. They were recorded for the Library of Congress in 1940, by University of Wisconsin music professor Helene Stratman-Thomas.

If the Pilsen Brass Band was as much at home parading down Main Street with its old-time instruments as it was in the dance hall, other local bands, influenced by mainstream dance bands in the era from the teens through the thirties, used instruments which were more modern but sometimes less mobile. A piano, saxophones, and a trap set of drums became common in groups like the Dan Zahorik Band, Gloe-Naidl Orchestra, and Cy Urbanek's Players, while the Lyric Orchestra included a trombone, a banjo, and a xylophone.

While the core repertoire of these ensembles remained the locally popular polkas, waltzes, and landlers of Czech and German origin, some Manitowoc bands also began to play contemporary American music. Art and Regis Brault were two members of the Lyric Orchestra, a largely Bohemian aggregation. They formed their own band, naming it Brault's Canadiens to celebrate their French-Canadian roots. They exclusively played popular music and spent months at a time on tour in the southern states. Another successful Manitowoc-based road band whose repertoire all but eschewed old-time music was Tiny Laude's Orchestra. These early groups paved the way for the 1940s Manitowoc popular dance bands of Bob Mlada and Duke Janda.

Romy Gosz, Polka King

While the road bands sought wider success by adopting modern music, it is ironic that the Manitowoc musician to achieve the most national acclaim was Romy Gosz, who stuck almost exclusively to the old-time sound. Gosz was born in 1910 in Rockwood, just north of Manitowoc. His musical precociousness is legendary. At the age of seven, Romy took his first piano lesson, but the following Saturday he notified his teacher, Mrs. Charles Kirchen, that he could not make it to the next lesson because he had to play for a dance.

In 1921, Romy's father Paul formed a unique entertainment combination, a family basketball team/dance band. Paul Gosz, along with sons Frank, Mike, George, and Romy, would play a local team and after the game would break out their instruments to make music for a social dance. This arrangement lasted until 1924 when Paul formed another band, Pauly's Playboys, leaving the boys on their own, under brother George's leadership. When George quit the band in 1928 to open a tavern, Romy took over at the tender age of seventeen.

Until 1931, Romy had been the band's pianist, but when a trumpet player was unavailable for a job, Romy switched to the horn that was to make him famous. Romy's piercing tone, iron lip, and prodigious volume became the trademark of the Gosz band. Romy's tone was so unmistakable that one of his sidemen once asserted, "In a twenty member trumpet section, you'd be able to pick him out" (Janda 1976). In the era before reliable amplification systems, Romy's band was able to play quite audibly in outdoor picnic groves and to jam-packed halls.

Romy Gosz (center with trumpet) and his band striking a barnyard pose amidst wedding festivities, Manitowoc area, 1950s ***Wisconsin Folk Museum Collection***

Romy had an uncanny ability to excite the big crowds without resorting to any flamboyant antics on the bandstand. The music itself conveyed such intensity that the dancers' spirits were lifted. But offstage Romy was known to cut up. At one point, he bought an old hearse to haul the band's equipment. It came complete with a siren and red flashing lights. Late one night, returning from a job, he tore through the little burg of Maribel, lights flashing and siren screaming. He quickly pulled in behind a tavern, went inside, and looked out the front window to see the locals run about trying to find out what the commotion was (Janda 1976).

Between 1933 and 1938 the Romy Gosz Orchestra recorded seventy-four sides for the Broadway, Decca, Okeh, Brunswick, and Columbia labels. His renditions of the best-known Czech folk tunes, like "Picnic in the Woods," "The 'Crying' Barbara Polka," and "Modre oci," became the definitive versions and many of his records featured incidental singing in the Czech language. It is another irony typical of ethnic sharing in rural Wisconsin that Romy was not Czech himself but of German-American background.

A humorous parody of one of his records has become a midwestern classic. In 1934, at a time when Gosz's waltz-tempo recording of the romantic Czech folk song "Svestkova alej" was very popular, the parody appeared. A *Milwaukee Journal* (April 9, 1945) article attributes its origin to the 1934 state American Legion convention, held in Green Bay. This ditty to the old Czech tune became widely known, competing even with "In Heaven There Is No Beer" as a favorite Wisconsin drinking song. Its new English lyrics:

> We left our wives at home,
> We left our wives at home,
> We left our wives with six other guys,
> We left our wives at home.

Years later, Romy recorded his own version of the parody.

More records were made in 1945 for Mercury. By then the wartime shellac shortage had eased. Pent up demand for his recordings was such that Mercury received eleven thousand orders for a Gosz recording, even before it was marketed.

Records brought national exposure and the Gosz band traveled as far as Texas, California, and New York, though they preferred to tour closer to home in the Midwest. Though national magazines like *Time* and *Coronet* declared him "the polka king" in the era prior to Frankie Yankovic's use of that title, Romy's most treasured recognition was a papal blessing from Pope Pius XII, given in recognition of his band's playing at the diamond jubilee celebration for St. Mary's Church in Tisch Mills (Ebner 1985 P).

Unfortunately, his musical success also had its dark side. Romy suffered from alcoholism. Like country music's Hank Williams, Romy Gosz was a brilliant and creative artist whose life ended much too early, in 1966 at age 55, owing to the deleterious effects of alcohol.

The Gosz legacy lives on. His son Tony kept the band going for a number of years, and after a hiatus the band is playing again with trumpeter Del Dassow, who many contend has an uncanny resemblance to Romy. His recordings are still popular and kept in print through the efforts of Greg Leider of Fredonia and his Polkaland record company. Moreover, numerous bands in the Manitowoc area and elsewhere in Wisconsin perpetuate his style. Tom Siebold's Brass Buttons, the Mark Jirikovec Band, the Harold Schultz Orchestra, the Bob Kuether Orchestra, the Larry Hlinak Band, Tuba Dan and the Polkalanders, and Jerome Wojta's Two Creeks Farmhands are some of the better-known bands actively playing the Gosz style in the 1990s.

Chapter 19

Wallonie en Porte: Door County Belgians

Program 19 Performances
1. Alfred Vandertie, "Nos-estans quites po l'Amérique"/"Au ciel i n'a pon.y bire." 2. Gladys Etienne Feron, "Mi feye, mi feye elle (av)ot frwed ses pids." 3. Alvina Fontaine, "Le jardin de Martin Plicotin." 4. Alfred Vandertie, "C'ést l'café, l'café" 5. Alfred Vandertie, "I Went to Market with a *pania volant.*" 6. Arthur "Zeke" Renard, "Dji m'fou d'ça." 7. Three Sharps, "Elle est byin trop crausse por mi." 8. Gene LeBotte, "Black Gypsy Waltz." 9. Ray Dorschner and the Rainbow Valley Dutchmen, "Kermiss Waltz." 10. Cletus Bellin, "La vieux gris caval."

Through Five Generations

On the southern end of Wisconsin's Door peninsula cluster small farm towns—Brussels, Rosiere, Namur, Duval, Missiere-dominated by century—old structures of brick fired from a local red clay. Their names as well as the predilection for brick attest to the local Belgian culture, which five generations have retained to an unusual degree.

While visiting an Antwerp tavern in 1852, a farmer from Brabant in central Belgium, Francois Petinoit, chanced to get hold of a pamphlet prepared by the then newly created Wisconsin Office of the Immigration Commissioner. The booklet was in Flemish and touted the availability of Wisconsin farmland for $1.25 an acre.

Belgium is the homeland of two distinct nationalities: the Flemish, whose language is closely related to Dutch, and the Walloons, who speak a French dialect. Petinoit, a Walloon who apparently could read and understand Flemish, convinced the heads of nine neighboring Brabant households to join him in founding a Wisconsin Walloon colony.

The colonists set out in May 1853, weathering seven stormy weeks at sea before finally settling on land in southern Door County. More Belgian immigrants followed, but by 1857 unfavorable reports of the hardships in the Wisconsin wilderness stemmed the tide of new arrivals. Nonetheless, natural growth eventually swelled the population of the Wisconsin Walloon colony to more than thirty thousand in Door and neighboring Kewaunee counties (Holmes 1944).

Fire destroyed the pioneer settlement of log buildings in October 1871; a thousand persons died and three thousand were left homeless. But the Walloons persevered, rebuilt in brick, and eventually prospered.

Through their good times and their trials, traditions have buoyed the Belgian community, especially religious traditions connected to their Catholic faith. A shrine at Robinsonville, known to the Walloons as Aux Premiers Belges, commemorates the apparition of the Blessed Virgin to a young Walloon, Adele Brice, in 1858. Well-attended processions are still held there on Rogation Day, in late May, to pray to the Virgin for abundant crops, and on Assumption Day, August 15, the anniversary of the apparition. But no holiday means more to the Wisconsin Walloons than the annual harvest festival, Kermiss, still celebrated in Rosiere and Brussels. In each town, on consecutive Sundays, after a special mass is celebrated in church, a procession with musicians moves down the street, pausing to dance in the dusty crossroads. Then, at a hall, the serious business of celebrating begins-dancing and consuming Walloon delicacies, especially the hundreds of Belgian pies prepared for the event. The Belgian prune and apple pies are unique. They contain custard and are topped with a thick layer of cottage cheese (Tlahac 1974).

Belgian pork sausages known as *trippe, kaset* (a seasoned and cured cottage cheese spread), and *jut* (a cabbage and potato concoction) are among the specialties. Nowadays, *booyah* (a thick chicken soup) is the best-known food symbolizing Belgian identity in Wisconsin. Booyah dinners at church halls and fireman's parks still raise funds for all sorts of charitable causes.

The Belgian fondness for traditional foods has been matched by their love of music, particularly the old Walloon songs. Although after five generations in America few fluent Walloon speakers are left, the Wisconsin Walloons nonetheless have produced some outstanding singers, several of whom were recorded for the Library of Congress in the 1940s. But for decades thereafter, Walloon singing received scant attention from outside the community.

Singing the Old Songs

In 1972, musicologist Francoise Lempereur journeyed from Belgium to northeastern Wisconsin. Her mission was to visit and record the traditional music of the far-flung colony of her compatriots. Upon her arrival in Green Bay, she set out for the rural Wisconsin village of Namur, the namesake of her home city. There she visited the Peninsula Belgian-American Club, meeting some of her own distant cousins in the process. When she inquired about singers of old Walloon songs, the club members directed her to their best singer: in the nearby port town of Algoma, tavern keeper Alfred Vandertie proved to be a song keeper as well (Vandertie 1989 I).

Alfred, who was born in 1911 on a dairy farm in southern Door County, spoke no English until he started school. The Walloon dialect of French was his first language. Alfred was always drawn to singing. During his childhood, singing was a constant part of socializing-around a farm kitchen table, in the church and church hall, on everyday occasions, and at grand feast days like the Kermiss harvest festival.

His taverns, at first in the rural crossroads town of Brussels and later in Algoma, were unofficial Walloon cultural centers. Until it closed in 1989, his Algoma bar had Belgian posters and crests and a large map of Belgium covering its walls. Interactions with his customers were occasions to learn and sing in the Walloon tradition. Francoise Lempereur recorded him and other Wisconsin Walloon

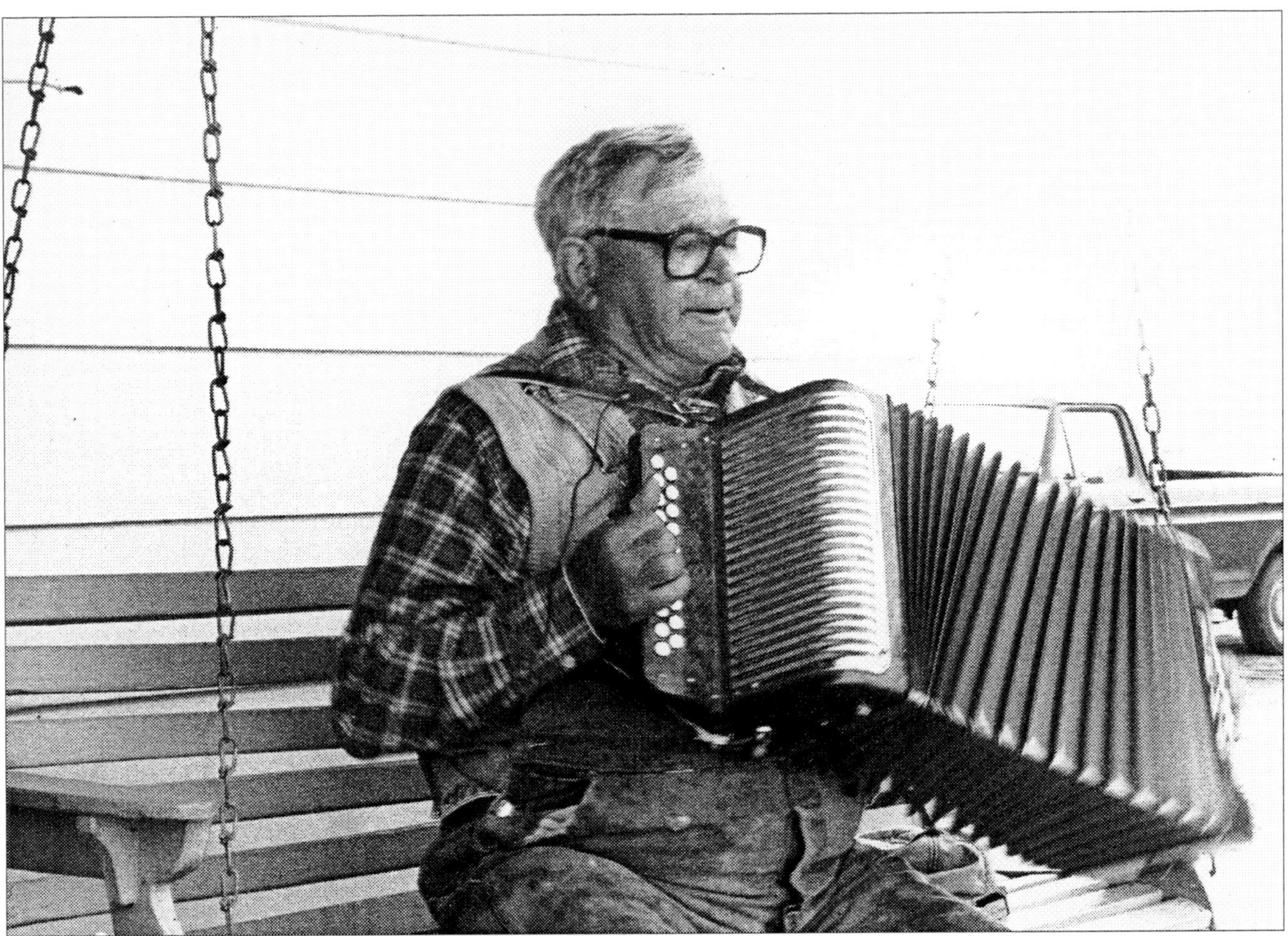

Arthur "Zeke" Renard, Duval, 1989 **Photo: Jim Leary**

singers, and back in Belgium produced radio programs and a record album of their songs. Alfred's powerful voice, acute pitch, and prodigious memory have made him admired in Belgium, where in the late 1970s he visited and had a chance to perform, and in Washington, D.C., where he appeared at the Festival of American Folklife in 1976, America's bicentennial. In 1989 he performed in a concert in Green Bay which was broadcast statewide over Wisconsin Public Radio to commemorate the anniversary of the "Simply Folk" folk music program.

There remain only a few younger fluent Walloon speakers, like Cletus Bellin, born in 1944, who also can sing the old songs. In instrumental music, the Belgians have generally adopted the Bohemian musical style of their numerous Czech neighbors. Benin, the station manager of radio station WAUN in Kewaunee, plays piano and sings in Jerry Voelker's Czech-style orchestra, singing phonetically in Czech with a very accurate accent. Gene LeBotte, whose forebear Theophile LeBotte played clarinet in the Rosiere band in 1858 at the very first Wisconsin Kermiss, is the leader of a Bohemian-style band which plays to a mostly Belgian crowd. Arthur "Zeke" Renard, whose one-man band employs button accordion, harmonica, kazoo, and bass drum, sings in Walloon and plays in a style all his own.

Their music has changed, but the customs and foodways have remained strong indicators of ethnic identity among the Walloons of Wisconsin.

Chapter 20

The Polish Fiddlers of Posen

Program 20 Performances
1. Cedar Swamp Boys, "Hupaj siupaj." 2. Jake Strzelecki, "Leaves Falling Down." 3. Felix Kania, "Wedding March." 4. Ed Kania, "Wedding March." 5. Joe Strzelecki, "Wedding March." 6. Tony Strzelecki and Tony Woczynski, "The Lice That Ate the Pants." 7. Tony Strzelecki and Tony Woczynski, "Turkey in the Straw." 8. Romel Brothers, "Factory Song." 9. Starlites, "Iron Foundry Polka." 10. Art Kole and Walter Bartolmiej, Unnamed tune. 11. Skowiak Brothers, "Oberek."

The Delight of Ethnologists

In the early 1870s, Poles from Poznan and Kashubia were lured by lumber companies to Presque Isle County, Michigan. There they cleared the rocks, stumps, and slashings from cutover acreage and established farms to grow rye and potatoes. They worked winters in the woods and labored in the limestone quarry on the nearby shores of Lake Huron. Some of their near neighbors were Anglo-Americans, but more were Low Germans—the Prussians and Pomeranians with whom they had rubbed shoulders in Europe.

Their relative isolation, rural occupations, and general conservatism combined with a regular influx of fellow immigrants escaping from Pennsylvania coal mines or Chicago factories to help them maintain many features of old-world culture well into the twentieth century. Konrad Bercovici, an immigrant journalist, visited Posen in the early 1920s. The United States had recently restricted immigration, the Prohibition legislation enacted by pious Wasps was in place, the Ku Klux Klan and other touts of "one hundred percent Americanism" were gaining influence. There was considerable public debate concerning the value of "foreigners" within the American fold. Bercovici stressed the intrinsic worth of old-world customs, while championing the immigrant contribution to American life, observing:

> The Pole is a very good farmer and a very good cattleman, but he believes in doing things as his father and grandfather did them. He, too, believes in small farm villages instead of a baronial estate for each farmer, as was [Thomas] Jefferson's original dream.
>
> (Bercovici 1925:124)

A decade later, the Federal Writer's Project workers who produced Michigan: A Guide to the Wolverine State (1941:484) emphasized only the archaism of a community which had preserved "intact its Polish culture" and therefore "was the delight of ethnologists." They were particularly struck by the vigorous celebration of life cycle rituals—especially weddings.

> Dinner for the wedding is provided by the father of the bride; the father of the groom supplies the musicians. Each male guest contributes to the bride's dowry in the ceremony of 'breaking the plate': a china plate is placed on a table in the middle of the room where general dancing is in progress.
> (ibid.)

At a specified time, the men threw silver dollars against the plate. When a plate was broken, the bride danced with the thrower-and kept the money. Marriage festivities continued "three days and three nights."

The chroniclers unaccountably ignored the essential participation of women, who prepared substantial traditional meals and, through a cycle of mournful songs, admonished the bride about the toil and anguish of married life. Their terse references to sustained dancing, meanwhile, only hinted at the contributions of a tireless corps of musicians with rich repertoires who kept revelers active for days. Posen's Polish musicians begin turning up in the printed historical record shortly after 1900, although they had been active from the first days of settlement.

From roughly 1908 until the early 1930s, Philip Lewandowski played violin

> along with Cash Lewandowski who also played the violin and Walter Pilarski, who was the drummer. This trio traveled to Rogers City, Metz, and Hawks and around the county, usually by the familiar horse and buggy, to play for the famous two-day weddings. (*Posen Centennial* 1970:98)

Felix Kania and Anthony Strzelecki were slightly younger than Lewandowski. Both men were born in Poland in the 1880s and both established farms in Posen, Michigan, in the early twentieth century. Felix Kania, a clarinetist, typically teamed up with a pair of violinists and a drummer to play for local weddings. Anthony Strzelecki, who had learned fiddling by ear from his father, Jacob, often teamed with a brother, Walter, who bowed chords on the bass fiddle (Kania 1989 I; Strzelecki 1989 I).

Up until the 1950s such men regularly escorted Posen wedding parties to and from the church with stately marches. And amidst the wedding dance—held in an empty barn or on a tent-covered outdoor platform—they favored crowds with polkas, waltzes, and such forms as the *oberek*, the *krakowiak*, and the *kujawiak*. But the supposedly "intact" culture that was "the delight of ethnologists" had been slowly evolving since the 1870s. These musicians, like their fathers, also played "Herr Schmidt" (a specialty dance of their German neighbors), a handful of American pop tunes, and an even larger share of square dance melodies acquired from the region's Anglo-Celtic settlers: "Devil's Dream," "The Irish Washerwoman," "Turkey in the Straw," and "Weevily Wheat."

Polish Ballads and Fiddle Tunes

Folklorist Alan Lomax, who visited Posen in 1938 while on a recording trip for the Archive of American Folksong in the Library of Congress, had doubtless been intrigued by the work of the Federal Writer's Project a few years prior, but he was perceptive enough to recognize cultural change. When Lomax recorded the wedding bands of Felix Kania and Anthony Strzelecki, he was most fascinated by the mixture of old-world and new-world sounds.

> A visit to Posen, Michigan, brought the Library an interesting collection of

Felix Kania, clarinet, leading a wedding band, Posen, Mich., 1920
Wisconsin Folk Museum Collection

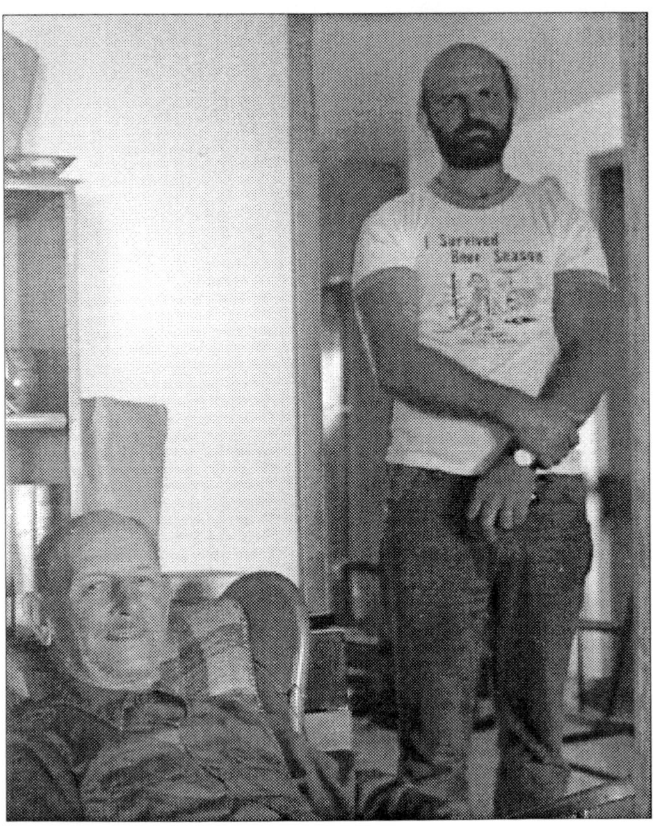

Sylvester Romel and his son, Bill, Posen, Mich., 1989 ***Photo: Jim Leary***

> Polish ballads and fiddle tunes. Many of the latter had been learned from local [i.e., Anglo-Celtic] fiddlers when the Polish settlers arrived and now among young people are passed under Polish names as Polish tunes.
>
> (Hickerson 1982:79)

In other words, although Lomax found thoroughgoing Polish songs and tunes, he also heard fiddlers bow square dance pieces in a syncopated improvisatory musical dialect that wed the *wiejska* or village orchestras of rural Poland to the string band tradition of British America.

In the late 1980s Ed Kania, Jake Strzelecki, and Joe Strzelecki, the sons of Felix Kania and Anthony Strzelecki, still maintained their community's fancy for both old-country couple dances and new-world hoedowns. Their amalgamated Polish-American repertoire has many parallels throughout the Upper Midwest. In the Weyerhaeuser area of Rusk County, Wisconsin, such small Polish bands as the Kassela Brothers flourished with a familiar instrumentation that included fiddle, bowed bass, and clarinet. Their neighbor, fiddler and dairy farmer Leonard Romanowski, was an ethnic-hillbilly regular on the "Polish Barn Dance," heard over Rice Lake's WJMC radio from 1939 to 1949 (Leary 1991a).

In Minnesota, meanwhile, Frank Chmielewski brought his fiddle from Poznan to Pine County in the 1880s. His son Tony took up the bow, and grandson Florian's musical memories of the 1930s are of "Dad playing at wedding dances with two violins and a [bowed] bass" (Leary 1990a:6). Florian's son Jeff, Frank's great-grandson, is a fiddler today with a fourth generation Chmielewski Brothers band.

Perhaps inevitably, Jeff Chmielewski draws upon both the distinct and the hybrid strands of his Polish-American musical heritage. He can fiddle Polish dance melodies in an old-time Polish style and put a convincing hoedown stamp on the tunes of Anglo-Americans. But why stop there? He can also make Polish pieces sound American and render American tunes unmistakably Polish. Jeff Chmielewski's deft playing, like Konrad Bercovici's impassioned words, asserts the enduring power of a musical identity that draws upon both the Old World and the New.

Chapter 21

Old-Time Music in Stevens Point

Program 21 Performances
1. Polka Stars, "Pytala sie panie." 2. Sosnowski Trio, "Wesoly goral mazur." 3. Polka Stars, "Stevens Point Polka." 4. Ray Konkol, "Varsuvienne." 5. Jolly Chaps, "Blackbird Waltz." 6. Norm Dombrowski and the Happy Notes, "Wonderful Life Polka." 7. Kaszuba Aces, "Tam pod Krakowem." 8. Polish Pride, "Sat on a Cow Polka." 9. Norm Dombrowski and the Happy Notes, "Swiss Boy."

Sawing Rhythm

Poles from Prussian-dominated Poznan and Kashubia began immigrating to central Wisconsin's Portage County in the late 1850s, settling on farms and in the city of Stevens Point. Their numbers increased in the early twentieth century as Polish workers fled the dangers of mines in southern Illinois and the congestion of Chicago and Milwaukee (Rosholt 1959:122,128). At least some of these newcomers were originally from the mountainous Galician region of southern Poland.

The historical record is sparse regarding old-time Polish music in Portage County, but certainly it abounded—especially at weddings. Historian Malcolm Rosholt reports that early weddings

> were often held in the barn in spring before new hay was brought in and *[sic]* which made it possible to dance on a temporary platform, or upstairs in the hayloft. One of the last of the Polish barn dances in Sharon occurred shortly after World War II. (Rosholt 1959:137)

Greg Zurawski (1927–1994), whose Polish-born grandfather played violin, recalled violin and concertina combinations at Polish weddings in the 1930s (Zurawski 1988 I).

In 1941 Robert Draves, a sound engineer working for the University of Wisconsin, made field recordings in Stevens Point of John Ciezczak, a fifty-six-year-old fiddler from mountainous southern Poland. Ciezczak had been active in old-country fiddle ensembles characterized by improvisatory lead and second violins, a bowed cello, and a syncopated "sawing" rhythm. His repertoire included tunes associated with Sabala, a renowned mountain guide, storyteller, and fiddler from the village of Zakopane who was documented and celebrated by Polish folklorists in the late nineteenth century (Spottswood 1977; 1982).

By the time Draves interviewed Ciezczak, however, his active days as a dance musician were over—not because he could no longer play, but because there was little interest in his old-world village sound. Perhaps he was bitter. Robert

Draves indicated as much when he wrote Helene Stratman-Thomas, his supervisor at the University of Wisconsin's School of Music, that locals had advised him Ciezczak would be unlikely to open up:

> I visited him in the morning and found him unwilling, saying that he couldn't sing any more, that he was too busy anyhow. But after a while he was telling me I had better record him 'cause I wouldn't find anything like it anywhere else.... After he got going, he was so enthusiastic there was no stopping him. (Leary 1987b:42)

While Ciezczak's Polish fiddle tunes were captured on wax and shipped off to the Library of Congress, other ethnic dance music dominated Portage County weddings.

Dutchman Disciples

In the 1930s German-Bohemian bands from southern Minnesota (Whoopee John, Six Fat Dutchmen) and Bohemian bands from eastern Wisconsin (Romy Gosz, Lawrence Duchow) established staunch regional followings through radio broadcasts, recordings, and incessant touring. Eventually they even spawned imitators in Polish strongholds like Portage County.

Dominic Slusarski, for example, was born on a farm west of Stevens Point in 1914. There were Polish-style concertina players around and Dominic took up the instrument. When he opened his Ritz Tavern in Stevens Point in 1941, however, the only Polish records available for the jukebox were by bands from faroff New York and Pennsylvania. The Upper Midwest's German and Bohemian sounds were more familiar. In 1947 Slusarski formed his own band, the Jolly Seven, that performed for dances and weddings until 1964. Their sound was very much in the vein of Minnesota's Whoopee John (Slusarski 1983 I).

Other Portage County polka bands of that era, although largely made up of ethnic Poles, likewise played German and Bohemian music. Malcolm Rosholt noted accordingly:

> Polish wedding customs in Portage County have changed in the last several decades.... About 11:30 a.m. dancing begins with an orchestra specializing in Bohemian polkas and waltzes, interspersed with Rock 'n' Roll. (Rosholt 1959: 135)

From the 1940s through the early 1960s, such bands included Benny Gagas and the Downbeats, Louie and the Old Timers, Johnny Laszewski, the Melody Makers, and others. From the 1960s through the present, still more Portage County Poles have followed a German-Bohemian lead, shifting their styles slightly from that of older Minnesota bands toward the contemporary Dutchman sound. They include the Jolly Chaps, the Jolly Polka Masters, the Polka Stars, and the Ray Konkol Band.

Li'l Wally's Renaissance

Despite their stylistic allegiance to German-Bohemian bands, these Portage County aggregations have always performed a few overtly Polish numbers at dance jobs. Meanwhile, just at the moment Malcolm Rosholt noted the proliferation of Bohemian music at Polish weddings, Polish music began a resurgence led by Chicago's Walter "Li'l Wally" Jagiello.

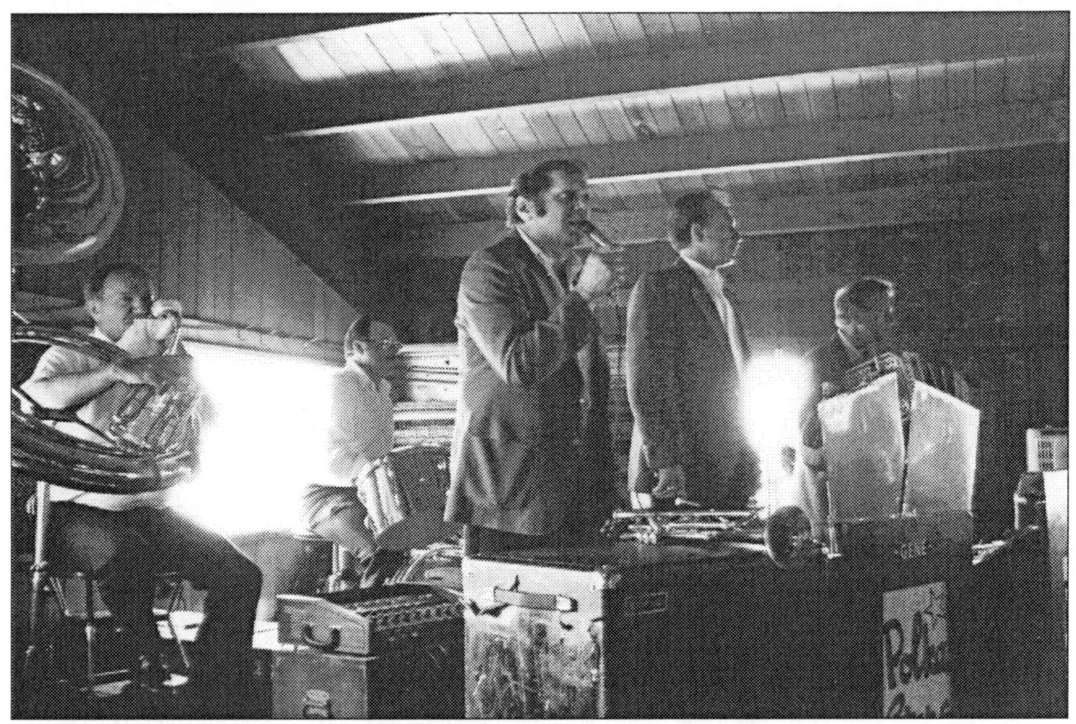

Gene Shulfer singing with the Polka Stars at the Red Barn Polka Festival, Evansville, 1988 **Photo: Jim Leary**

Norm Dombrowski and the Happy Notes, Stevens Point, 1985
Wisconsin Folk Museum Collection

Improvising concertina players, village or *wiejska* style fiddle bands, and old folk songs persisted in the densely populated neighborhoods of Chicago's working-class Poles. By the late 1940s the teenage Li'l Wally was combining his loose, rollicking concertina with heartfelt vocals at Windy City taverns. While high-toned critics regarded these performances as artless, even bad, older Polish-Americans hailed Jagiello's revitalization of the songs they had grown up with. Li'l Wally's rise also coincided with the larger American success of country, rock, and folk musics—all of them "natural" forms that challenged the arranged and mannered performances of popsters. Not surprisingly, younger Poles, like Portage County's Norm Dombrowski, saw parallels between Li'l Wally and rock's Little Richard, between Polish and Presley.

Born in 1937 in rural Portage County, Norm Dombrowski found the German-Bohemian bands that dominated the dance scene boring, but he was smitten by Li'l Wally in the late 1950s. He listened to records and traveled to Chicago, where he saw other Polish bands play, like Marion Lush, the Naturals, and the High Tones. Taking up the drums and lead vocals, Dombrowski formed the Happy Notes in 1960 with Jerry Halkowski, Ron Gruna, and Marv Stencil. More than thirty years later, the Happy Notes consist of Norm and his grown children (Dombrowski 1988 I). Their continued popularity and the subsequent emergence of other bands—the Kaszuba Aces, the Cavaliers, the Polish Edition, the Nutrels, the Dynasounds—have reinstated Polish music as the requisite sound for Portage County weddings in the late twentieth century.

Chapter 22

Pulaski Is a Polka Town

Program 22 Performances
1. Alvin Styczynski, "Pulaski Is a Polka Town." 2. Dick Rodgers, "Dan's Dizzy Hop." 3. Dick Rodgers, "Chocolate Soda Polka." 4. Alvin Styczynski, "Hup Sadyna." 5. Polka Dimensions, "Merka, merka," 6. Maroszek Brothers, "Kujawiak." 7. Steve Rodgers and Friends, "Down on the Corner." 8. Polkatown Sound, "I've Just Seen a Face."

Polka Town

On a long weekend at the end of July every year a transformation takes place in the northeastern Wisconsin dairy-farming village of Pulaski. Wire-and-lathing snow fences enclose the city park just past the small downtown commercial strip. Tent-covered dance floors and beer bars appear, food stands exude the aroma of Polish sausages on the grill, and Pulaski becomes, as promised in local musician Alvin Styczynski's song, the quintessential "polka town."

> Pulaski is a polka town
> With loads of boys and girls around.
> It's very plain to see, they're singing merrily
> Dancing and hopping up and down.

Pulaski Polka Days are the biggest of many local dance events. Polka enthusiasts from miles around more than double the town's population of under two thousand. From midday until late each night, at least two bands-one in the pavilion, the other in the tent pump out polkas and an occasional waltz, *oberek,* or *kujawiak.* As the trumpets, concertinas, electric bass, and drums blare at the ear-ringing level to which modern sound systems have inured us, dancers whirl about the floor in sweeping counterclockwise circles. The dancers are old and young, teenagers in blue jeans and tee shirts, and farming folk sporting seed company baseball caps, print dresses, and billowy blouses and slacks. The most serious dancers wear polka club outfits-frequently vests in shades of red, trimmed with rickrack and bearing the club's insignia on the back-worn with matching slacks or skirts over rustling crinolines. The polka dancing styles are as diverse as the crowd. As they execute jitterbug swings, the heads of the hottest club dancers bob up and down like pistons in double time to the music, while the more casual dancers glide or hop in one-step, two-step, or heel-and-toe polkas. Somewhere among the dancing throng, gaudy golden plastic crowns glisten on the festival's king and queen.

It takes a lot of bands to keep the two dance floors filled for three days. Most of the bands each year are from the Pulaski area—Chad Przybylski, the Polka Sweethearts, the Maroszek Brothers, Alvin Styczynski, Steve Rodgers, the

Polkatown Sound, Mike Ryba and the Changing Times Orchestra, Eldon Otto, and the Polka Dimensions. Nationally known "name" bands are also a must for the big event—Eddie Blazonczyk's Versatones out of Chicago always appear, guarding their status as the number one purveyors of the modern Polish-American "Dyno" style. Former Chicagoan Lil' Wally Jagiello, who originated the rootsy "Honky" style revolution in Polish-American music, comes back up north from Florida. Appearances by hot younger performers like Scrubby Seweryniak and the Sunshine Band from Buffalo or the Toledo Polkamotion give the crowd a chance to meet the bands from far away whose synthesis of rock with polka has been making waves on local polka radio shows. Some years even Cleveland's Frankie Yankovic, a living legend pushing eighty but still touring, is a big draw despite the fact that his trademark Slovenian-style polka is not the prevalent sound at this Polish music-oriented event.

The polka scene in Pulaski has retained a few of its local peculiarities—circle two-steps, non-hop style polka dancing, and the older fans' appreciation for the northeastern Wisconsin Bohemian style of music—but increasingly it manifests the national Polish-American polka culture. For instance, Mike Ryba's band is a proponent of Lil' Wally's Honky style, and most of the other local bands mentioned above perform in the Dyno style of Eddie Blazonczyk, arguably the most influential Polish-American musician and a man with personal connections to northeastern Wisconsin.

It is not surprising that nationally popular Polish music styles are now favored in Pulaski. Pulaski's Poles have long been part of a midwestern, if not national, ethnic network. The Polish settlers in Pulaski did not come directly to northeastern Wisconsin from a single isolated village or region in Poland. Rather they are the descendants of immigrants from various parts of Poland who worked in American mines, mills, or lumber camps and who may have lived in several Polish-American communities before they accumulated the wherewithal to purchase farmland in this corner of Wisconsin. Many have relatives in Chicago, Milwaukee, Detroit, or other large urban Polish-American centers.

Well into the 1940s the Pulaski community enjoyed village music from Poland in instrumental trios or quartets combining fiddle, concertina, clarinet, and bowed string bass at local weddings and festivities. The music was appropriate to their rural conditions and stemmed from their peasant roots. Pulaski had no large Polish-American orchestral groups like those based in New York and other cities of the eastern United States, though some of the 78 rpm records of these groups certainly found their way to this rural outpost of Polonia. When a larger polka band was formed in the 1940s by a local Pole, Dick (Rodzicak) Rodgers, it followed the model of the Bohemian bands popular in their region.

From Honky to Dyno

In the 1950s Lil' Wally began to record and tour, playing Honky, his updated American version of the raw village music of Poland. This style immediately attracted devotees among northern Wisconsin's Polish musicians like Pulaski's Alvin Styczynski and Stevens Point's Norm Dombrowski. By the mid-1960s, a second revolution in Polish-American music was effected by Eddie Blazonczyk.

Blazonczyk was born in Chicago to a family which hailed from the southern Tatra region of Poland around the city of Zakopane. His mother Antonina was a community cultural activist who led a *goral*, or Polish highlander, folk music

The Polish Sweethearts of Pulaski, 1985 ***Wisconsin Folk Museum Collection***

and dance ensemble. His father was a tavern keeper, who exposed his young son Eddie to Honky music by hiring musicians like Steve Adamczyk and Marion Lush. When Eddie was still a boy, the elder Blazonczyk purchased a tavern in the northwoods hamlet of Hiles, Wisconsin, about a hundred miles northwest of Pulaski. As a student at Crandon High School in the late 1950s, Eddie formed a rockabilly band that covered the hit tunes of the likes of Carl Perkins and Gene Vincent. By the time they left high school in the early 1960s, the band became known as Eddie Bell and the Hillcroppers, a reference to the musicians' other occupation-timber workers in a pulp lumbering operation.

Blazonczyk's musical aspirations drew him back to Chicago, where he started a band. From 1962 to 1964 he worked a day job for the Mercury Record Company with the expressed purpose of learning everything he could so that he could start his own record business. In 1964 he launched the Bel-Aire record label to record his own Versatones as well as the other Polish bands of the Windy City.

The trademark sound of his band's Dyno style spread rapidly and soon became the standard for younger Polish-American musicians. The archetypical Dyno band features two trumpet players, one or both of whom can also handle reeds. They play mostly unison or parallel melodic parts. A concertina player is required for melody, countermelody, and slightly dissonant fill chords. Three players provide rhythm: an accordionist who scarcely needs a right hand since rhythmic chordal "bellows-shaking" on each eighth note of the 2/4 polka measure is the main task; Blazonczyk's own highly amplified electric bass guitar (Eddie's bass is so live that he rarely uses his right hand to pluck the strings—the notes ring out from his "hammering on" the strings with the fingers of his left hand), and a drummer with a full trap set playing in the characteristic Polish style with lots of rim shots and syncopation.

Over the years the Dyno style has evolved, taking on more rock elements in one direction, or reviving aspects of the more contrapuntal Honky style. Some bands have even resurrected the fiddle as a conscious "old-timey" Polish element, which paradoxically has made it possible also to "Americanize" their sound by introducing trendy Nashville country or Cajun musical quotations into the Polish polka.

The musicians jamming and the dancers twirling at Pulaski Polka Days are affirming their connection to a broader Polish-American polka scene. The most ambitious Pulaski bands like the Maroszek Brothers and the Polkatown Sound follow the latest trends in Polish-American music and through their recordings and appearances at other polka festivals around the Midwest contribute to the ongoing artistic evolution of the Polish-American polka.

Chapter 23

The Tamburitza

Program 23 Performances
1. Zagreb, "Tamburitza Airs." 2. Tom Marincel, "Na levoj strani kraj srca." 3. Vila, "Ti Marička peglaj." 4. Zagreb, "Popefke sem slagal." 5. Elias Serenaders, "Na selo." 6. American Croatian Silver Strings Tamburitzans, "Mariner marš." 7. Sarajevo, "Daj mi čašu rakije." 8. Rick March (live performance), "Kola na dangubi."

Tamburitza Extravaganza

High-spirited celebrants pack the hotel room, sitting on all available chairs, beds, and tables, standing shoulder to shoulder, spilling into the hall. Some squeeze through the crowd to fetch beers from the bathroom's icefilled tub. Some carry on a running argument with hotel management about the noise level. It could be after hours at any convention of car salesmen or the brass widget trade association—except for one thing. While half the men and women are holding beer cans or glasses, the others are picking or strumming tamburitzas, and all are bellowing, "Bdi Ksenija, kčeri moja mila" (Mind, Ksenija, my dear daughter). This is the yearly Tamburitza Extravaganza.

Three annual events show the scope of the tamburitza tradition in North America: the Croatian Fraternal Union's Junior Cultural Federation convention, in which more than two dozen youth orchestras participate; the Tamburitza Extravaganza, where twenty to thirty professional tamburitza combos perform for and jam with each other; and the Tamburitza Festival, a gathering of adult amateur tamburitza orchestras recently created in 1986, also sponsored by the Croatian Fraternal Union. The tamburitza players, mostly of Croatian and Serbian background, hail from western Pennsylvania, all the Great Lakes states, Ontario, and St. Louis. A few are from South Slavic outposts farther west, in California and the Mountain states.

The vigorous and growing tamburitza tradition, transplanted to North America from the Balkans, was named after its chief family of instruments. A tamburitza is a fretted stringed instrument. It comes in five sizes, from smaller than a mandolin to larger than a string bass. Though it might include a violin or accordion, the group is still called a tamburitza combo or orchestra.

The original instrument was Middle Eastern—a basic long-necked lute with a small pear-shaped body—brought by the Ottoman Turks into the Balkans in the fifteenth century. The original type is still played today, especially by the Slavic Moslems of Bosnia and the upland Albanians. In other areas, the Middle Eastern form was modified and the frets were adjusted to suit Western scales and European design concepts.

Although orchestras of various sized tamburitzas must have existed a few decades earlier, the first one to receive notice in historical literature was that of Pajo Kolaric, a Croatian alderman from the town of Osijek in eastern Croatia. In the mid-nineteenth century his patriotic anthems aroused Croatians to oppose Hungarian hegemony and forever associated the instrument with Croatian national identity (Kolar 1975). Fine musicians of other nationalities in the same region, Serbians and Gypsies in the Vojvodina province, also play the tamburitza, but the instrument does not have as profound a symbolic value to those ethnic groups.

By the end of the nineteenth century, tamburitza orchestras were firmly established in Zagreb and other large Croatian towns and cities. The most renowned classical composers in Croatia, Ivan Zajc and Bozidar Sirola, also composed music for the tamburitza orchestra. Music and politics were thoroughly intermeshed. According to the prevailing romantic nationalist ideas, through playing music that sought to present an "elevated" version of Croatian peasant culture, the ensembles were promoting the concept of the equality of the subject Croatian nation (and by extension, the other Slavic nationalities) with the two dominant nations of the Austro-Hungarian Empire.

Hapsburg repression made it difficult to form overtly political groups, but *cultural* groups, usually including a choir and a tamburitza orchestra, could function. National sentiments could be expressed by singing in the native Slavic tongue, by giving patriotic titles to instrumental pieces, and by playing anything at all upon the symbolic national instrument, the tamburitza.

By the early 1890s Croats and Serbs had begun to emigrate to North America in large numbers prompted by the combination of bad economic conditions in the homeland and the demand for unskilled industrial laborers in the United States. The tamburitza orchestra or, more frequently, smaller rustic tamburitza combos that played at weddings or in village taverns were already a well-established part of the musical life of immigrants.

From Village Tavern to Immigrant Saloon

In America, the village tavern was replaced by the immigrant saloon. Trusted saloon keepers performed many of the services of a banker and travel agent as well as a translator and counselor. Although it is not clear when the first tamburitzas were brought to America—there are reports of singing and dancing to the tamburitza aboard ship on the transatlantic crossings—the immigrant saloon, like the village tavern, was a natural setting for small informal tamburitza combos.

The immigrants faced difficult and insecure living and working conditions, since the dominant society ostracized and discriminated against them, and death and dismemberment were daily hazards in mining and heavy industry. So they joined together in mutual protective societies for burial and life insurance, and in singing societies and amateur tamburitza orchestras for spiritual and cultural uplift. Indeed pressures analogous to those which prompted the proliferation of cultural societies in Austria-Hungary also existed in the United States. On both sides of the Atlantic, Croats and Serbs felt the need to resist the denationalizing forces of their governments and sociocultural environments. The immigrants often named the American choirs and orchestras after those in the Old World: for example, the Zora ("dawn") singing society established in Chicago in 1902 was named after its counterpart in Karlovac, Croatia.

The Gogebic Range Tamburitzans led by Mike Orlich (center), Ironwood, Mich., 1979
Wisconsin Folk Museum Collection

Tamburitza orchestras—whose members also learn to sing in chorus and dance choreographed medleys of folk dances—continue to flourish, as an ethnic educational institution for Croatian youth. The Croatian Fraternal Union has organized a CFU Junior Cultural Federation to coordinate and assist their activity on a national level. Moreover, excellent musicians or dancers in the youth groups can aspire to the tamburitza "big leagues": to become one of the thirty members of the Duquesne University Tamburitzans, collegian performers who receive full scholarships to that Pittsburgh Jesuit university and tour nationally and internationally. The formation of more adult orchestras, mostly comprising alumni of the youth groups, has been stimulated by the CFU since the early 1980s.

Serbian communities have similar youth groups who sing, dance, and play, but recent Serbian immigrants have promoted a newer musical style, the accordion-based *narodni orkestar* (folk orchestra) which has flourished and largely replaced the tamburitza. Serbian tamburitza orchestras have managed to hold on only in a few localities like Duluth, Minnesota, and Ironwood, Michigan, where there has been little recent immigration from Europe.

But whether among Serbians or Croatians, the real breeding ground of the future professional tamburitza combo musicians is in festivities which follow the performances of youth orchestras. At these events, informal combos of orchestra members play by ear for social ethnic dancing. Some of these young combo players go on to form semiprofessional groups playing for weddings, picnics, and dances. Thus the formal orchestras provide a training program to ensure a continuing supply of Croatian and Serbian ethnic musicians.

Chapter 24

Sjajno more ("Shining Sea") Lake Michigan: Tamburitza from Gary to Sheboygan

Program 24 Performances
1. Sinovi, "Pjesma Žumberka." 2. Continentals, "Oj djevojko mala." 3. Popovich Brothers, "Mene majka jednog ima." 4. Mike Radicevich, "Čačačko kolo." 5. Old Town Strollers with Peter Roth, "Jovano, Jovanče." 6. Old Town Strollers, "Donesi vino, Krčmarice." 7. Sinovi, "Dedin poklon."

Strollers and Sons

Mike Radicevich is a young Milwaukee musician who for nearly two decades has made tamburitza music in his family's restaurant, the Old Town Serbian Gourmet House. True to their name, the Old Town Strollers drift from table to table entertaining the well-dressed and well-mannered restaurant patrons as they enjoy a *paprikaš* or *burek* dinner. The musicians play an eclectic European cafe repertoire—a Hungarian *csardas,* a Russian gypsy melody, a Neapolitan air, or even a French chanson from the repertoire of Edith Piaf—along with their Serbian *starogradske pesme* (old town songs) or kolo (dance tunes). Their skillful, understated renditions lend musical grace to the dining experience.

The instruments in the ensemble are also international. Mike is the only player of tamburitza: his wife Dawn plays violin, and they may be joined by some combination of a guitarist, a string bass player, and either a Hungarian *cymbalum* (large hammer dulcimer) player or a chromatic button accordionist. Dawn may sing a few songs, but most of their cafe repertoire is instrumental.

Another musician, Chicagoan Joe Gornick, is a founding member of Sinovi (sons), a tamburitza combo. The nucleus of the band, from the musically talented Gornick and Kirin families, are indeed the sons of noted Croatian-American tamburitza players. For more than a decade, Sinovi has played the circuit of Croatian picnics, weddings, anniversaries, pre-Lenten dances, ethnic lodge Christmas parties, and fish fries, just as their fathers did. On any weekend they may be in western Pennsylvania, Ohio, Indiana, Illinois, Wisconsin, Missouri, and occasionally in the far-off Croatian communities of California and the Mountain states. At their gigs, Croatian Americans and their friends consume lamb with green onions, work up a sweat alternately dancing kolo line dances or hopping to a polka beat, and crowd around the band beside the bar—singing until hoarse, between gulps of beer from plastic cups, old country songs whose words they may now scarcely understand. Joe, a strong singer in Croatian and English, is usually the string bass player, while the remaining musicians play a full complement of the tamburitza family of instruments—the *prim*, *brač*, *čelo brač*, and *bugarija* (the soprano, tenor, and baritone melodic voices and the rhythm instrument)—and also sing. Like the Old Town Strollers' tunes, Sinovi's repertoire is eclectic. It is what their audience wants to hear: old Croatian folk songs as well as the latest hits from Zagreb, Macedonian tunes, Slovenian polkas, a few classic rock numbers by the likes of Simon and Garfunkel or the Beatles, and even some pop-rock-tamburitza originals.

A Question of Audience

Mike Radicevich and Joe Gornick are both tamburitza players in their thirties who make a portion of their livelihood from playing music and are both from industrial cities near Lake Michigan. The shores of Lake Michigan from Gary, Indiana, to Sheboygan, Wisconsin, have been a regional hearth to the tamburitza tradition in America. Mike and Joe both partake of the Lake Michigan region's rich tamburitza scene though they represent the two entirely different directions tamburitza music has taken in the United States: Mike plays a cosmopolitan eastern European music for the general public who patronize his family's Serbian restaurant; Joe plays the eclectic musical mix requested by Croatian Americans at ethnic gatherings.

These two directions were present in the earliest tamburitza ensembles in North America. In Steelton, Pennsylvania, an immigrant from Karlovac, Croatia, Frank Hoffer, and two of his daughters established a tamburitza quartet in 1891. They played by ear on homemade instruments. Although a tamburitza history notes a couple of memorable concerts they performed for the general public (at a vaudeville review in nearby Harrisburg and at the 1893 Chicago World's Fair), most of their playing was for their own ethnic community, about which, except for their distinction of playing at the first convention of the Croatian Fraternal Union held in 1894 in Cleveland, the history is silent (Kolar 1975:38).

Only a few years after Frank Hoffer's family quartet got their fellow immigrants hopping, the Croatian tamburica orchestra Sokol began to contribute their music to the American scene. Led by Ivan Ocvarek, this very accomplished seven-piece orchestra was originally organized in the 1890s in Sisak, Croatia. Before coming to the United States in 1900, the group performed in Paris at the Folies-Bergere, as well as at the Grand Opera House, in the Kaisergarten of Dusseldorf, and for the proverbial Crowned Heads of Europe: in the castle of the Grand Duke and Duchess of Luxemburg, and at Sandringham for a gathering which included Emperor Franz Jozef of Austria and ex-Queen Isabella of Spain, hosted by the Prince of Wales.

In New York City, Frank Zotti, the noted Croatian immigrant banker, acted as their agent, putting out an advertisement in English which plainly stated, "The purpose ... is to introduce to the Public the Instruments which interested so much H. R. H. the Prince of Wales, and the other nobility of Europe" (ibid.). Their prestigious U.S. performances included a 1900 engagement at the Roof Garden of the Waldorf-Astoria Hotel in New York and a performance for President William McKinley on September 5, 1901, at the Pan American Exposition—the day before he was assassinated!

Frank ("Poncho") Majdak Jr. playing at the annual Croatian Fraternal Union picnic, Mukwonago, 1984 ***Photo: Jim Leary***

The band toured the United States, going at least as far as Galveston, Texas, and is reported to have settled in Buffalo, New York, where for several years they played regularly at a locally noted German restaurant.

Through the twentieth century, a majority of *tamburashi* (tamburitza players) in America have been immigrant factory workers and miners who played at a tavern or church hall, or their descendants, who have perpetuated the music at picnics, weddings, and ethnic doings. But another important component of the tamburitza tradition has involved ensembles who, seeking professional status, have devised strategies to target an elite or a wider American audience.

For a number of years, the vaudeville and Chautauqua circuits provided a way. Two very significant ensembles were quite active in vaudeville. Zvonimir, an ensemble named for an eleventh-century king of Croatia, was formed in Steelton, Pennsylvania, in 1906 and toured actively until 1928. Over the years, personnel turned over continually, but the musicians included several of the most influential tamburitza musicians of all time: Rudolf Cernkovich, John Plasay, John Gajski, and Peter Savich. A second group, Sloga ("unity") was formed by Fabian Charles Koss in Farrell, Pennsylvania. The tuxedo-clad Sloga toured from 1910 to 1933. Koss, whose emphasis was to present a respectable, high-toned image for tamburashi, was joined in Sloga in 1925 by tamburitza great Paul Perman.

A third group, the Elias Serenaders, was a family band, formed in Milwaukee by Charles Elias in 1924. They toured extensively on the more educationally oriented Chautauqua circuit, often appearing in school auditoriums. Upon the death of the elder Elias in the mid-1930s, his son, Charles Jr., continued to tour the group until 1945. Their final travels were as part of a USO-sponsored tour of the Pacific to entertain American servicemen. The younger Elias remained active in tamburitza music, notably as the director of southern Wisconsin's American—

Croatian Silver Strings youth orchestra, from 1957 until his death in 1984.

Since Elias's death, Joe Gornick has been directing the Waukegan, Illinois, youth orchestra, a group similar to the one in which he learned the tamburitza tradition. Joe's music offers evidence that the tamburitza and its music remain a potent symbol of ethnic identity among South Slavs and a vital expressive medium within the ethnic community. Mike Radicevich's group continues the other aspect of the tradition: playing a variety of Continental European music for a general audience.

Chapter 25

Echoes of Slovenia

Program 25 Performances
1. Hank Magayne with Rick March, "Slovenian Waltz Medley." 2. Frankie Yankovic, "Dance, Dance, Dance." 3. Louie Bashell, "Won't You All Come Dance with Me?" 4. Frank Pakiz, "The Clap Dance." 5. Richie Yurkovich, "Top of the Hill." 6. Barich Brothers, "Pod mojim okincem." 7. Mike Rydeski and the Polka Jacks, "Treba ne." 8. Lojze Slak, "Veseli kletar." 9. Chicago Button Box Club, "Na mostu." 10. Barbara and the Karousels, "El Rio Drive."

Squeezebox City

A recent Friday night in Milwaukee offers a glimpse at the full range of the city's Slovenian-style polka scene. Lojze Slak, the Earl Scruggs of the Slovenian button accordion, was in town, on tour from Slovenia. At the Schwabenhof picnic grounds on the outskirts of the city, couples danced to the polkas and waltzes delivered by the ten accordions of the Chicago Slovene Button Box Club. In the West Allis neighborhood, in a bar across from the Allis Chalmers tractor plant, Gary Frank played piano accordion, while at the Blue Canary Ballroom, concertina player Don Gralak, a Polish American, swung through tunes ranging from "Under the Double Eagle" to "The Theme from Benny Hill," all in the Slovenian polka style.

Today, Slovenian polka includes two musical styles: a multiethnic contemporary music typified by Frankie Yankovic and the assertively ethnic music of the Slovenian button box clubs. The roots of both styles can be traced to the small nation in the eastern Alps that in 1991 became independent from Yugoslavia. Slovenian villages organized religious and secular choirs as well as marching and dance bands (March 1985[1989]).

Music was a part of everyday life for the Slovenian immigrants who came to North America around the turn of the century. The corner tavern and the home—the two centers of immigrant social life—were filled with music, and the button accordion was the instrument that Slovenians preferred. Frankie Yankovic, the accordionist who revolutionized American polka music, described in his autobiography his home in the Collingwood section of Cleveland in the 1920s:

> [Max] Zelodec, who worked as a mechanic, would invariably pick up his squeezebox after supper and the boarders would start singing. My father

This article is drawn with modifications from Richard March, "Slovenian Polka Music: Tradition and Transition," John Edwards Memorial Foundation Quarterly 21, *nos. 75-76 (spring/summer 1985): 47-50 (published in spring 1989). With permission.*

> would always join in. I'd sit there as quiet as a churchmouse and listen to them. They all had good voices. The more they drank, the better they sang.
> (Yankovic and Dolgan 1977)

Button boxes were treasured. They were brought over by immigrants, purchased eagerly from instrument makers like Cleveland's Anton Mervar or Milwaukee's George Karpek, or ordered from Europe by mail. A good new accordion could cost as much as two hundred dollars in the 1920s, a big investment in those days. Yet many Slovenian families clearly felt it was worth the money. Accordionists had status in the ethnic community.

Contact with other ethnic groups and their music, with American popular music, and with school music classes broadened the horizons of many young Slovenian-American musicians. They felt the urge to create a music reflecting their own experience, much as the immigrant music reflected that of their parents. The button box suited the style of music played by Slovenian immigrants. But their children wanted a different, more versatile sound.

The melodic reed blocks of the button accordion produce only a diatonic scale while the left hand chords and bass notes are set up to accompany tunes with two or three basic chords. It is nearly impossible on the button box to play satisfying renditions of the jazz-influenced popular music of the 1930s and 1940s. In contrast, the piano accordion offers a full chromatic scale to get those "blue notes" and a more than adequate array of chord buttons and basses. By the 1930s, younger ethnic musicians turned in great numbers to the piano keyboard accordion. A new musical idiom was taking shape.

A One-Man Crusade

Frankie Yankovic was the key figure. Much as his contemporary Bill Monroe codified a distinctive bluegrass style out of traditional roots, Yankovic created a lively, modern music rooted in Slovenian traditions. And like Monroe, Yankovic has unceasingly barnstormed bars and dance halls across the country—a oneman crusade for the musical style that carries his strong imprint.

Yankovic's basic band included a piano accordion—solovox or cordovox (electronic accordions)—playing melody, a second accordion, and a four-string banjo playing rhythm. Piano, bass, or drums might be added for more rhythm, and in some bands (although not in Yankovic's) a clarinet or sax might be used for more melody.

Although Slovenian, Yankovic and his fellow musicians were not greatly interested in promoting their ethnicity. Rather they sought to be accepted as contemporary musicians. Yankovic led the way. His band tended to wear suits or tuxedos-not ethnic costumes—and played modern instruments—not the ethnic button box. They also sang newly devised English lyrics to Slovenian tunes as well as to melodies borrowed from such other cultures as Italian or Czech.

English lyrics set to a Slovenian tune were not usually translations but whole new sets of words. The Slovenian *Bod' moja, bod' moja, bom lesnikov dal* (Be mine, be mine and I'll give you a hazelnut) in English is sung, "She told me she loved me but oh how she lied."

Richie Yurkovich in his basement recording studio, Willard, 1988 ***Photo: Jim Leary***

Although the innovators of the Yankovic style were primarily Slovenians, their music soon found an enthusiastic following especially among the first American-born generation of central and east European ethnic groups. Like the bluegrass or urban blues of the period, Slovenian-style polka attracted largely working-class people who were enjoying unprecedented economic well-being in the years following World War II. With more leisure time and disposable income, they were eager for a music that mediated between their parents' roots and their contemporary experience.

"I'd like to think of myself as the blue collar worker's musician," Yankovic has said. "I'm proud of that. After all, this country was built on the blood and sweat and guts of the blue collar man" (Yankovic and Dolgan 1977). In some areas, such as the south side of Milwaukee or the east side of Cleveland, Yankovic's sound became the local music of blue collar bars and dances. And though it was played and enjoyed by people of diverse ethnic backgrounds, the name—"Slovenian style"—stuck.

Within the Slovenian-American community, too, the Yankovic style enjoyed wide acceptance. The piano accordion became the most popular instrument, overshadowing the button box.

In the 1960s and 1970s, as American society became more accepting of symbols of ethnic diversity, communities renewed interest in their traditional arts. In the early 1970s, Slovenian Americans began to revive the more "traditional" button box as an important ethnic symbol. Button box orchestras with ten to thirty members began to form in many communities around the country. The recordings of button box virtuoso Lojze Slak, imported from Slovenia, stimulated interest. Older players who had set aside button boxes since their youth took up the

instrument again, and ethnic teenagers began to learn it as well.
Button box orchestra members typically wear Slovenian folk costumes or at least ethnic vests at public performances, play older Slovenian folk tunes, and sing in Slovenian. Unlike the tight Yankovic-style professional bands, the clubs also have a place for musicians who are not so accomplished. Here the ethnic involvement outweighs purely musical concerns. Nonetheless there is incentive to strive for virtuosity. Button box competitions award trophies and cash prizes.

The button box revival has had an influence also on the Yankovic-style bands. Recognizing the growing popularity of button boxes, many of them now include a couple of numbers on the button box in a dance set or on an album.

But whether the band is Yankovic style or a button box group, the music is dance music and the dancers never seem to get enough. As Raymond Podboy, leader of the Chicago button box club says, "My dad always said about this music, 'If you're dead you gotta get up and dance'" (Podboy 1985 I).

Chapter 26

The Milwaukee Polka

Program 26 Performances
1. Joey Klass, "Peppy's Polka." 2. Louie Bashell, "Dad's Polka." 3. Joey Zingsheim, "We Love Our Wives (But Oh You Gals)." 4. Richie Ostrowiecki and the Polka Pals, "Don't Cry, Anna." 5. Richie Michalski, "No Beer Today." 6. Don Gralak, "Lori Lynn Ländler." 7. Verne and Steve Meisner, "Meisner Magic." 8. Straight and Fuzzy Band, "Kramer's."

Germans, Poles, and Slovenes

"Beer from Milwaukee, the very best in town. . ." is the first line of "The Milwaukee Polka," a Frankie Yankovic hit celebrating the city's best-known product. Despite the efforts of high-toned local boosters to pro mote a cosmopolitan image and eliminate the beer and bratwurst associations of the city, Milwaukee retains a strong cultural particularity based on the European origins of much of its population. In this "German Athens" of America, the descendants of nineteenth-century immigrants still proudly proclaim their Pomeranian, Saxon, or Bavarian roots in *liederkranz* choirs, *schuhplattler* dance groups, and brass *kapelle*.

While the Germans dominated the north side of the city, the Poles have been everywhere, especially on the south side. From the soaring dome of the St. Josephat basilica to the Polish Falcons and Polish Legion of American Veterans halls, the immigrants from the lands between the Tatras and the Baltic Sea have made their own indelible imprint on their part of Milwaukee. Aside from the big populations of Germans and Poles, Milwaukee has dozens of other ethnic communities, many from central or eastern Europe. Most of them have retained such ethnically specific musical traditions as church choirs and instrumental ensembles, and these play in the ethnic group's domain or represent the group at international folk fair events.

Aside from the overtly ethnic music, there is also polka—urban vernacular music emblematic of Milwaukee. Despite the vast numerical superiority of the Germans and Poles among Milwaukee's European-Americans, the music of Slovenia, a tiny European country of two million people, has become the dominant Milwaukee polka style. While much has been written on the ethnic history of Milwaukee and the city's tendency to maintain old-world traditions, symbolized today by the summer-long succession of ethnic festivals on the lakefront, scant attention has been paid to the ethnic impact on the grassroots vernacular music of Milwaukee, its rich polka tradition.

Milwaukee along with a handful of other American cities—Buffalo, Cleveland, Chicago, Pittsburgh, and Youngstown—claims to be a Polka Town. Some polka traditions, such as the Nebraska Czech style or the southern Minnesota

Dutchman style, are rural based. The urban traditions, however, have been supported since the late nineteenth century by the children and grandchildren of immigrants from central and eastern Europe who labored in the smokey, grimy industrial towns of the Great Lakes and East Coast.

The Silk Umbrella Man

The immigrants carried on their old-world musical traditions in their primarily blue collar ethnic neighborhoods. For example, Joseph Bashell, a Slovenian immigrant and the father of Milwaukee's most influential polka musician, Louie Bashell, kept a tavern in the Walker's Point neighborhood. Besides making good wine and beer, Bashell played Slovenian folk music on the diatonic button accordion, an ability that drew customers to his tavern. Immigrant families lived in crowded apartments, often made more so by boarders from the homeland. So they socialized and put on family festivities at the corner tavern run by a compatriot.

By the time Joseph's son Louie was seven, about 1921, he was helping out, sitting on a table with a button accordion on his lap, while the elder Bashell tended to other matters. Bashell's was a Slovenian tavern, but in dozens of other corner taps across Milwaukee, German or Polish or other ethnic music was playing.

Growing up in Milwaukee, children of immigrants experienced the influence of their own ethnic heritage, but they were also in contact with other ethnic groups. Neighborhoods solidly populated by only one nationality were rare indeed. In Walker's Point in the 1910s and 1920s, Slovenians lived among numerous Poles, Greeks, and Croatians and some Germans, Irish, and Italians. Louie grew up speaking English to these kids, each of whom might have spoken a different native language at home.

He learned the Slovenian music from his father, and friends hired him from time to time to play Slovenian folk songs for their parties. But he also studied music at Boys Tech High School, heard American popular music on the radio, and had a chance to hear the sounds of other ethnics. He shared the experience of growing up ethnic in a blue collar neighborhood with all the other local youth of his generation. When the time came for him to make his own music, it reflected all of these influences.

Still in high school, he formed a popular trio with a drummer and a reed player, and they made some records in the 1940s on Milwaukee's Pfau label including Bashell's signature tune, "Zidana marela [Silk umbrella polka]," a Slovenian folk song. But Louie's bands have also played Polish polkas and obereks, Viennese waltzes, Scandanavian schottisches, "The Twelfth Street Rag," "The Oklahoma Boogie," Swiss ländlers, an Italian tarantella, and whatever else his multiethnic Milwaukee fans have wanted to hear.

By his late twenties, Louie was married, had two of his four children, and opened his own tavern in another primarily Slavic neighborhood, near the Allis Chalmers tractor plant in West Allis. His polkas figured significantly in the tavern business, but ultimately he gave up the bar to devote himself exclusively to music.

Although his training at Boys Tech qualified him to be a plumber, he only worked briefly in that trade. Demand for his musical skills kept him employed full time all of his life. For over thirty years, the Bashell orchestra was the most influential band

Louie Bashell, Milwaukee polka king, Milwaukee, 1987 **Photo: Milwaukee Journal Sentinel. Used with permission.**

in town. Bands like Roman Haines and Louie Byk made their own contribution to the Bashell style. Dozens of accordionists patterned themselves after Louie, and a good many, like Ferd Buchele and Johnny Drozdibob, served an apprenticeship in Bashell's band before striking out on their own. Milwaukee accordionist Gary Frank has said, "Sure I took lessons, but I really learned about polkas by going and listening to Louie. You won't find a polka musician in the Midwest that Bashell hasn't influenced" (Zurawik 1975).

Other polka styles had their Milwaukee adherents—Max and the Merrymakers, Polish-American musicians who played in the Minnesota Dutchman style, entertained for years at the Wisconsin Roof Ballroom; Sammy Madden (né Salvatore Madence), of Italian extraction, headed a very popular Milwaukee band playing Bohemian-style polka. These styles linked Milwaukee to the sounds most popular in the surrounding countryside. Nonetheless, through Bashell's influence, the typical Milwaukee polka became a Slovenian sound, and the typical Milwaukee polka band had a multiethnic repertoire with plenty of tunes to a jitterbug swing.

Chapter 27

The Hartmann-Meisner Polka Dynasty

Program 27 Performances
1. Verne and Steve Meisner, "Meisner Magic." 2. Gordon Hartmann, "Dorf Music." 3. Steve Meisner, "Burgettstown Polka." 4. Gordon Hartmann, "Happy Polka." 5. Gordon Hartmann, "Polkaholic." 6. Steve Meisner, "Blue Island." 7. Gordon Hartmann, "Friends Forever." 8. Steve Meisner, "Jammin' Polkas." 9. Gordon Hartmann, "Finger Rapids Polka."

True to Frankie

"In Wisconsin we've been more true to Frankie's sound than anywhere else, even more than in Ohio, where he's from. We appreciate him more here" (Meisner 1991 I). Steve Meisner is referring to Cleveland's Frankie Yankovic, whose modern polka style rooted in traditional Slovenian music has been especially strong in Milwaukee and the surrounding area of southeastern Wisconsin. In the 1980s and 1990s Steve, a young polka band leader, and his cousin Gordon Hartmann, also a band leader, have been among the most important promoters of Yankovic's style of Slovenian polka music.

Since the European-American population of Milwaukee and vicinity is predominantly of Germanic and Slavic origin, the Slovenian music had a particular resonance there. The striking but simple melodies have Slavic soul, and the chord progressions have a tight symmetrical structure, similar to the music of the Bavarians, Austrians, and Swiss, the Germanic peoples with whom the Slavic Slovenians share the Alpine region.

From his musical cultural base in the large Slovenian community of Cleveland, Yankovic emerged in the late 1940s as a nationally known recording artist with a modern, popular polka style that has been widely emulated by other bands. In the Milwaukee area these included the bands of fellow Slovenians like Frank Bevsek, Spike Micale, and Hank Magayne, but Yankovic also had devotees of other nationalities. Barbara Kaszubowski Flanum-Lane, Al Roberts Gostomski, Bill Savatski, Louie Byk, and Don Gralak are but a few of the leaders of Milwaukee area Slovenian-style bands who are of Polish extraction, while Verne Meisner, Normie Dogs, Joey Klass, Tony Rademacher, Gary Frank, and Norbie Baker are a few of their counterparts of German descent.

The polka bands led by Slovenians and those led by others differ in some ways, but they also have a lot in common. In the Slovenian-led bands, one notices a stronger ethnic grounding: they usually draw upon a broader base of musical sources, give greater prominence to those Slovenian tunes best known by

Slovenians, and preserve more original song lyrics. However, the similarities between the repertoires and styles of the polka bands led by Slovenes and those led by non-Slovenes now outweigh the differences. The recordings of Yankovic and other Clevelanders, like Johnny Pecon and Kenny Bass, and the folios of sheet music—especially those of the Yankovic recordings—soon became the authoritative source from which all of the "Yankovic style" bands forged a core repertoire and helped define the modern Slovenian-style polka scene.

Accordion Prodigies

Having been crowned America's Polka King at a "battle of the bands" in the Milwaukee Civic Auditorium in 1948, Yankovic was wildly popular throughout southeastern Wisconsin in 1949 when the Austrian-German parents of elevenyear-old Verne Meisner bought their son a piano accordion. Verne had been born in Milwaukee, but spent a good part of his early childhood in North Dakota, where his father had worked on farms. The family moved around a lot, eventually returning to southeastern Wisconsin, settling in their forebears' home town, Whitewater. The twelve lessons included with that purchase of the accordion proved to be all the instruction Verne required to launch an influential musical career that is still going strong.

Musically talented, Verne was taking professional playing jobs as soon as 1950 with his group Verne Meisner and the Polka Boys. He swiftly became well known around southern Wisconsin as an accordion prodigy. By fifteen, he was already touring regionally and in 1957, at nineteen, he made his first of many recordings, a 45 rpm single featuring two original tunes. One of them, "Memories of Vienna," was the first of numerous original Meisner tunes to have an impact on the polka scene. Others, such as "El Rio Drive" and "Ukrainia," have entered the polka tradition and are now performed by many bands.

A professional musical career is often difficult to combine with a stable personal life. Verne has had to fight and has recently overcome the alcoholism which nearly derailed his career, and his first marriage did not withstand the strains of a musician's lifestyle. Nonetheless, Verne's musical career has now lasted more than forty years, a significant contribution to the polka tradition. His band's style of play continues to be influential: the clean melodic lines and Verne's renewal of emphasis on the saxophone as a second voice in the Yankovic style have become widespread in Milwaukee area polka bands.

About the time Verne was taking up the accordion, his cousin Ron Hartmann, also of Whitewater, was showing his own musical talents. As teenagers in the 1950s Ron and Verne kept southeastern Wisconsin dance halls hopping to a Yankovic style Slovenian sound, but in later years, Ron's band adopted a German-flavored sound, using brass and a less frenetic tempo than the Slovenian style. Until his early death in the 1980s, Ron continued to provide music, primarily in the surroundings of Whitewater.

Steve Meisner, the son of Verne, and Gordon Hartmann, the son of Ron, are continuing their family tradition as polka band leaders. Steve still resides in Whitewater, while Gordon has relocated a few miles to the northwest in Madison. They were both born at the beginning of the 1960s and, like their fathers, were musical prodigies. Both of their bands play in the same modern Slovenian style,

Verne and Steve Meisner with their Baldoni accordions, Whitewater, 1985 ***Wisconsin Folk Museum Collection***

both play a lot of original material. Hearing only a few bars, it is possible to mistake one band for the other. Yet the underlying emotional expression in the music of the two bands is markedly different, reflecting the differing life experiences of the two young men.

Steve, whose relationship with his father was complicated by divorce, received an ambivalent message from Verne when he first showed an early interest in music. As a seven-year-old, Steve's entreaties to his father to teach him to play were at first rebuffed, and then Verne thrust a momentous decision upon his young son: "If you begin to play, you have to promise that you'll never quit." Steve leapt to the challenge without a safety net and made it. Only a year later his father began to bring Steve along to play some jobs with the Meisner band, often placing the diminutive kid on a box so he could reach the microphone.

Gordon seems to have had more security in his move to take part in his family's music making. Gordon recalls that his father and mother approvingly eavesdropped through the heating ducts on his efforts at age seven to find his way around on a little 50-bass piano accordion. Moreover, Gordon recounts that everyone in his extended family seemed to make music in some way—to play an instrument or sing well. It just seemed natural to him to give it a try. Gordon also had opportunities to play gigs with his father's band and became the leader of his own band shortly before his father's death. Gordon's first recording is dedicated to his father's memory and includes a Ron Hartmann original tune which Gordon had to plumb from the depths of his memory.

While the Gordon Hartmann band plays a jazzy, technically demanding, modern polka style that seems to be fully imbued with the *joie de vivre* polka enthusiasts regularly cite as the essence of the music, Steve Meisner's compositions range between polka joy and the sort of melancholy brooding usually associated with country music. Songs like "Sincerely We're Through" and "Don't Sweetheart Me" ironically combine a perky polka sound with a less than joyful theme.

Cousin Gordon's compositions extol his band's efforts to "whip this party into a polka friendzy" (the misspelling is deliberate), and he makes light of his own particular "polkaholic" addiction—"I need a polka to get me through the day." Steve escapes into fantasies of a romantic "Blue Island" "where the women always smile..." or sings the polka blues about less than ideal intimate relationships.

> I always thought the only man to light your fire was me.
> But then I hear when word gets round, it's burning constantly.

Steve Meisner and Gordon Hartmann, the second-generation polka prodigies, are now mature performers creating sounds which will likely prove to be some of their most significant music. Let us hope they can sustain their innovative approach to the tradition, maintain their virtuoso performance standards, and, especially, continue to create original material which uses the polka idiom to express their thoughts and feelings.

Chapter 28

Old-Time Dance Music in Madison

Program 28 Performances
1. Sammy Eggum with John Schermerhorn, "San Antonio Rose"/ "Hoop-de-do" (theme song from *Dairyland Jubilee).* 2. Bruce Bollerud, "Stegen vals." 3. Emerald Isle Ceili Band, "Kesh Jig." 4. Joey Tantillo, "Accordion Polka." 5. Rudy Burkhalter, "My Swiss Girl." 6. Madison Maennerchor with Lawrence Duchow's Red Ravens, "O Tannenbaum." 7. Lawrence Duchow, "Our Mike Polka." 8. Rhythm Kings (Don Ring), "One Has My Name, the Other Has My Heart." 9. Uncle Julius and His Boys, "Helena Polka." 10. Wanta Dance Band, "Dutch Festival Waltz."

Wonderful Madison

For several years during the 1980s, if on a Friday night you had stopped at the Club de Wash, a tavern in the old Washington Hotel beside Madison's Milwaukee Road railway depot, you would probably have heard an original humorous song by the accordion-guitar duo Peter and Lou Berryman teasing Madisonians for their cosmopolitan pretensions: "Wonderful Madison, jewel of Wisconsin," they sang, "...more than one high school...five hundred lawyers and cable TV."

As the state capital, Madison boasts a gleaming granite capitol dome dominating the narrow isthmus between lakes Mendota and Monona. As the home of the University of Wisconsin, a feature of Madison has been the campus, with its venerable stone edifices, Camp Randall Stadium, and a sprawl of utilitarian rectangular buildings and dormitories, a city within a city for more than forty thousand students.

So many newcomers are attracted to Madison that you can spot bumper stickers proclaiming Madison Native. The university has drawn people from around the world and spawned a professorial community concentrated on the near west side and a countercultural bohemian community centered on the near east side. Civil servants from every corner of the state live all over the metropolitan area. But intermingled with "the state" and "the U," there is also a small upper midwestern city, with the main offices of regional insurance companies and typical midwestern industries serving agriculture, especially dairy farming, or engaged in meatpacking and machinery making.

Ethnic Connections

This intermingled small midwestern town is as tuned in to regional and ethnic traditions as the university community is to cosmopolitan trends. As elsewhere in the Upper Midwest, ethnicity is a major organizing principle in local cultural activities. The most numerous and longest-established ethnic groups in Madison's cultural matrix are the Germans, Norwegians, Swiss, Italians, and Irish.

Except for the Italians, each of these Madison ethnic groups interacts with a sizable southern Wisconsin rural community of their compatriots or cousins, most of whom came to the United States on the same nineteenth-century wave of migration. The Germans have ties to Waunakee, Jefferson, Waterloo, Roxbury, and Sauk City; the Norwegians to Stoughton, Mount Horeb, and Hollandale; the Swiss to Monroe, New Glarus, Honey Creek, and Monticello; and the Irish to Pine Bluff, Ridgeway, and Darlington in southwestern Wisconsin—to name only a few. These interactions have stimulated both townsfolk and farmers. Madison Germans happily hop to polka bands at Waunakee's Volksfest and Jefferson's Gemütlichkeit Days, and Madison Norwegians flock to Stoughton's Syttende Mai and Mount Horeb's Song of Norway. The Green County Swiss may be the best-organized rural ethnic group in southern Wisconsin: numerous large annual events—like New Glarus's Heidi and William Tell festivals and Monroe's Cheese Days festival—feature heavy doses of Swiss music.

The city cousins join the efforts to set up ethnic events by taking part in Madison's single- or multiethnic fests like Festa Italiana, the Holiday Folk Fair, and the Triangle Ethnic Fest. Through his accordion school and the annual Accordion Jamboree, Madison's Rudy Burkhalter, a cultural leader of Swiss Americans, helped perpetuate his own and a host of other central and northern European musical traditions in Wisconsin. Moreover, some of the Madison-based ethnics host performers from the old country: the Shamrock Club has brought from Ireland Wexford's Gertrude Walsh dancers and Dublin's Barley Bree.

The Madison Maennerchor is the oldest continuously functioning musical organization in Madison. Singing mainly arrangements of German folk songs, this German-American men's choir began in 1854 as an affiliate of the local *Turnverein,* or gymnastics society. Serving the mind, body, and spirit, the Turners, as they are called in English, combine exercise and gymnastics with educational and cultural activities like the choir. The instrumental side of the German musical heritage is maintained by the Max Drexler Band, a brass band or *Kapelle* of twelve to eighteen members who perform marches, polkas, and waltzes and occasionally sing in German. The Uncle Julius Orchestra, a fine German dance band with Dutchman-style leanings, played all the big dance halls in the 1940s and 1950s; and Madison still has a fair number of GermanAmerican polka bands such as the Steve Franzen and Gordon Hartmann orchestras, though they play nowadays in the Slovenian polka style popularized by Frankie Yankovic.

The Norwegians also have a long-established men's chorus, the Grieg Choir, named for the famed composer. Like the Maennerchor, they sing arranged folk songs. The Norwegian instrument of choice has tended to be the fiddle—either the conventional four-string violin or the elaborate and ornate Hardanger fiddle, whose five additional strings are never bowed but sound only in sympathetic vibration. Rural Dane County, especially its southeastern section, has been known as a hotbed of Norwegian fiddling. One of the most influential of oldtimers was Henry Everson. A second noted fiddler was Hans Fykerud of Stoughton, whose brother Lars was a legendary fiddler in Norway.

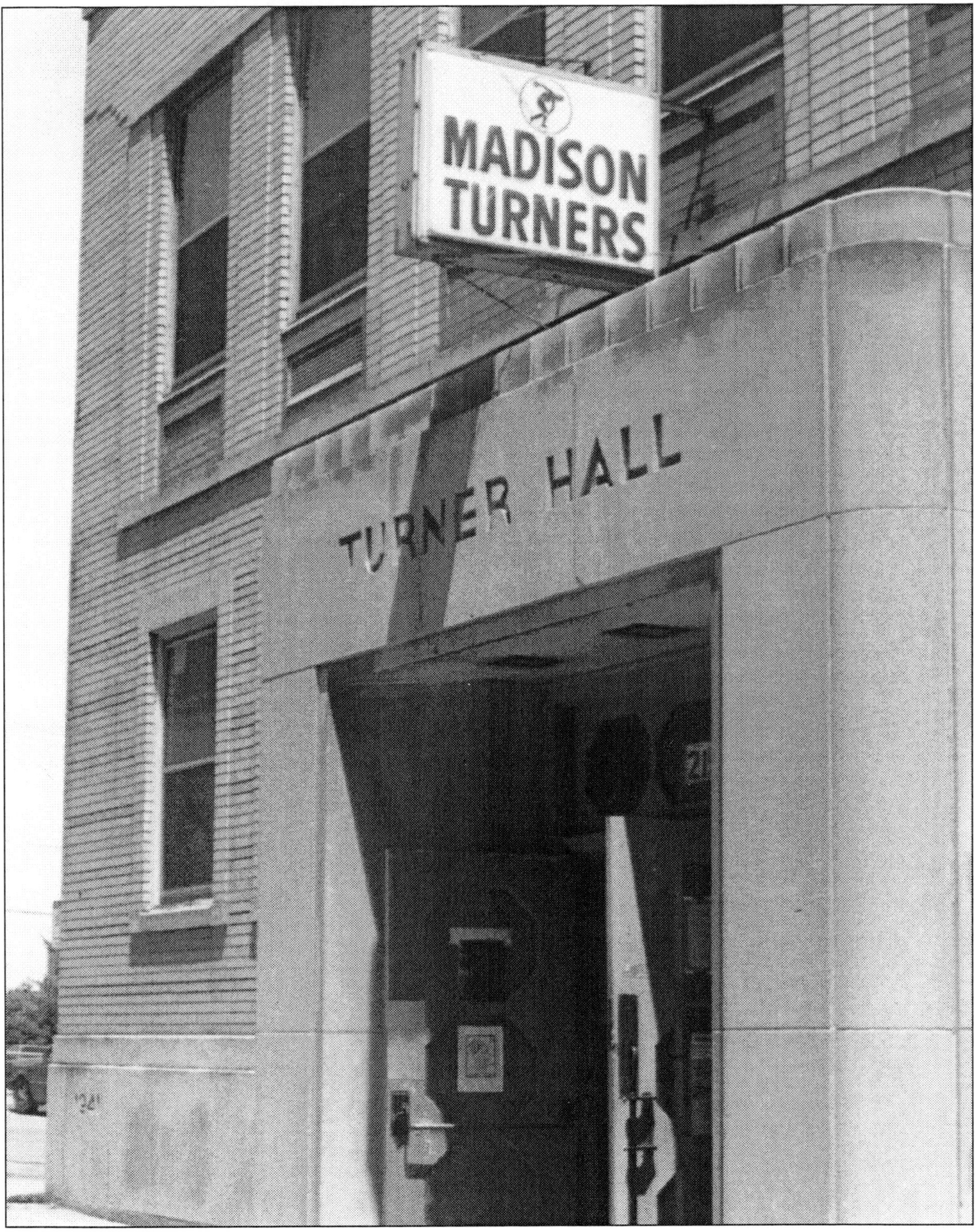

Madison's Turner Hall, site of many old-time dances, 1994 **Photo: Richard March**

Dane County was a major center of Hardanger fiddling, especially in the 1920s and 1930s, when its sheriff, Harald Smedal, was a leader of the local Hardanger fiddlers' club. The members included both male and female musicians. Dagny Quisling, whose family established a well-known Madison medical clinic, was one of the most outstanding players. Nowadays, the Hardanger fiddle is played by Scandinavian-American enthusiasts, who may belong to the Hardanger Fiddle Association of America-based in Sioux Falls, South Dakota—and keep in touch through the newsletter *Sound Post*—published in Minneapolis. Dane County still has the important distinction of being home to one of the rare Hardanger fiddle makers, Ron Poast of Black Earth.

Norwegian music remains vital in the Madison area. Since the mid-1980s, fiddler Walter Landerud of McFarland has organized the Spelmanslag, an annual gathering of fiddlers and accordionists. Blue Mounds likewise hosts a Scandinavian fiddlers' event in July. Stoughton High School boasts a fine Norwegian dance troupe-it may be the only public high school in the United States where Norwegian dancing satisfies the physical education requirement.

Folklore Village Farm in Dodgeville has been a hub for folk dance enthusiasts, including many from Madison. Wiscandia, an accomplished ensemble playing traditional Scandinavian music, comprises Folklore Village participants who learned to play at folk dances.

The lively Swiss-American musical scene in Green County and the contributions of Madison's Rudy Burkhalter are covered in another essay. Nonetheless, it bears mentioning that modern Swiss polka bands have enthusiastically embraced Frank Yankovic's Slovenian style. Indeed, the Swiss and Slovenians share similar Alpine music traditions in their European homelands. Roger Bright, who for over a decade has played every weekend in the New Glarus Hotel, did a stint as second accordionist in Yankovic's band. Keith Zweifel's Stateline Playboys and the Greg Anderson Band are two more Slovenian-style bands lead by younger Swiss ethnics.

The Italians came to Madison a bit later than the Germans, Norwegians, Swiss, and Irish, in the early twentieth century, the largest contingent immigrating from the Calabrian village of Pianna degli Albanesi. The village name, "Plain of the Albanians," refers to its ethnic makeup. Descendants of Albanians who in the fifteenth century fled the Ottoman invasion of their homeland, crossing the Adriatic Sea to southern Italy and Sicily, have remained a distinct ethnic group in Italy, retaining the Albanian language and devotion to the Eastern Orthodox church. Those Albanian Italians settled in Madison, especially in the near west side Greenbush neighborhood. They formed the still active Italian Workmen's Club and—not finding an Orthodox church in Madison at the time—an Italian Methodist church.

Italians Joey Tantillo, an accordionist, and Tony Salerno, a violinist, led successful polka bands that played a mixed repertoire of popular and ethnic music reflecting Madison in general. Unfortunately, little specifically Italian music is performed in public by this community. Dance, however, has persisted. The Italian Workmen's Club has put together an ensemble of youthful folk dancers who perform to recorded music.

The Irish likewise tended to enthusiastically adopt the region's multiethnic music.

The Shamrock Band, lead by Francis McMahan, performed Wisconsin old-time dance music for many years during the 1950s and 1960s, appearing regularly on television. Jim Kilkelly is a dance promoter who has hired some of the finest Dutchman-style bands for dances in the Hollandale Ballroom. In the last two decades, the Shamrock Club, a bastion of Madison's Irish, has provided a basis for Irish-specific cultural activity—a singing group, the Irish Folk Singers, directed by Francis McMahan, a dance group directed by Ginny O'Brien, and the Emerald Isle Ceili Band, led by Mike Doran.

Irish musicians like the Chieftains and the Clancy Brothers instigated a revival of traditional Irish instrumental music and singing. The ethnic community-based Emerald Isle Ceili Band, and Irish music enthusiasts connected to the university like Boxty and the Irish Brigade, have created an active Irish music scene in Madison.

Chapter 29

Swissconsin

Program 29 Performances
1. Betty Vetterli and Martha Bernet, "I Want to Be a Cowboy's Sweetheart." 2. Louis Alder and His Swiss Yodelers, "Mountaineer Song." 3. Moser Brothers, "Jodler Ländler." 4. Rudy Burkhalter, "My Swiss Girl." 5. Robbie's Yodel Club, "Teach Me How to Yodel." 6. Betty Vetterli and Martha Bernet, "Yodel Polka." 7. Gottfried Wenger and Burnette Kubly, "Wenger's Delight." 8. Alphorn Trio, "Alphorn Melody." 9. Clayton Streiff, "Talerschwingen."

Yodelers in Dairyland

In 1845 nearly two hundred Swiss immigrants journeyed from the economically strapped canton of Glarus toward south central Wisconsin's present-day Green County. Two decades before, a handful of Swiss had settled just westward around the villages of Shullsburg and Gratiot; and by 1842 Swiss from the canton of Graubunden were ensconced to the north in what would become Sauk County's town of Honey Creek. Some Honey Creek newcomers soon traveled up the Mississippi to homestead in LaCrosse County and especially in Buffalo County's Waumandee Valley.

Wisconsin's Swiss were overwhelmingly German-speaking Swiss, and they tended to settle adjacent to other German speakers. The 1880s marked the peak of Swiss immigration to the United States, a span that coincided with the expansion of the dairy and cheese-making industries in Wisconsin. By the turn of the century, nearly eight thousand Swiss, mostly farmers, had dispersed through all but a half dozen of Wisconsin's seventy-two counties. By the 1930 census, Wisconsin, America's Dairyland, was the state with the highest per capita concentration of Swiss. Green County was and remains the cultural heart of Swiss Wisconsin (Hale 1984).

Swiss dance bands—with some combination of button accordions, clarinets, zithers, and violins—were common at Green County's nineteenth-century Swiss dances. Citizens of New Glarus celebrated *kilbi* Mondays—annual celebrations to raise funds for the church—each September with dances "at three or more different halls, and all are crowded" (Luchsinger 1884:636). No doubt some whoops and yodels filled the dance halls, but Swiss yodeling in Wisconsin was not reported until the 1890s.

Yodeling (the nonverbal falsetto performance of melodies involving polyphonic shifts from "chest" to "head" singing) has been used for centuries in the central

This essay was condensed from J. P. Leary, 1991, Yodeling in Dairyland: A History of Swiss Music in Wisconsin *(Mount Horeb: Wisconsin Folk Museum). With permission.*

European Alps by cowherds to signal one another and to call and calm their livestock. The influx of Swiss to 1880s Wisconsin included natives of Appenzell and Bern, cantons noted for the strength of their yodeling traditions. Betty Vetterli of Monroe recalled that many of her older rural neighbors still "yodeled while milking the cows" in the 1930s and 1940s. Vetterli herself learned the rudiments of yodeling by listening to her grandmother Kneubuehl and her grandmother's sisters, late-nineteenth-century immigrants from Bern (Vetterli 1989 I).

The latter half of the nineteenth century was also a period when the folk and a cappella *naturjodel* was complemented by the *jodellied* or *gsatzli,* new compositions in a folk style that combined wordless solo yodeling with singing, often to instrumental accompaniment. Many Jodellied practitioners formed choral-singing groups. The most popular of these alpine groups from the late 1830s on were the singing families who not only won sustained followings in their native Alps, but also enjoyed vogues throughout Europe and even in the United States, where they played to opera house audiences, inspired popular composers, and influenced the southern duet singing that remains an important element in country music.

At least three yodel clubs were founded in Monroe and New Glarus, Wisconsin, in the 1920s. The Monroe Yodel Quartet began curiously in 1921, when a Swiss mountaineer used subterranean walls, instead of alpine peaks, for an echo chamber.

> Fred Boesiger was entering a tunnel leading to an underground cheese storage cellar and couldn't resist yodeling to see if there would be an echo. To his surprise, there was a clear yodel reply from the other end. Charles Jenny and Mr. Boesiger ran to meet each other and to finish their song. The Quartet was formed by the addition of Louis Alder and Fred Ritschard.
>
> (*28th Swiss-American Songfest Program* 1976:13)

The group traveled to Richmond, Indiana, in 1929 and, with Alder performing on zither, recorded three songs for the Gennett label as Louis Alder with His Swiss Yodelers.

No Swiss group had a greater impact on Wisconsin than the Moser Brothers, Albert, Paul, and Alfred. Natives of Bern and noted musicians in Switzerland, the Mosers toured Wisconsin extensively from the mid-1920s through the 1930s. Local newspapers heralded their coming with photographs showing the brothers, clad in Bernese garb, holding their instruments against a painted mountain backdrop. In typical fashion, the *Rice Lake Chronotype* of April 28, 1926, remarked, "Some of their best selections have been recorded by the Victor company and may be purchased in this city." The Mosers recorded at least thirty-six sides in Victor's New York studio from 1925 to 1927. Their records, which can still be found in the collections of Wisconsin's Swiss, include singing, yodeling, accordion solos, accordion/violin/bass trios; marches, waltzes, ländlers, polkas, slow airs; paeans to romance, cows, mountains, flowers, rural life, and assorted Swiss homelands (the Bern highlands, the valleys of Emmental and Grindelwald).

The Biggest Accordion Band in the World

Rudy Burkhalter, the dean of Wisconsin's Swiss musicians, traveled with

Monroe Yodel Quartet: (L-R) Fred Ritschard, Fred Boesiger, Louis Alder, Charles Jenny, late 1920s ***Wisconsin Folk Museum Collection***

the Mosers from 1928 through 1936. Burkhalter was born in Basel in 1911. His father and several uncles were accordion players, and Rudy won his first accordion contest as a nine year old. When he was twelve, a Basel distributor for the Odeon label took him to a Paris studio to make records for the Swiss market. At eighteen he was leading a Swiss dance band and working as a travel agent when the Mosers hired him to barnstorm through America.

By 1938 Burkhalter had married an American and, although he was leading a successful band in Switzerland, war loomed and Wisconsin beckoned. "Many times I remarked to the Moser Brothers if I ever should be so lucky as to settle down in the United States this [Madison] is one place where I'd like to live." Once settled in Wisconsin, Burkhalter played in numerous dance bands and, with the aid of his wife, Frances, established a circuit of accordion schools that persisted until 1960.

> We would descend upon a community in a radius all around Madison. Advertise a free accordion lesson program. Two month free lessons and we furnish the accordion. I imported two hundred small piano accordions from Switzerland especially for beginners. We handed those out and people would come and sign up.... We drove up to Baraboo, to Reedsburg, to Richland Center, to Beaver Dam, to Watertown, to Dodgeville, to Darlington, New Glarus, Monroe, all around. (Burkhalter 1987 I)

Although Burkhalter taught a wide range of tunes, he also favored a Swiss repertoire and many of his Swiss charges, like Betty Vetterli, carried on Swiss music.

Rudy Burkhalter's musical presence coincided with the rise of Green County tourism as visitors sought Swiss culture in the communities of Monroe and New Glarus. To the ambience of Brown Swiss cattle, cheese factories, chalet architecture, an annual Wilhelm Tell pageant, and Swiss shops, he added alpine accordion and yodeling vocals. Burkhalter led "the Biggest Accordion Band in the World" in Cheese Days parades, entertained in Bernese attire at a restaurant, coached yodel clubs, organized traveling programs of yodelers, flag throwers, and cowbell ringers for the National Folk Festival, and composed songs—one of which, "Teach Me How to Yodel," figured in a Disney feature.

Today, thanks to Burkhalter, his students, and other musical descendants of immigrants, Swiss music can be heard year round at numerous Green County hostelries and festivals.

Part 4

Instruments and Infrastructure

Chapter 30

Women Polka Band Leaders

Program 30 Performances
1. Aunt Sharlene and Cousin Eleanor, "Dick's Polka." 2. Lenore Berg and the Rhythm Badgers, "Oskar Carlson's Waltz." 3. Concertina Millie, "Broom Dance." 4. Concertina Millie, "Red Raven Polka." 5. Renata and Girls, Girls, Girls, "Honky Time Medley." 6. Marge Ford and the Alaska Polka Chips, "Two Sisters Polka." 7. Joanne Hawkins, "Joanne's Polka." 8. Barbara and the Karousels, "Growling Mickey's Polka." 9. Lenore Berg and the Rhythm Badgers, "Finska Waltz."

Domestic Players

Women have always been an integral part of the Upper Midwest's polka scene. Indeed the very term *polka* may derive from the Czech word for a Polish woman. Yet polka women have been generally less recognized than men. They have been constrained by roles that determined where, in what company, and even what instrument they would play. While most women have worked within these boundaries, a few, like Viola Turpeinen (see chapter 15), have pushed beyond them.

In keeping with the German proverbial phrase *kinder, kuche, kirche* (children, kitchen, church), women have been most prominent as domestic players—confining their music to evenings at home, Sunday afternoons, or the occasional house party. Besides entertaining in these contexts, women have often transmitted their musical knowledge to the next generation. When Stan Stangle, an eventual stalwart in Ashland, Wisconsin's Bohemian Brass Band, was a boy in the 1920s, his mother, Ludmila, "played one of these button accordions. And, of course, a mouth organ came later" (Stangle 1980 I). Similarly, Barbara Portner Wilfahrt's singing of old German songs did as much as her husband's concertina playing to influence the eventual bandleader "Whoopee John" Wilfahrt (Rippley 1992:12). Many sons and grandsons of such women went on to form bands.

When women have "played out" for polka dances, however, it has typically been as part of a family band—a veritable extension of domestic music into a public milieu. Rosemary Korger Menard (1916-1987) was one of seven children born to Anton Korger and Rose Rada Korger in the Eau Claire area. The elder Korgers loved to sing and play, and all their children followed suit. In the 1930s Rosemary played violin in a band that featured her father on button accordion, her paternal uncle Herman on clarinet, and Herman's daughter Gertie on piano. Known simply as the Korgers, the band played "all around the countryside" at Farmers Union halls and rural get-togethers (Menard 1985 I). When the group dissolved after a few years, Rosemary resumed her role as a domestic player, performing for her own children, for school programs and "home talent" nights.

Lenore Greenwald Berg (b.1929) likewise grew up in a musical family. Of seven sisters and brothers, "all but one is musical." Although her siblings favored country music, Lenore was attracted to the Scandinavian old-time dance tunes of her parents' generation. She was also influenced by a local trio of accordion-playing Swedish brothers, Gust, Carl, and Erik Berg. Lenore eventually married Carl Berg and began playing piano and accordion with Erik's band in the early 1950s. When Erik Berg died in 1960, Lenore formed the Rhythm Badgers and kept right on playing. "The two guys played what I wanted. We never had problems" (Berg 1989 I).

Lenore Berg's musical skill, her long tenure with a family band, and, perhaps, her chosen instruments contributed to her success. Polka fans will always dance to good players, male or female, but polka culture is conservative. Although public polka dances have always involved drinking and courting, they have also been places where moderate behavior prevailed and where entire families might gather. Women who lead bands which are clearly not family bands have often stressed family connections in ways both subtle and obvious. Lenore Berg's surname echoed the old Erik Berg Band, and her husband, Carl, often traveled with her to dance jobs. Concertina Millie, Concertina Tillie, Concertina Patty, Aunt Sharlene, and Cousin Eleanor have likewise assumed stage names that suggest girlishness and kinship.

I Held My Own

Girlish innocence and domestic images, not surprisingly, have been the trademarks of a number of all-female dance bands in the Upper Midwest. In the 1920s Betty's Melody Makers, a Sheboygan band, posed for publicity postcards in a parlor outfitted with a baby grand piano. The Schmitz Sisters Orchestra, meanwhile, draped the top of their upright piano with lace doilies (Corenthal 1991:218,221). In the 1970s, the Swiss Girls shared billing with Rodney Ristow, bandleader and patriarch. And in the 1980s, Renata and Girls, Girls, Girls (not women, women, women) traveled with Renata Romanek's father as manager and chaperone.

Instruments too convey messages. While women at home have, like Ludmila Stangle, played "simple" instruments like the button accordion and harmonica by ear, others, like Rosemary Menard, have been encouraged to take lessons on the violin and, especially, the piano. Expensive, associated with classical music, and appropriate to a well-off family's spacious parlor, the piano was and continues to be a sign of status. Familiarity with its intricacies, morever, has been acquired typically through schooling. Even in the late twentieth century, and certainly in the recent past, a young lady who was able to cook, sew, and master a parlor instrument might be considered well bred indeed. The portable, only slightly less pricey, piano accordion, with its similar keyboard, likewise bore genteel connotations. In the 1990s, women polka musicians still generally play some kind of keyboard or squeezebox.

Those who played outside of family bands and who favored horns have had a more difficult time. Born into a Montgomery, Minnesota, Czech community in 1922, Blanche Havel Zellmer was attracted to the saxophone. The grain seeder on the Havel farm had rubber tubes, and young Blanche would pretend that they were the mouthpieces of saxophones. Her dad played "the old Czech tunes" on

Lenore Berg in her music room, Barron, 1989 ***Photo: Jim Leary***

violin and trumpet. Blanche began to play trumpet by ear as an eight year old, then learned to read notes while in high school. While the trumpet or cornet is her main instrument, she soon became competent on the saxophone, the clarinet, and the rotary valve flügelhorn.

Despite her skill, she was to discover that "music is still a man's world." Her band director told her at fifteen that she ought to "march with the *kolačky* girls" in the community's annual Kolacky Days parade instead of playing with the concert band. But she stood her ground. Once out of school, she found that "a woman piano player was always welcome," but it was difficult for a woman horn player to gain acceptance: "I was always very self-conscious about playing with the men because it wasn't a woman's place to do these things." Eventually she discovered that if she really wanted to play she had to organize her own band. As the leader of Blanche and the Waltz Kings, she could say, "I held my own" (Zellmer 1990 I).

The difficulties that Blanche Zellmer encountered still confront women who approach polka music in an unorthodox manner. But women continue to do just that and, like Blanche Zellmer, they hold their own. In the 1990s, upper midwestern polka bands led by women—Barbara and the Karousels, Becky and the Ivanhoe Dutchmen, and LaVerne and the Starlights—are no longer a novelty but a norm.

Chapter 31

Midwestern Ethnic Radio

Program 31 Performances
1. Detroit Croatian Radio Program, "Lijepa naša domovina." 2. Balkan Serenaders, "Domovina zovi nas." 3. Anton "Speedy" Beringer (1985 I), A Musical Remembrance of Heinie and His Grenadiers. 4. Heinie and His Grenadiers, "Tiroler Holzhacker Buab'n." 5. Mad Man Michaels, "Czarnina Kid"/"Lincoln Avenue." 6. Indianhead Rendering Company ad on the Eric Berg radio show followed by Eric Berg, "Chillicothe Schottische." 7. Famous Lashua, "Won't You Share Your Love with Me?" 8. Sunny Brown, "Spanish Two-Step."

The Station That Speaks Your Language

Radio has always had a place for idiosyncratic freebooters who start up local stations, or special interest groups who buy or borrow odd hours of air time from established stations. All it takes to put a radio broadcast on the air is a transmitter and a little basement studio, a business or a church to purchase some Sunday morning air time for a meagre sum, or a part-time producer with a program idea and a couple of sponsors. Broadcasters outside the medium's mainstream have often relied on traditional music to serve their particular subcultures. Although largely overlooked, their diverse efforts contribute significantly to the history of American radio.

Radio was in its infancy in the 1920s when programs offering ethnic and regional folk music were first broadcast. Because radio could be heard in the countryside, the regional folk music appreciated by ruralites was put on the air. In 1922, WSB in Atlanta, a station owned by the *Atlanta Journal*, featured Fiddlin' John Carson and Rev. Andrew Jenkins, probably the first southern country musicians on the air. Shortly thereafter, WBAP in Fort Worth, Texas, produced the first radio barn dance show, a format that was quickly imitated by Chicago's "National Barn Dance" on WLS and Nashville's "Grand Ole Opry" on WSM (Malone 1974).

In northern urban areas as early as the 1920s, some stations broadcast programs in the plethora of (mostly European) mother tongues of the new immigrants. In 1927, WEVD began in New York with the later-imitated slogan "the station that speaks your language." It had competition from WBNX in the Bronx and from WHOM, a Jersey City station begun in 1920. In other listening areas, multilingual broadcasting could be heard over WRAX in Philadelphia; WBRE in Wilkes-Barre, Pennsylvania; WJAY in Cleveland; WBVM in Utica, New York; and WJBK in Detroit, to name a few (Greene 1992).

The Voice of Croatian Americans

The Croatian Radio Program sponsored by the Croatian Radio Club from 1939 to 1952 is a good example of the radio efforts of urban ethnic groups in the middle of the twentieth century. In 1939 Croatians formed a radio club with the explicit purpose of creating a Croatian radio program in the Detroit area. My aunt, Agnes Grbac Daniels, who had immigrated as a teenager from her native village on the northern Adriatic island of Losinj to the south side of Chicago and in 1941 had relocated with her husband to Detroit, became the program's second regular announcer. Mrs. Daniels recalled, "The committee people came to me at a picnic and asked me to be the radio announcer. At first I didn't think I should say yes but they said, 'Sure you can do it, you'd be good'" (Daniels 1991 I). She was known to have a good voice and stage presence from her background as an active member and soloist in Slavuj, Detroit's Croatian singing society. Moreover, having immigrated at a young age, she had attended school in the United States and spoke English fluently and more confidently than many of her European-raised compatriots.

The Croatian Radio Club raised funds to launch the program. Station WJBK already broadcast other ethnic programs, so the club simply had to obtain a suitable time slot, organize the program content, put the program on the air, and continue to raise funds to keep it going. The broadcasts began in May 1939 with the theme song "Lijepa ňasa domovina," the Croatian national anthem, played from a recording of a tamburitza orchestra and choir. On a typical program, the station's announcer introduced Mrs. Daniels as the program's hostess. She would then greet the listeners in English and Croatian. Most of the hour was devoted to Croatian folk music. For ordinary programs, a technician cued up 78 rpm recordings of tamburitza combos from Croatian communities around the United States. (See the chapter on tamburitza.) For special programs, such as Croatian Radio's anniversary, "live" music was broadcast from a larger studio. A Detroit tamburitza combo, the Balkan Serenaders, led by Marko Kramarich, was the house band. They played and sang and also accompanied guest vocal soloists—such as Marko's daughters Helen and Violet—in folk songs as well as some classically inspired material. Helen Kramarich sang Schubert's "Ave Maria" for a special request, and Mrs. Daniels herself performed "Dalmatinski šajkaš" (Dalmatian boatman), a showpiece of vocal virtuosity from a wellknown Croatian operetta.

Besides announcing the music, Mrs. Daniels read summaries of the news in Croatian and announcements of social events and club meetings. Events were many because in Detroit Croatians from particular regions (Dalmatia or Lika or Zumberak) had clubs that put on their own dances, picnics, and banquets, and broadly based groups like the Croatian Fraternal Union also had activities. During World War II, Mrs. Daniels read dispatches on the situation in Croatia, and she frequently mentioned the war relief efforts of Detroit Croatians. Meanwhile the Croatian Radio Club played a significant role in two multiethnic Slavic-American congresses held in Detroit and Chicago to support the war effort.

Most Croatian Radio Club members and program listeners first encountered radio in America, since most of them had arrived in the United States before radio had spread widely. Thus they modeled their program on the American musical variety show, using the Croatian language and material of interest to Croatians. On the show Mrs. Daniels and other occasional speakers pronounced *radio* "REY-dee-

A Swiss band on radio in Racine, postcard, late 1920s ***Wisconsin Folk Museum Collection***

oh" as it is in English, even when speaking Croatian, instead of "RAH-dee-oh" as it is in Croatian. For thirteen years the program helped tie the community together.

Most Croatian immigrants were poorly educated villagers who came to America with few assets to work in the burgeoning heavy industries of North America. In the first decades of the twentieth century, in mines, factories, and steel mills, they experienced labor strife. Many were organized into militant unions such as the United Mine Workers, the United Steel Workers of America, and the United Automobile Workers, affiliated with the Congress of Industrial Organizations (CIO). Labor militancy, opposition to the Serbian monarchy dominating their homeland, and generally left-leaning politics characterized the views of many Croatian Americans before World War II. Of course, their leftist tendencies also were tempered by widespread devotion to the Catholic Church.

During World War II, the Soviet Union was a U.S. ally and the Communist-led Partisans were the most effective anti-Axis force in the Balkans, so there was considerable sympathy for Tito and his followers. Echoing this sympathy, U.S. news broadcasts announced labor and socialist-oriented activities. At the end of World War II, with the Cold War, the U.S. political climate changed and left-leaning "foreigners" suddenly were suspected of being potentially treasonous radicals, just as had happened after World War I during the notorious Palmer Raids. Rumors circulated that the foreign language broadcasts might be carrying coded messages to Communist spies. The "Croatian Radio Program" was canceled by WJBK in 1951—at the behest of the FBI, Mrs. Daniels reckons. The club found a station in the nearby college town of Ann Arbor and continued the show for several months. But Mrs. Daniels began to feel intimidated. She was tailed by presumed FBI agents en route to and from Ann Arbor. In a climate of fear the members of the Croatian Radio Club gave up their efforts and shut down the program.

While this program ended, in subsequent years Croatian and other ethnic broadcasting has burgeoned in Detroit as well as in many other upper midwestern cities. WNZK, WCAR, and WPON are three Detroit stations that devote all or much of their air time to ethnic programs. The newer waves of immigrants have changed the relative mix of the programs. In Detroit, Arabic, Pakistani, and Indian programs; programs in East Asian languages; and Spanish programs—reflecting a variety of Latin American cultures—now are broadcast cheek by jowl with eastern and southern European programs. Ethnic radio is alive and well in the Upper Midwest.

Chapter 32

In Tune with Tradition: Wisconsin Instrument Builders

Program 32 Performances
1. Ray Polarski, "Schottische." 2. Andrea Een, "Bruremarj etter Ola Mosafinn." 3. Lou Prohut, "The Boomba Polka." 4. Fred Benjamin, "Moccasin Game Song." 5. TRAILS Drum, "Intertribal." 6. Louis Webster, Medley (loon song, Oneida song, western song). 7. Wang Chou Vang, *Tan blai* [flute] solo. 8. Alfonso Baldoni, "Spring Polka." 9. Jerry Minar and Friends, "Bev's Polka."

One-Man Shops and Woodland Sounds

In 1944 twenty-two-year-old Anton Wolfe, a farmer in Wisconsin's Bayfield County, bought his first concertina. It was a used Wunderlich model manufactured in Germany. And with a war on he was not likely to get a new one (Wolfe 1985 I).

World War II was a hard time for German-Americans, including ethnic musicians. Syl Liebl of LaCrosse changed his band's name from the Jolly Germans to the Jolly Swiss Boys. The militaristically titled Heinie and His Grenadiers dissolved until after the war. Minnesota's "Whoopee John" Wilfahrt was accused of being a Nazi spy. His band's travels, the ridiculous rumor contended, were a front for surveillance of the American war machine; meanwhile his drummer son Pat was alleged to tap out code messages to spies at dance jobs (Rippley 1992). And false gossip concerning Milwaukee's Peters Brothers, players and purveyors of German concertinas, reckoned they were smuggling orders from *der Führer* in their squeezeboxes.

When Anton Wolfe's concertina broke down, he fixed it himself. And when he could not buy a new German model to match the old, he began to make one. Today Wolfe is one of the foremost suppliers of concertinas to Dutchman-style polka bands.

Similar instrument makers abound in one-man shops throughout the Upper Midwest. While a few fashion custom models of commonly available instruments, like guitars or banjos, most are craftsmen of necessity whose products otherwise would not be available. With a few exceptions, their instrument making is linked with an evolving tradition of ethnic music.

Portions of this essay were derived from J. P. Leary,1990, "Wisconsin Folk Musical Instruments: Objects, Sounds, and Symbols," in In Tune with Tradition, *ed. Robert T. Teske and James P. Leary, 13-28 (Cedarburg, Wis.: Cedarburg Cultural Center). With permission.*

Woodland Indians of the nineteenth century played a narrow array of traditional instruments on ceremonial occasions. Rattles accompanied the songs of medicine men in curing and ritual. Young men courting played love songs on wooden flutes. Water drums were exclusive to the medicine lodge, and hand drums were used for doctoring, gambling, and war.

The large dance drum mainly in use at contemporary powwows emerged in the late nineteenth century in connection with the Grass Dance movement on the Great Plains (Vennum 1982). Today's singers and players of the dance drum, called Drums themselves, travel an annual powwow circuit. Some play modified marching band drums, but many rely on instruments constructed by men like Joseph Ackley—and only handmade drums are ritually invested with a spirit and a name. The demand for traditional drums is paralleled among native peoples by a renewed interest in hand drums, medicine games, and the old courting flute.

Fiddle Makers

While Woodland Indians lacked stringed instruments, European settlers brought them in abundance. The fiddle—important in folk music throughout Europe by the eighteenth century—was the primary traditional instrument made and played in nineteenth-century Wisconsin. Fiddles were especially popular in the lumber camps, where jacks of all backgrounds mingled and were often expected to contribute to a weekend's entertainment. Some loggers carved fiddles from cigar boxes with a jackknife. Others, like Ray Polarski, whittled wooden fiddles as kids but graduated to sophisticated tools and jigs to craft melodious fiddles.

By the latter part of the nineteenth century the accordion and the related German concertina had begun to challenge the fiddle's place as the most prevalent instrument in the Upper Midwest's European-derived folk music. Accordion and concertina importers and builders established stores in Milwaukee and Chicago. Despite ups and downs in popularity, they have been distributing squeezeboxes throughout the region ever since.

Norwegians, however, have remained stubborn holdouts for the fiddle, perhaps a legacy of those immigrants from the districts of western and southern Norway where the *hardingfela,* or Hardanger fiddle, was prominent. From the late nineteenth century through the early 1920s, Norwegian newcomers included virtuoso players and makers of this ornate and difficult eight-stringed instrument. The late twentieth century formation of the Hardanger Fiddle Association of America, based largely in the Upper Midwest, has lent support to a new generation of Hardanger fiddle makers like Ron Poast of Black Earth, Wisconsin.

Innovating Immigrants

The post-World War II era in particular has seen an influx of newcomers seeking work in mostly urban areas of the Upper Midwest: Europeans, Hispanics from the American Southwest, Mexico, and Puerto Rico, southern-born African Americans, and Southeast Asians. Often settling in enclaves, they have established social and cultural institutions that include traditional musical performances and demand specialized instruments.

The Hmong, a mountain people from northern Laos, were allied with the United States during the Viet Nam war and, in the wake of that conflict, were driven by the Pathet Lao to refugee camps in Thailand. Those arriving in Wisconsin, for example, have settled in extended family groups in such medium-sized cities as

Hardanger fiddle components at Ron Poast's shop, Black Earth, 1990
Photo: Jim Leary

William Schwartz and his Stumpf Fiddle, Sheboygan, 1990 **Photo: Jim Leary**

Appleton, Eau Claire, LaCrosse, Madison, Menomonie, Sheboygan, and Wausau. Immigrant parents have stressed the importance of their children's education and "Americanization," but they have also tried to preserve elements of their culture, including music and musical instruments.

Like Anton Wolfe, cut off from the war-torn homeland, they have often lacked appropriate instruments or even the materials to make them. Wang Chou Vang of Menomonie was unable to find bamboo of the sort grown in Laos to make resonators for the two-stringed violins (*ncauj nrog ncas*) he once made and sold to fellow Hmong. He experimented with a metal patio lamp before discovering a gourd that would work. Other Hmong have used Ovaltine tins and coconuts for the sound boxes of their violins.

Just as Vang has had to search for new materials, he has also had to struggle to find new uses for his instrument. In the old country, young men used their violins to court women, a function that has vanished in America. Other instruments and their makers have faced the same dilemma. William Schwartz of Sheboygan has turned the "stumpf fiddle," once a noisemaker reserved for pre-Lenten carnivals, into an all-purpose party instrument. Since young Menominees no longer play love songs outside their sweetheart's wigwams, Louis Webster has incorporated the sound of his courting flutes into rock 'n' roll, while Ojibwa flute maker Frank Montano trills New Age compositions.

As for Vang, he has sometimes played his violin at Hmong New Year's celebrations where he and others offer reenactments of bygone cultural traditions for the edification of their children. Perhaps, with the passing of his generation, such violins will be forgotten. It is a dark thought. But perhaps they will be venerated as important cultural symbols of the past to be displayed prominently in ethnic homes. Or perhaps, most optimistically, the next generation of Hmong will find a way, as other peoples have, to work old instruments and sounds into their new music. If that is so, then surely some younger artisan will make the *ncauj nrog ncas* when Wang Chou Vang is gone.

Chapter 33

The Accordions

Program 33 Performances
1. Cousin Fuzzy, "Why Don't You Squeeze Me." 2. Tom Marincel, "Croatian Kolo." 3. Richie Yurkovich, "Marička pegla." 4. Arthur "Zeke" Renard, "A la fête." 5. Louie Bashell, "South." 6. Hank Magayne, "Barking Dog Polka." 7. Jerry Schneider, "Emil's Polka." 8. Tuba Dan and the Polkalanders, "Flutaphone Polka."

Accordion Jamboree

For the past fourteen years on the Sunday after Easter, two or three dozen accordion players have gathered at the Chalet St. Moritz, a Swiss restaurant surrounded by dairy farms just west of Middleton. In front of two or three hundred listeners, these men and women spend a long pleasant afternoon taking turns on stage at the Accordion Jamboree. For many years, Rudy Burkhalter, the patriarch of Swiss music in America, was master of ceremonies. The accordions' variety and appearance are striking: little one-row button boxes have big onionshaped handles on the stops; two-, three-, and four-row button boxes are encased in gleaming red plastic from Germany or intricate inlaid wood from Slovenia; piano keyboard accordions are bejeweled with rhinestones, with a phalanx of rectangular stops labeled Trumpet, Clarinet, Musette; chromatic button accordions have a dizzying array of black and white dots flanking ribbed bellows emblazoned with a kinetic diamond pattern; electronic cordovoxes are technical wonders running on electricity, not air, the bellows but vestigial reminders of their lineage; and a few other squeezeboxes are not even accordions at all, but concertinas and a bandoneon.

The players play only the southern Wisconsin sampling of the diverse ethnicities and musical styles of the accordion world: Swiss ländlers, German and Slovenian polkas, Polish obereks, Finnish hoppwaltzes, Irish and Scottish jigs, Norwegian schottisches, French-Canadian reels, Italian operetta overtures, Czech waltzes, a few jazz numbers, and some country and western tunes.

Squeezebox Typology

One of the most successful musical instruments in history, the accordion is played on all inhabited continents of the earth and has become central to numerous musical traditions. The various contemporary types of accordion result from the tinkerings of nineteenth-century inventors who sought to create new sounds and to automate the playing by using a cluster of mechanical levers and springs—the latest technology of the Machine Age. The accordion relies upon the basic principle of the free reed to produce its tone. Earlier European reed instruments such as the oboe, clarinet, pipe organ, and bagpipes use "beating reeds," that is, reeds that produce a sound by vibrating against another surface—

another reed, the player's mouth, a mouthpiece, or a metal pipe. The free reed, in contrast, is fitted into a tight frame, but is attached to it or touches it at only one end. When air is forced through a passage containing the reed, the air in escaping makes the reed move or vibrate in the frame, and so produces a sound.

Although the idea of the free reed was certainly known earlier, it was not until 1777 when a French Jesuit missionary, Father Joseph Amiot, sent to Europe a Chinese free reed instrument, the *tcheng*, that European inventors began to take a keen interest in developing new free reed instruments. The first innovation was the reed or parlor organ, devised to replace earlier, less practical attempts to produce a portable pipe organ.

In 1821 a German named Buschmann invented a basic harmonica, a mouthblown free reed instrument that he called the *aura*. The next year, he devised the *handaeoline*, a harmonica blown by a small bellows pumped by the left hand with a keyboard of buttons to be played by the right. Like the harmonica, a different chord is produced depending on whether the bellows is pushing air out or drawing air in through the reeds. In essence, this was the origin of the righthand melodic side of the accordion. In 1829, it occurred to Cyril Damian, an organ builder from Vienna, that the left hand could do more than just pump the bellows. He added a second box to the left side of the handaeoline with two levers to play an accompanying bass note and chord for each direction of the bellows. Damian dubbed his innovation "accordion" after the German word *akkord* (chord). It was a one-row diatonic button box—an instrument that is still manufactured and played today.

Other inventors, mainly French, improved upon Damian's patent and added more buttons, rows, basses, and chords in an effort to increase the accordion's versatility. Button accordions of various sizes and designs proliferated and became very popular, even integral, to the musical traditions of many nationalities, like the Swiss, Bavarians, Austrians, Slovenians, and Czechs of central Europe; the Mexicans in northern Mexico and the American Southwest; the Cajuns in southern Louisiana; the Irish; and the Dominicans and Haitians of the Caribbean.

Button accordions are often mistakenly called "concertinas" by the uninitiated, sharing as they do buttons and bellows and free reeds. The concertina, however, has no single buttons producing pre-set chords, and it stems from a completely separate lineage. The octagonal English concertina was invented—also in 1829—by English physicist Sir Charles Wheatstone. His invention is a chromatic instrument with uniform tone regardless of the direction of the bellows. Around the same time German technicians in Chemnitz began to develop a larger, basically rectangular diatonic concertina.

The first fully chromatic accordion with uniform tone was created in 1892 by a Belgian inventor, Armand Loriaux. These button chromatics are widely played by contemporary musicians in Europe and many contend that they are the most versatile type of accordion. The button arrangement was developed in 1882 by the Hungarian inventor van Janko, who proposed that it should replace the piano keyboard. Since the fingerings for all scales are identical, a player has to learn only one scale and and can easily transpose keys. Though pianists were not persuaded to abandon their traditional keyboard, the buttons caught on among European accordionists.

Alfonso Baldoni posing with a Baldoni button accordion in his Milwaukee store, 1990
Photo: Jim Leary

In 1909 accordions with a piano keyboard arrangement for the right hand and the 120 bass Stradella left hand were introduced. These came to predominate in the United States, where the chromatic button accordion is still a relative rarity. Although the diatonic button box was already ingrained in the musical traditions of a number of American culture groups, by the 1920s. many players were drawn to the modernity and versatility of the piano accordion. One of the first virtuosos on the piano accordion, Pietro Deiro, popularized the instrument not only among his fellow Italian Americans, but also for the general public. Dick Contino, Lawrence Welk, Pee Wee King, Frankie Yankovic, and Myron Floren are some of the most influential players, who helped incorporate the piano accordion into popular dance band and western music and created a 1950s polka fad.

After the emergence of rock 'n' roll in the later 1950s, the accordion became less popular, although it remained crucial in various ethnic traditions. Today, as pop musicians seek to incorporate some of the ethnic sounds of Cajun, Zydeco, and Texas Norteno music, the squeezebox is enjoying a robust revival. Although it is unlikely ever to challenge the popularity of the guitar, the accordion has shown up recently in the bands of pop musicians Bruce Springsteen, Tom Waites, Ry Cooder, and John Cougar Mellencamp. Buoyed by the recently increased visibility of the accordion in mainstream media, the many accordionists of Wisconsin and the Upper Midwest can be proud that they never lost the faith!

Chapter 34

The Concertina

Program 34 Performances
1. Karl and the Country Dutchmen, "Mississippi Valley/Chicken Polka." 2. Peters Brothers, "Alte deutsche Melodien." 3. Hans Wilfahrt ("Whoopee John"), "*Kinder* Polka." 4. Irving DeWitz, "Ländler." 5. Alvin Styczynski, "Krakowiak." 6. Syl Liebl and the Jolly Swiss Boys, "Heime Polka." 7. Karl [Hartwich] and Brian [Brueggen], "Green Is Green." 8. Art Altenburg, "Wedding Dance." 9. Karl and the Country Dutchmen, "Chopsticks."

Seven Roads out of Hustisford

Irving DeWitz was born on a farm in 1896 in heavily German Dodge County, Wisconsin, near Hustisford. His parents, Frank and Emma, were good dancers who strutted their stuff at local halls and house parties. Frank even played violin by ear, and Irving liked the sound. But he was completely captivated when he heard a neighbor named Griebe play the concertina. While jostling dancers in a cramped kitchen faced the music, DeWitz squeezed behind Griebe so he could see the man work buttons and bellows. The hours went by, he recalled, and "I fell asleep looking over his shoulder." Young DeWitz dozed, the music persisted. Irving remembered that "it stayed in my head two, three days" (DeWitz 1985 I). Soon Irving DeWitz had a chance to get a second-hand concertina, but he insisted on a new one and his skeptical father put up the money.

In 1913, DeWitz played for his first dance. He only knew a waltz, a two-step, and a square dance. "A woman flew out the window during the square dance." Undaunted, Irving played on.

He took lessons from a local player named Haack, then traveled to Chicago for an intensive course from Henry Silberhorn. In his first year he earned enough money to pay back his dad; in the second year, he was able to purchase a new wardrobe; and, with the third year's proceeds, he bought a new Ford Runabout. "There were seven roads out of Hustisford, and I drove on every one to play dances." By the late 1920s he was playing over Poynette's WIBU radio. He had also begun to sell concertinas, sponsor public programs featuring traveling concertina virtuosos, give lessons to local students, and form his charges into a club that, from 1937 to 1952, entertained the public with an annual program. By the 1970s Irving DeWitz had taught some five hundred men and women to play concertina—many went on to form their own bands.

Irving DeWitz's involvement with the concertina exemplifies that instrument's varied history in the Upper Midwest. The boxy "German concertina," as distinguished from the hexagonal "English concertina," was given its modern form by Carl Friedrich Uhlig (1769–1874) of Chemnitz, Germany. A portable

Irving and Lucille DeWitz, Hustisford, 1929 ***Wisconsin Folk Museum Collection***

instrument of the reed organ family, the concertina has two reed-filled boxes with exterior buttons that are joined by a bellows. When a push-pulling player "works" the bellows and buttons, the air forced against select reeds produces tones. The right hand conjures melodies, while the left offers bass accompaniment. And like the related button accordion, the concertina is diatonic with different notes on the "push" and the "pull."

Concertina Evangelists

Never as popular as the accordion, the concertina was nonetheless well established among the immigrants from eastern Germany and Poland who fled war-torn central Europe in the late nineteenth century. Most who brought concertinas were content to play them amidst informal family and neighborhood doings, but others had greater ambition. Henry Silberhorn, a German immigrant to Chicago, was a veritable concertina evangelist. In the early decades of the twentieth century, Silberhorn imported and sold instruments. More importantly, he also gave lessons, encouraged the formation of concertina clubs, and

Art Altenburg in his Concertina Bar on Milwaukee's south side, 1988 ***Photo: Jim Leary***

produced a series of instruction booklets and collections of tunes arranged for the concertina.

Henry Silberhorn's Instructor for the Concertina (Silberhorn 1910) eschewed musical notation for a tablature format that was aimed specifically at those who wished „to learn to play the concertina without having previous knowledge of music." Once competent, a concertina player could teach others. And once a basic stock of tunes had been mastered, there were other Silberhorn books to buy: three volumes of a *German Song Album* (1910–1913), *Fifteen Children's Songs and Games with Words* (1928), and numerous arrangements of "international" and American tunes. Meanwhile Silberhorn kept up with his clientele, which included Irving DeWitz, through a concertina-boosting periodical, the *Booster*.

Concertina lovers in the Upper Midwest were similarly inspired by such barnstorming musicians as the legendary Peters Brothers, whose itinerary included both urban centers and rural communities like DeWitz's Hustisford. Max, Wilhelm, and Helmut Peters were teenagers when their parents, Paul and Anna, immigrated to the coal mines of Henrietta, Oklahoma, in 1912. The boys worked in the mines, but a local theater owner heard them play at a birthday party and offered them a job. From 1912 through 1941, the Peters Brothers worked the vaudeville circuit clad in lederhosen and plumed alpine hats. World War II and the decline of vaudeville ended their travels, but Max Peters settled in Milwaukee where he played regularly until his death in 1983 (Peters 1981 I).

Two wars with Germany not only stifled public concertina players like the Peters Brothers, but they also curtailed the concertina supply. The instrument, however, would not be denied. Thanks to concertina-playing immigrants, promoters like Silberhorn, and disciples like DeWitz, the concertina had already become essential to the Upper Midwest's Polish and Dutchman polka styles, and it was the focal point of concertina clubs throughout the region. The periodic unavailability of Arnold, Lang, and Wunderlich concertinas from the old country, meanwhile, stimulated the rise of American-made concertinas: Patek, Pearl Queen, and Star in Chicago; Brown and Hengel in Minnesota; Karpek and Wolfe in Wisconsin.

In the 1990s, concertina players throng to Art Altenburg's Concertina Bar on South 37th in Milwaukee, one of several regional squeezebox centers. Concertinas of various makes line shelves, an entire wall is covered with photographs and clippings of active concertinists, and players jam there each Thursday night. Altenburg is an enthusiastic supporter of the World Concertina Congress, which, not surprisingly, is based in the Upper Midwest. Predictably, Henry Silberhorn was a charter member of that organization's Hall of Fame, and Irving DeWitz joined his company in 1978.

Part 5

Sacred Traditions

Chapter 35

Crying Holy unto the Lord: Midwestern Sacred Musical Traditions

Program 35 Performances

1. Gymanfa Ganu Choir, "Crug y bar." 2. Moses Morgan, "Uncle Joe." 3. Lee Morgan, "Uncle Joe." 4. Charles Karye and Lempi Luoma, Finnish Apostolic Lutheran hymn. 5. Bethany Swedish Baptist String Band, "Lofven Gud." 6. Ruth Zemke Flaker, "Liebster Jesu, wir sind hier." 7. John Kezele, "Radujte se narodi." 8. Bernice Barnak and Mary Stelmach, "Pojdzmy wszysy do stojenki." 9. Alvin Styczynski, "Pojdzmy wszysy do stojenki." 10. Father Frank Perkovich, "We Offer Bread and Wine." 11. Alfred Vandertie, "Estîz là, quand." 12. George Dybedol, "Den store hvite flok vie se."

Songs, Cycles, Seasons

In the 1920s and 1930s, when Alexei Siedlecki and Pete Suminski were young men in the east side Polish neighborhood of Ashland, Wisconsin, christenings, weddings, and wakes all demanded religious songs. Babies were welcomed at backyard gatherings, married couples were feted in the Polish hall, and souls were sent off in the parlors and kitchens of survivors. At the wake for Alexei's uncle, Frank Chmielewski,

> they had three fellows up from Duluth that sang songs all during the wake at night—*all* night. And then they come out in the kitchen, they had a table and it was just full of food. And they got drunk and sober and fed and everything else at the wake. You've heard of the Irish wakes? The Polish wakes were right next door. ...All songs in Polish—religious: on death and where they were going to go. (Siedlecki 1981 I)

The childhood neighbors of Alexei Siedlecki and Pete Suminski, Bernice Barnak and Mary Stelmach, likewise attended such events. All four looked forward to house visits and Polish carols during the Christmas season, and to the egg decorations and songs of rejoicing that accompanied Easter (Barnak 1981 I; Stelmach 1981 I).

Elsewhere across the Upper Midwest, European-American Christians sang sacred songs in their native tongues. Catholics and Eastern Orthodox adherents, in keeping with the natural orientation of their liturgy, celebrated life cycle and seasonal rituals. Protestants observed these occasions with equal enthusiasm, but they were also likely to possess a wider range of devotional songs and to sing them at gatherings outside the cycle of life rituals or seasons. Some of the religious verses favored by ethnic Upper Midwesterners were folk songs, others were the work of prominent composers; some were learned by heart from another's singing, others were acquired through songbooks; some have persisted into the present, others have been forgotten or replaced by newer compositions. And they have been performed in a wide range of vocal and instrumental styles.

Singing in the Spirit

The Welsh Presbyterians and Calvinistic Methodists who settled southern Wisconsin in the 1840s and 1850s brought the tradition of the *gymanfa ganu* (hymn-singing festival) to such communities as Oshkosh, Neenah, Wild Rose, Red Granite, and Cambria. Theirs was a choral tradition that relied on hymnbooks with both words and music, four-part harmony, an organist and, often, a singing master or director.

The journalist Fred Holmes who roamed ethnic Wisconsin in the 1940s, was mightily impressed by what he heard at the Peniel church in rural Winnebago County.

> Assembled in and without the country church were 400 men and women arranged in groups—sopranos, altos, contraltos and basses—all eagerly responding to the directions of the choir-master who had been brought from some distant city for the event. As noonday approached the people warmed to the occasion. Greater enthusiasm became manifest. Then, like the quick whipping about of a wind, an exultant participant turned the orderly singing into an encore, repeating one of the [English] verses already sung except in the Welsh tongue. Words no longer soared from the lips but from the heart. The whole congregation burned with renewed spirit. The purity of natural voices scored new heights. Again and again other verses were repeated until it seemed the singers' voices would break in the wildness of enthusiasm. The organist and chorister must always be alert to renewed outbursts once this *hwyl* (spirit) appears. Pausing only for meals, served picnic style from huge baskets, the festival proceeded. Darkness fell at last to send the people home. (Holmes 1944)

Holmes's description might easily have served for Cambria's Gymanfa Ganu of October 1989. Olwen Morgan Welk and her brother, Lee Morgan, whom we recorded for Down Home Dairyland, were among many who were at both events and have helped maintain their ancestral tradition.

The contemporary choral singing of Finnish Apostolic Lutheran congregations in northern Wisconsin is equally compelling in its power, and it is similarly combined with a dinner on the church grounds. Yet its style is quite distinct. The Finnish Apostolic movement emerged in the northern regions of Sweden and Finland in the mid-nineteenth century when Lars Laestadius, a Lutheran minister, "underwent a spiritual awakening and started a fervent campaign of preaching contrition and repentance" (Swanson 1970:2). In Finland, the movement has remained within the state Lutheran Church, but in the United States the Apostolic Lutherans have broken away from the official Suomi Synod and have further subdivided into numerous sects.

In the early 1980s, the Pollarite Apostolic Lutherans in the Marengo-Highbridge area of southern Ashland County, Wisconsin, held services the last full weekend

The Polish Conversation Class singing Polish carols in Holy Family Catholic Church, Ashland, 1980, with Bernice Barnak and Mary Stelmach (second and third from the left) **Photo: Jim Leary**

of each month. Gathering in an old school building, resembling the plain parish halls preferred by old-country Apostolic Lutherans, the Wisconsin faithful sang both during formal liturgical services and informal song services. Spurning organs as "worldly" and disdaining the arrangement of voices into discrete parts, the Apostolic Lutherans sang unaccompanied, with unrestricted volume, and in unison. Their words were preserved in such regionally published songbooks as *Uskovaisten Lauluja* (1948) and *Uskovaisten Virsia* (1953), but tunes were maintained entirely through oral tradition.

Charles Karye, whose parents had been cantors both in the old country and America, had mastered many religious songs as a three-year-old in 1906 and, in his role as hymn singer for the Marengo congregation, eventually expanded his repertoire to 328 songs. This number hardly exhausted the body of songs active among Apostolic Lutherans, especially since new ones were being composed all the time. Richard Kumpula, a full-time meat cutter and a part-time preacher at the Marengo church, did not claim to be a songwriter, but reckoned "sometimes songs just come to me" (Kumpula 1981 I). Although not incorporated into liturgical services, Kumpula's Finnish-language songs, circulated in mimeographed form, were an active part of song services—as were Finnish versions of such nineteenth-century English-language gospel songs as "Rock of Ages."

Similar changes—both from within the ethnic community and as a result of cross-fertilization with religious features of larger American life—have occurred throughout the Upper Midwest. Parlor bands relying on autoharps, guitars, and violins were common among Scandinavians in the late nineteenth century. The parallel country gospel string-band tradition of Anglo-Celtic southerners, promulgated through radio and recordings since the 1920s, won immediate converts among Scandinavians. African-American quartet singing, likewise disseminated through mass media, inspired ethnic interpretations like Alfred Vandertie's Walloon rendition of "Were You There When They Crucified My Lord?" Meanwhile the guitar-based "folk mass" that emerged in the Catholic church in the 1960s prompted first Slovenians and then Czechs, Germans, and Poles to compose squeezebox-driven polka masses. These remarkable syntheses have kept sacred traditions of the Old World vital in the New.

Chapter 36

Gospel in Wisconsin

Program 36 Performances
1. Gill Singers, "On and On with Jesus." 2. Madison Gospelaires, "I Know I Am a Child of God." 3. Corinth Missionary Baptist Church with Joanne Moore, "You Don't Have to Move a Mountain." 4. Madison Gospelaires, "Guide Me." 5. Happy Harmonizers, "Happy with Jesus." 6. Richard Jones, "Shake My Mother's Hand" 7. Jannie Lee Burton, "Will You Pay a Price?" 8. Vocalaires, "Be Careful with Your Soul." 9. Independence Gospelettes, "Save My Soul."

Dr. Watts Transformed

African-American gospel is an immensely complex phenomenon. It encompasses music, ceremony, text, and theology. Millions of churchgoers in many denominations sing gospel—for example, African Methodist Episcopal (AME), Baptist, Church of Christ (Holiness), and Pentecostal or Apostolic Faith churches. The music is absolutely central to the worship. Often the singer in an African-American church can rival the minister. "'I heard somebody say the minister's the man because nobody ever got saved off singing,'" says a disgruntled Roberta Martin Singer. "'That's not so, singing has saved many souls'" (Heilbut 1985).

Music has been integral to the Christian religion of African Americans since slavery. In the 1700s slaves attended and were influenced by the revival meetings of the Great Awakening, set in motion by firebrand preachers like Cotton Mather and Jonathan Edwards. The slaves combined eighteenth-century English revival hymns with African stylistic preferences to create the form of lead-andresponse congregational singing usually called "Dr. Watts singing." The style is named for Isaac Watts, a composer of stern Calvinist hymns, born in Southampton, England, in 1674, who along with John Wesley, William C. Doane, and John Newton was a noted hymn writer. His *Hymns and Spiritual Songs*, first published in 1707, has been so influential that even his colleague John Newton's best-known composition, "Amazing Grace," often may be called a "Dr. Watts hymn" by African Americans (Spencer 1990).

In the Dr. Watts style, as in Anglo-Celtic southern white church singing, a minister or song leader "lines it out," that is, chants a line which the whole congregation then repeats in a slow free meter. The slow tempo and straightforward melody allows each singer to extensively improvise embellishments and riffs that parallel the vocal techniques of secular field hollers and work songs. Typically there is no instrumental accompaniment. The oppression and uncertainty African Americans have faced found a voice in the melancholy tone and resonance of such stark Watts lyrics as ". . . death may soon disrobe us all/Of what we now possess" (from "The Day Is Past and Gone").

The venerable Dr. Watts style still persists in some rural southern churches as well as in the urban communities of former ruralites. However, a succession of newer musical and song styles have swept African-American churches. In the late nineteenth century, upbeat hymns without lining out, like "What a Friend We Have in Jesus" and "Pass Me Not, O Gentle Savior," offered a more optimistic sound and theological vision in congregational singing. Small groups also emerged in the "quartet" style, performing either *a cappella* or with a nonintrusive rhythmic backup.

Quartets and Conventions

The term *quartet* refers to the four-part harmony a group of singers employs, although the group may feature five, six, and occasionally even ten singers. Traveler's accounts mention slaves singing in "quartettes" as early as 1851, and Reconstruction-era traveling minstrel shows began to feature secular black quartets. Reminiscing about his 1890s Florida childhood, noted musician and scholar James Weldon Johnson stated, "Pick up four colored ... young men anywhere and the chances are ... that you have a quartet. Let one of them sing the melody and the others will naturally find the parts" (Johnson 1929).

As Johnson noted, quartet singing, sacred and secular, has long been a widespread and popular tradition among African-American men. Like the preacher's and deacon's roles, quartets used to be an exclusively male province. Female quartets are a more recent phenomenon, and women quartets still tend to call their highest singers "tenors" and the lowest "bassos."

Quartets managed to find a foothold in popular culture quite early. Columbia recorded the Standard Quartette on cylinder in 1895. In 1902 the Victor catalog listed "Negro Shouts by [the] Dinwiddie Colored Quartet ... sung as only negroes can sing them" (Broughton 1985). The industry took until the 1920s to begin recording African-American folk music—blues, jazz, sermons, and quartets-more extensively. By the later 1920s gospel quartets were being broadcast "live" along with hillbilly musicians, dance bands, and comedians on southern radio.

Tidewater area groups like the Silver Leaf Quartet and the Norfolk Jubilee Singers of Virginia were among the pioneers, and by the 1930s the Soul Stirrers from Texas and the Famous Blue Jay Singers from Alabama were gaining fulltime professional status. But the group to have the most influential popular career in the 1930s and 1940s was the Golden Gate Quartet of Norfolk, Virginia. They developed a rhythmic, infectious style described by Willie Johnson, founder of the group, as "vocal percussion." Using polyrhythmic, syncopated vocal backup, they popularized the biblical fables of the jubilee songs. Many quartets later emulated their exciting practice of switching lead voices during a song. Their career included regular broadcasts on the NBC radio network and performances at the White House and New York's Cafe Society.

The quartet tradition has continued to proliferate and evolve, as influential groups like the Swan Silvertones, the Dixie Hummingbirds, and the Highway QC's emerged in the postwar era. Perhaps Take 6, whose jazzy harmonies truly stretch the boundaries of quartet singing, may become the Golden Gate Quartet of the 1990s, crossing over to a broad popular audience.

Although nowadays people frequently refer to all the above-mentioned styles of religious singing as "gospel," many older singers reserve the term for only

The Happy Harmonizers (L-R: Ardella Herron, Geneva Herron, Shirley Herron, Bertha McMillan), Milwaukee, early 1980s ***Wisconsin Folk Museum Collection***

the style created by Thomas A. Dorsey, who coined the term *gospel.* Born in 1899, the son of a Baptist minister, Dorsey was raised in Atlanta. In his teens and twenties he was a blues pianist. As "Georgia Tom" he accompanied blues greats Ma Rainey and Bessie Smith. In 1921 he was "saved" but continued to divide his attention between blues and religious music until 1929 when he devoted himself totally to gospel.

Profoundly influenced by the songs of C. A. Tindley, a Philadelphia Methodist minister, Dorsey was especially prolific in the 1930s. During the Depression he combined the good news of gospel with the melodies and rhythms of blues. Through sales of his sheet music, his annual National Gospel Singers Convention, first held in 1932, and his ceaseless touring from 1932 to 1944, Dorsey imbued African-American churches with his gospel sound and created the music which made possible the solo careers of the singers he trained, like Sallie Martin, Willie Mae Ford Smith, Roberta Martin, and Mahalia Jackson. His classic song, "Precious Lord," composed while grieving the deaths of his wife and child in 1932, is one of the most powerful and best-loved gospel numbers and a showpiece for the noted gospel stylists. Another Dorsey song, "Peace in the Valley," is best known from the recordings of Red Foley and Elvis Presley.

Dorsey's Gospel Convention has served as the model for gospel workshops now held around the country. The most notable recently was James Cleveland's annual Gospel Music Workshop of America. Local chapters make sure gospel continues to grow and prosper as young singers and musicians learn to perform in choirs as soloists, choir directors, or instrumentalists.

Although Wisconsin is on the northern periphery of the gospel heartland, the gospel heard in the Dairyland is a part of an influential and growing nationwide tradition. From a cappella quartets like the Happy Harmonizers to contemporary stylists like the Vocalaires, Wisconsin groups perform the various styles of gospel at musical gatherings throughout the Midwest—and even beyond.

Part 6

Newcomers

Chapter 37

Borinquén suelo querido: Puerto Rican Music in Wisconsin

Program 37 Performances
1. Sabor, "Consencias." 2. Trulla Navidena, "Danza." 3. Trulla Navidena, "La banta negrita." 4. Bentetu, "Plena Bentetu." 5. Bentetu, "Bomba Medley" 6. Andando Solo, "En la vida todo es ir." 7. Trulla Navidena, "Cortando cana."

Three Kings' Day

Dominoes were clicking in the basement of Centro de la Comunidad Unida in Milwaukee on the twelfth day after Christmas, Three Kings' Day, the Epiphany. To the initiated the sound is as evocative of home as the croak ing of *coqui*, the Puerto Rican frog. Hundreds of men and women had gathered to celebrate one of their most important holidays with dominoes, a popular game on the island. The room was filled with the aroma of *arroz con gandules*, a dish of rice and unique small beans, and a cascade of voices spoke Spanish with a Caribbean lilt. From one corner came music—the strumming of a guitar, the tremolo of a *cuatro's* strings, and the rhythmic scraping of a *guiro*. Instead of the snow and ice of January in Wisconsin, I could almost imagine that outside was Borinquen, as the celebrants affectionately called their tropical homeland.

The Caribbean island of Puerto Rico was a Spanish colony until Americans took it as a U.S. territory early in this century after the Spanish-American War. As U.S. citizens, Puerto Ricans were free to immigrate and soon did, seeking work in larger mainland cities, especially New York.

Puerto Ricans have diverse origins. The Taino were the indigenous people. In the sixteenth century, the Spanish arrived as colonizers. Later, the Africans arrived, brought as slaves to work on sugar plantations. So the genetic and cultural background of most Puerto Ricans combines two or three of these sources—indigenous, Spanish, and African.

For over fifty years a small but growing population of Puerto Ricans have become established in Wisconsin, primarily Milwaukee. Most arrived after World War II and many of the early arrivals had previously lived in other mainland cities like New York. By the late 1950s more Puerto Ricans, from rural areas or medium-sized towns like Caguas, Ponce, and Mayaguez, came directly to Milwaukee. Manufacturing jobs in the foundries and machine shops were the lure and Puerto Rican neighborhoods soon developed, first in the Holton Street area on the city's northeast side and in Merrill Park on the near west side. Later, an increasing number of Puerto Ricans settled on the south side, often in the same neighborhoods where Mexicans had begun to settle. (An important aside:

Although they are often lumped together by outsiders as "Hispanics," Puerto Ricans and Mexicans are culturally quite distinct. Their Spanish dialects differ, as do customs, foods, and traditional musics.)

From the Mountains to the Coast

About twenty thousand Puerto Ricans live in Milwaukee. Most come from village or working-class origins, and they tend to prefer the *jibaro* style of traditional music. A few hundred live in Madison, the only other Wisconsin city with a large group of *borinqueños*. Most are middle-class people—university students or faculty or those working permanently in the city. In Madison, a number of young players play in the *bomba y plena* musical style, which originated in the lowland plantations and spread to the urban areas.

Jibaro and *bomba y plena* refer to a major distinction within Puerto Rican musical culture. *La musica jibara*, music originating in the upland rural areas of central Puerto Rico, emphasizes stringed instruments—the guitar and the cuatro, a small Caribbean ten-stringed, guitar-shaped instrument, played melodically with a pick in the manner of a mandolin. *Jibaro* means villager or peasant and carries all the concomitant ambivalence in attitude about ruralites.

In a jibaro group, the cuatro is usually the lead melodic voice and is emblematic of la musica jibara. Recently, cuatros have become easier to obtain in Milwaukee since instrument maker Miguel Cruz has set up shop making and repairing cuatros. Beginning by scavenging wood from discarded furniture and repairing instruments in his small apartment, Cruz now is turning out solid cuatros in a store front in Walker's Point.

Bomba y plena, characteristic of coastal areas, has more African musical influence. The emphasis is on call and response singing to the accompaniment of various percussion instruments, for example, congas—large wooden vase-shaped drums, played without drumsticks—and pleneras—smaller hand-held drums, resembling tambourines without the jingles. Like the blues, *bomba* refers to a common type of improvised song, replete with realistic and sometimes wry commentary on life and love.

Instrumentation in jibaro and bomba y plena overlaps. Congas or guitars may show up in either type of ensemble, and both styles prominently feature the guiro, a percussion instrument of Taino origin made from a small notched gourd which is scraped with a stick or nowadays an Afro comb.

Salsa has become the accepted term in the past twenty years for the most publicized form of Puerto Rican music, the jazz-influenced modern style based on traditional Puerto Rican sounds. In salsa, modern instruments dominate—saxophones, trumpets, and synthesizers—but congas, metal versions of the guiro, and occasionally even a cuatro link salsa instrumentation to Puerto Rican tradition. Relying on *cumbias*, *meringues*, and other tropical rhythms, salsa has become less specifically Puerto Rican and more of a contemporary Latin American sound shared by all Latinos. Cecil Negron and Toty Ramos are prominent exponents of salsa in Milwaukee, and there are always a few excellent salsa bands to play for a range of community events.

In contrast, Wisconsin has no organized jibaro ensemble. Dozens of jibaro players in Milwaukee come together to jam, particularly during the Christmas

Miguel Cruz with one of his homemade cuatros, *Milwaukee, 1990* ***Photo: Jim Leary***

season when it is traditional for informal groups to make the rounds (called *parrandas*), dropping in on friends to sing Christmas songs. It was exactly this sort of group, led by Ruben Garcia, that I encountered at the dominoes tournament. To record this evanescent music, I urged the group into a quieter room and with one microphone and a Nagra recorder captured the flavor of their jam session. On the occasion of being recorded, they decided to name themselves Trulla Navidena (Christmas carollers), but they were essentially an informal aggregation.

Nor does bomba y plena have much in the way of formally organized groups. Orlando Cabrera, a meteorologist for the Wisconsin Department of Natural Resources and otherwise a member of Sotavento—a pan-Latino ensemble playing improvisatory, contemporary music using some Hispanic traditional instruments—wanted to play and demonstrate specifically Puerto Rican folk music in educational settings. To this end he organized Bentetu, a nascent group composed of some Puerto Rican students in Madison. So far, their main activity has been to hold jam sessions in the multicultural center at the University of Wisconsin's Memorial Union, bringing together a number of musically talented students from Puerto Rico.

In Milwaukee and Madison, Puerto Rico is in the hearts and music of these relatively new Wisconsinites. *Borinquén suelo querido* (Puerto Rico, beloved land) is not just a song title and the name of this "Down Home Dairyland" program, but a deep emotion shared by the borinqueños of Wisconsin.

Chapter 38

The East in the North: Southeast Asian Music in Wisconsin

Program 38 Performances
1. Voices of Hmong, "Hmoob zha." 2. Wang Chou Vang, *Tan blai* solo. 3. Nao Chay Yang, *Qeej* solo. 4. Sophea Mouth, Tro solo. 5. Bayon Dontre, Wedding music. 6. Bayon Dontre with Chanda Ra, "Memories of Lost Love in Michigan."

Khmer Musical Traditions

To most Americans, the culturally diverse Southeast Asian nations have been relatively little known. The memory of World War II campaigns in Burma and Malaya had begun to fade by the 1960s when the United States became engaged in the undeclared war in Vietnam. In the neighboring countries of Laos and Cambodia, the war was conducted for several years in secret, but by the beginning of the 1970s, the conflict in these lands became too intense to remain cloistered. A part of this secret war was the recruitment of upland tribes in Laos by the Central Intelligence Agency to disrupt the supply lines running from North Vietnam through Laos to the Viet Cong-controlled areas of South Vietnam. These groups were known as the Montagnards, a name stemming from the French colonial period when Laos, Cambodia, and Vietnam were lumped together as "French Indochina." Occasionally the media referred to the hill tribes as "Meo tribesmen"—*meo*, "savages," is a Chinese term. Their name for themselves, *Hmong,* "free people," has only started to become better known in the United States.

In Southeast Asia a sharp social and cultural distinction is made between the lowland peoples and those of the hills. The lowland Vietnamese and the Khmer of Cambodia (and the Han Chinese to their north) cultivate rice in irrigated paddies on the fertile plains, live in permanent settlements, and are part of the dominant national culture, linked to national "great traditions" maintained by cultural institutions in the urban areas (Crystal 1983).

Thus the Khmer musical traditions carried on by the Cambodian refugee community in Janesville had the benefit of formal institutions in Cambodia to support music education and performance. Moreover, in Cambodia, music is viewed as essential in a host of social settings. Foreigners visiting Phnom Penh have been astonished to note that musical performances were a required feature even at boxing matches (Mao and Ho 1969). Before the match, music (played by male, rarely female, flutists) invokes the spirits; during the match, music accompanies and keeps pace with the action, stopping only between rounds or when a boxer winds up prostrate on the mat.

Music at boxing matches is but one indication of a Cambodian's lifelong involvement with music. From a mother's lullabies, through haircutting ceremonies, weddings, traditional festivities, and finally funerals, live musical performances are viewed as essential. Cambodians in the United States feel strongly that the wedding ceremony above all requires traditional music.

Sophea Mouth—a refugee from western Cambodia who has lived in Lake Geneva, Janesville, and is currently a student in Madison—had formal music lessons as a child in Cambodia. Although the ensemble Sophea Mouth led until recently, Bayon Dontre, would use electric guitars, synthesizers, and a modern drum set to play contemporary Cambodian pop music, when they played for wedding ceremonies they used traditional instruments: the *tro* (a two-stringed Southeast Asian violin), the *chapei* (a plucked fretted lute-type instrument), and the *roneat* (a bamboo xylophone). A Cambodian wedding is serious and solemn. Even among the most humble families, weddings cannot be celebrated without music. A particular tune to which wedding participants sing the appropriate words must accompany each phase of the ceremony, from the cutting of the hair, the adornment with flowers, the calling forth of the bride, the saber dance, and the viewing of the bride and groom to the final phase when the groom follows the bride to the nuptial chamber.

Because of the formal nature of musical education and performance in Cambodia, Sophea Mouth compares Cambodian music to Western classical music. The Cambodian tradition, however, does not rely on written music, and musicians improvise and vary the tonality a great deal within either the five-tone or the seven-tone scale—the ones most frequently used.

Hmong Music/Sacred Speech

The Khmer traditions typify the lowland culture, while the Hmong, the largest group of Southeast Asian refugees in Wisconsin, are highlanders. In their homeland, they are but one of a number of distinct hill tribes who practice slash and burn agriculture, periodically migrating when the fertility of the soil is exhausted, and who maintain separate tribal cultural traditions, often as distinct from other neighboring hill tribes as from the lowland culture.

Coming from a nonliterate society, the Hmong had not only to learn English, but also to learn the concept of a written language. Semi-nomadic highland tribespeople suddenly had to learn to navigate the cities of an urban, industrial society.

Hmong music is expressive and powerful, although not as complex and refined as the Cambodian urban tradition. It shares many characteristics with that of the neighboring Lao, employing some similar singing styles and many of the same instruments (Miller 1985).

Unlike the Cambodians, the Hmong do not typically play traditional music in ensembles of diverse instruments. They emphasize soloistic playing, though in recent decades Hmong rock bands have brought a form of ensemble play to Hmong culture. The traditional instruments may be as simple as a leaf, the edge of which is held taut by the lips to produce a musical tone. The Hmong also play a two-stringed fiddle, similar to the Khmer tro, and like the Lao, their word for it is *saw.* They use many wind instruments, flutes like the *tan blai,* and the instrument which is afforded the most significance within the culture, the *qeej*

Wang Chou Vang playing the tan blai in his Eau Claire home, 1988 ***Photo: Jim Leary***

(pronounced "kaeng").

Qeej music is produced by metal free reeds fitted within bamboo tubes. The ends of the tubes are gathered in a wind-chest into which the player forces air through a blowpipe. The joints are made airtight with an insect product similar to beeswax. The reeds only sound when the player's finger covers an air hole on the particular tube, forcing the stream of air through the reed. Historical studies often mention this type of instrument as a forerunner of the accordion. While Lao players tend to hold the bamboo tubes in a vertical position, Hmong qeej players tend to hold the tubes horizontally, near the ground, swinging the instrument and performing dance motions while they play.

One type of motion stems from a tradition of martial art contests between qeej players in which each musician, while playing, attacks his opponent using the feet. Qeej player Joe Bee Xiong of Eau Claire asserts that in the distant past such battles could be fought to the death, the coup de grace being a kick that would drive the opponent's blowpipe through his palate into the brain. In the United States, such battles are only symbolically represented by two young qeej players rhythmically circling and kicking at each other's feet.

According to Sheboygan qeej player Vue Yang, the playing during the mock battles is "just music" (Yang 1990 I). But there also exists another category of qeej playing, where the music has a lexical meaning in the tonal Hmong language: a musical rendering of a sacred text. Here, the musician is actually a shaman, a religious leader who takes spiritual journeys to guide or cure the souls of his compatriots. The Hmong funeral has remained one of the most important rituals for which a qeej player is required. The musical text and the slow dance motions of the player guide the soul of the departed back to the resting place of the ancestors. Thus playing the qeej is only the surface manifestation of a demanding process requiring that one learn numerous sacred texts to be "played" through the instrument, and know the appropriate situation in which to invoke the particular text.

The Hmong and Cambodian communities of the Upper Midwest continue to grow and their vital and compelling musical traditions have become a permanent part of the region's cultural mosaic.

Part 7

Recorded legacy

Chapter 39

Small Labels, Big Music

Program 39 Performances
1. Bernie Roberts, "Flying Saucer Polka." 2. Fritz Bechtel and the Jolly Ramblers, "When the Sun Comes over the Brewery." 3. Marvin Brouchoud, "Raise the Window Down." 4. Syl Liebl and the Jolly Swiss Boys, "Baby Waltz." 5. Cavaliers, "Chubby Mama's Oberek." 6. Fendermen, "Heartbreak Special." 7. Zakons, "Wasted." 8. Royal Lancers, "Badger." 9. Earl Hooker, "Two Bugs in a Rug." 10. Singing Souls, "When I'm Gone." 11. Independence Gospelettes, "She's Gone (Will the Circle Be Unbroken?)."

The Foreign Market

Commercial recording companies never set out to document traditional music. Like other businesses, they sought to make a profit. Yet they made and marketed thousands of remarkable sound recordings by traditional musicians, a feat unmatched by scholars. By the second decade of the twentieth century, commercial giants like Victor and Columbia began to discover there were substantial regional and "foreign" markets for rural and ethnic music. People wanted to hear performers from their own ethnic group. Since the companies were based in the greater New York City area, their initial attempts to reach new customers depended upon either immigrant musicians dwelling in New York City or those from the hinterlands who were willing to travel to the eastern metropolis.

The Big Apple was undaunting to the Upper Midwest's Scandinavian performers. Some were recent immigrants who had passed through Ellis Island. Others were veteran ethnic vaudeville performers working a circuit that stretched from Brooklyn's Scandinavian enclaves to Seattle. Hjalmer Peterson, a Swedish singer and comedian based in Minneapolis, made a trial recording for Victor in March 1914. Apparently the company showed little interest, but two years later Peterson recorded four sides for Columbia in New York City. Using the stage name Olle i Skratthult (Ole from Laughtersville), Peterson would, between 1916 and 1929, record more than seventy sides for Victor and Columbia. Ethel and Eleanora Olson, Norwegian singers and dialect comedians from Minneapolis, likewise traveled to New York City in 1918 to make records for Victor (Spottswood 1990:2627–2631, 2713–2718).

Perhaps because bringing their own band was prohibitively expensive, perhaps because of the recording company's or the musicians' union's insistence, both Peterson and the Olsons were accompanied by a house or studio orchestra on their Victor recordings. The orchestra leader, Nathaniel Shilkret, was one of the fledgling industry's most active "session men," backing up countless ethnic performers, whether Dutch, French, German, Italian, Jewish, or Swedish. While a fine musician, Shilkret nonetheless provided a polished generic sound that differed considerably from the saltier musical dialect of the performers back home.

By the mid-1920s, improvements in recording technology and continued demand prompted the major labels to send out field recording teams to regional centers, including upper midwestern cities. Meanwhile new record companies with national ambitions began to attract the region's traditional and ethnic musicians. Jozef Sosnowski, for example, took his Polish trio from Milwaukee to Chicago to make records for Columbia, Mermaid, and Okeh between 1925 and 1929. Minnesota's Whoopee John Wilfahrt first recorded for Okeh in Minneapolis in 1927. Louis Alder and His Swiss Yodelers journeyed from Monroe, Wisconsin, to the Gennett studio in Richmond, Indiana, in 1929.

The tide of regional ethnic recordings that marked the 1920s was effectively stemmed by the Depression. Except for a few uncommon performers—like Whoopee John, Romy Gosz, and the Viking Accordion Band—the Upper Midwest's ethnic musicians all but disappeared from major labels for most of the 1930s. A resurgence toward the decade's end by Heinie and His Grenadiers (Milwaukee) and Ted Johnson and His Scandinavian Orchestra (Minneapolis) was interrupted by World War II, restrictions on the shellac from which records were made, and labor disputes.

Electronic Entrepreneurs

Major record labels showed very little interest in pursuing regional and ethnic markets in the postwar era. Neither the musicians nor their audiences had diminished, however, and small entrepreneurs saw their chance. Many were tinkerers with electronic equipment who relied on contacts with local musicians; others were musicians themselves who wanted to get their sound heard on radio, jukeboxes, and home turntables. All demonstrated a willingness to learn-as-you-go. Between the mid-1940s and the mid-1950s, companies producing ethnic 78 rpm recordings in Wisconsin included Broadcast, Kittenger, Pageant, Pfau, Pointer, Polka Dot, Polkaland, Potter, Tell, and probably many others.

Only Polkaland has survived the ensuing decades and the technological shifts from 78s to 45 rpm "singles" to 331/3 rpm "long play" recordings to cassettes. Dave Bensman began Polkaland in Sheboygan in the early 1950s. His entrepreneurial odyssey began when he bought a system to provide amplified sound and advertisements for dances, fairs, and other public events. A fascination with electronic equipment led him to open an appliance store. Soon polka bands in the heavily German and Bohemian locale approached him to fix their equipment and record demos. Bensman built a makeshift studio, began making records, then worked with a jobber and established his own radio station (WSHE) to promote his product. After Bensman's death in the 1960s the label was sold to Greg Leider of Fredonia, Wisconsin, who has continued to issue new recordings, while transferring older Polkaland titles to cassette (McHenry 1991 I).

While Polkaland's efforts have been confined to a regional market and a stable of polka bands, the Cuca label of Sauk City, Wisconsin, registered a few national hits (notably the Fendermen s "Muleskinner Blues" in 1960), while expanding its mostly polka-oriented catalog to include rockabilly, blues, and gospel sounds. Another youthful tinkerer, Cuca founder Jim Kirchstein, eventually earned an acoustic engineering degree from the University of Wisconsin, with coursework in electronics. His recording studio included a three-layered ceiling of original

German or "Dutchman" albums issued between the 1950s and the 1980s by small record companies in Minnesota and Wisconsin ***Photo: Jim Leary***

design, and he ran a pressing plant that could produce several thousand albums daily and a like number of 45s (Kirchstein 1992 I).

Since Cuca's demise in 1972, however, the economics of the small companies that produce the Upper Midwest's ethnic recordings have altered radically.

Whereas Polkaland and Cuca once underwrote the cost of records that they would subsequently promote and sell, today's labels are essentially recording services. Bands put up their own money for studio time and they purchase a stock of recordings which they market themselves. The recording company (often a one-person operation) provides the sound engineering and production for a master tape, offers cover design services, acts as a liaison with the pressing plant (often somewhere outside the region), and lends its label name.

While this latter-day arrangement might seem a simple exchange of cash for expertise, the most successful ethnic labels in the Upper Midwest are run by working musicians who—by virtue of their personal tastes, skills, and ongoing relationships with other musicians—have attracted particular clienteles and produced distinctive sounds. Roger Bright's Bright Productions of New Glarus lures Swiss performers. The sax-accordion Slovenian flash of greater Milwaukee emanates from Don Hunjadi's HG studio in Franksville, while a button box and chordovox Slovenian sound characterizes many titles issued by Richie Yurkovich's RY records of Willard. "Polka Joe" Wojkiewicz of Green Bay has issued many recordings by northern Wisconsin's Polish bands on North Star Appli. Followers of the concertina-tuba-dominated Dutchman style generally cross the border to New Prague, Minnesota, where Jerry Minar runs JBM Productions.

The studios run by these musicians and engineers are all sidelines. There will probably never be big money in recording the old-time ethnic sounds that persist in the Upper Midwest. But while the labels are small, the music is big.

Chapter 40

Saving the Sounds of Tradition

Program 40 Performances
1. Bob Mathiowetz, "Concertina Gallop." 2. Agnes Sullivan, "The Queen of England." 3. Ted Ashlaw, "Driving Saw Logs on the Plover." 4. Charlie Patton, "Pony Blues." 5. Dachauer Bauern Kapelle (Dachau peasant band), "An der Moldau." 6. Warde Ford, "Keith and Hiles Line." 7. John Hermundstad, "The Waltz the Devil Danced Himself to Death With." 8. Matt Radosevich, "Mladi kapetani." 9. Al Kolberg, "Lauterbach." 10. Einard Maki, "Orpo pojan valssi."

Pioneer Field Recordists

Thomas Edison's cylinder recorder was a scant thirteen years old in 1890 when Jesse Walter Fewkes, a Harvard anthropologist, recorded songs and stories from the Passamaquoddy Indians of Calais, Maine (Hickerson 1982). And, by the early twentieth century, commercial recording companies like Edison, Victor, and Columbia were issuing the music of traditional performers on cylinder and disc. Anthropologists, folklorists, ethnomusicologists, record producers, electronics buffs, and enthusiasts have been capturing traditional music ever since.

Frances Densmore was the first to make field recordings of traditional music in the Upper Midwest. Born in Red Wing, Minnesota, in 1867, she was inspired by Alice C. Fletcher's pioneering work, *A Study of Omaha Indian Music* (1893). In 1907, equipped with a bulky Edison Home Phonograph, Densmore commenced recording the music of her region's native peoples: first among the Ojibwa on reservations in White Earth, Leech Lake, and Red Earth, Minnesota, and Lac du Flambeau, Wisconsin; then among Wisconsin's Menominee and Winnebago peoples. Her Ojibwa recordings alone number nearly five hundred songs (see Densmore generally and Vennum 1989).

Densmore's work was supported by the Bureau of American Ethnology at the Smithsonian Institution in Washington, D.C., and was part of the Bureau's broader effort to document the "fading" cultures of native peoples. Beyond recording a wide array of courting, hunting, healing, gambling, war, and dream songs, Frances Densmore took photographs of musical instruments, singers, and events, set down performers' biographies and details about the use and meanings of their songs, and carefully described nonmusical aspects of Woodland Indian life. Her *Chippewa Customs* (1929) remains a classic.

While the anthropological impulse and institutional sponsorship spurred Densmore, a passion for poetry and an artist's wanderlust moved Franz Rickaby. Born in Springfield, Illinois, in 1889, Rickaby, the descendant of musicians and teachers, was a violin-playing dance band leader and published versifier while in his teens (D. Greene 1968). In 1917, after graduating from Knox College and earning an M.A. from Harvard, Rickaby took a position in the University of North Dakota's English Department.

Harvard had been the seat of American ballad study since the mid-nineteenth century, so it was not surprising that one of the first courses Rickaby offered was "Balladry: English and American." His journal of 1919 reveals a particular fascination with the works of another Harvard graduate, John Lomax.

> February 4 ... I have become enamored of the ballad! The condition began with a hasty survey I began some weeks ago of Lomax's "Cowboy Songs."
> (D. Greene 1968:325)

That summer Franz Rickaby went "auto-tramping" across the northern reaches of Minnesota, Wisconsin, and Michigan in search of lumber-camp ballads. Although he garnered but a few examples, he persisted and, prior to his death in 1925, recorded the fifty-one texts, tunes, and variants that comprise *Ballads and Songs of the Shanty-Boy* (1926).

Rickaby's book is especially valuable for the first full portrait of a composer of lumber-camp ballads, William N. Allen of Wausau, Wisconsin. Allen was born in St. Stephens, New Brunswick, in 1843 to Irish immigrant parents and traveled with them to the Upper Peninsula of Michigan and then Wisconsin in the 1850s. At seventeen young Billy apprenticed to a timber cruiser in Green Bay, and at twenty-five he was cruising in the Wausau area where he remained.

About 1870 he began composing songs and poems of logging life, drawing upon traditional tunes, language, and verse structures. He also performed his logger ballads in lumber camps and several entered oral tradition, including "Driving Saw Logs on the Plover," with its admonition that farming is a safer occupation than logging.

Allen was still active in 1928 when eleven of his poems were published under the pen name "Shan T. Boy" in Lake Shore Kearney's *The Hodag*. While all treat logging and the woods, a few political ditties reveal the sharpness of Allen's Democratic wit. "I Do Not Choose to Run" pillories President Calvin Coolidge for fishing on an oil magnate's Brule River estate while shunning the lumberjacks who are kept outside with a "ten pound padlock." Playing upon Silent Cal's oft-quoted decision not to seek another term, Allen places the GOP leader in the path of a legendary woods beast, the dinosaurlike Hodag.

> When Calvin roams the northern wood,
> On Lake Superior's shore,
> Should [he] meet a Hodag seeking food
> And hear his awful roar.
> He'll throw away his fishing rod,
> His reel and fancy gun
> And whisper to himself, "My God,
> I think I choose to run."

The Wisconsin Chair Company

While Calvin Coolidge, the man who said "the business of America is business,"

Czech sheet music at the home of Clara Sveda, Ashland, 1981 ***Photo: Jim Leary***

found his way into a folk poet's verses, upper midwestern businessmen preserved folk music through commercial recordings. In 1915 the Wisconsin Chair Company of Port Washington expanded its product line to include "phonographs and phonographic records." Soon it was issuing recordings on Puritan and Paramount labels (Calt 1988). Both labels featured second-rate pop performers that the bigger recording companies had rejected, but Puritan, in keeping with the immediate area's large German population, offered a string of recordings by German male choruses and peasant bands. In 1921 Paramount also provided record-pressing services to Milwaukee's fledgling Polonia Phonograph Company, but their product was defective and resulted in a suit.

The inability of the Wisconsin Chair Company's subsidiaries to command stellar pop artists and to provide a product of consistent quality for the region's ethnic musicians resulted in a shift in orientation to black artists and audiences who would consider low pay and technically shoddy records better than nothing. As Otto Moeser, the Chair Company's president from 1935 to 1955, blithely recollected: "We could not compete for high class talent with Edison, Columbia, and Victor, and we had inferior records; so we went to race records." Nonetheless Paramount was responsible for recording some of the finest Delta blues players, including the legendary Charlie Patton, who traveled from Mississippi to Wisconsin in May 1930 to record such classics as "Pony Blues" (Palmer 1981: 82–83).

Since the pioneering efforts of Frances Densmore and Franz Rickaby, and the serendipitous blundering of the Wisconsin Chair Company, others have sought to preserve the traditional music of the Upper Midwest's diverse peoples. Sometimes supported with government funds, equipment, and a sense of mission, sometimes embarked upon their own self-financed vision quest, sometimes driven to turn a profit, they have all contributed to saving the sounds of tradition.

Folklore Institutions in the Upper Midwest

The Center for the Study of Upper Midwestern Cultures

901 University Bay Dr., Madison, WI 53705. Phone: (608) 262-8180.

The Center is committed to the languages and cultural traditions of this region's diverse peoples. CSUMC fosters research and the preservation of archival collections, while producing educational and outreach programs for a broad public audience. The regional center also assists community groups, classrooms, and independent scholars with projects involving Upper Midwestern cultures.

Folklore Program, University of Wisconsin–Madison

306 Ingraham Hall, 1185 Observatory Dr., Madison, WI 53706. Phone: (608) 265-3514.

The UW-Madison Folklore Program began offering courses in Fall 1983. The Program's approach is comparative and interdisciplinary, with a concern for genre, theory, performance, ethnography, archiving, and responsible public presentation of folklore through exhibits, festivals, media productions, and other modes of representation. The University has one of the largest concentrations of foreign language and area studies programs in the nation and the Folklore Program is particularly strong in African, Asian, and European folklore. Offerings in American folklore, including American Indian Folklore, place a special emphasis on the surrounding region. The Program is the teaching arm of the Center for the Study of Upper Midwestern Cultures.

Wisconsin Arts Board

101 E. Wilson St., First Floor, Madison, WI 53702. Phone: (608) 266-2513

Offers folk arts grants, technical assistance, internships, and public programs. Co-produces traditional music CDs and documentaries and folk arts education curriculum such as the websites Wisconsin Folks and Wisconsin Weather Stories, and the books Kids' Field Guide to Local Culture and Teachers' Guide to Local Culture.

Wisconsin Music Archives, University of Wisconsin–Madison

Mills Music Library, B162 Memorial Library, 728 State St., Madison, WI 53706. Phone: (608) 263-1884

Maintains a research collection of Wisconsin and regional musical materials, with strong holdings in traditional and ethnic music. The archives always strives to increase its collection, which includes commercial and field recordings, sheet music, books and pamphlets, and correspondence and papers. The special collection contains more than 25,000 items representing all Wisconsin musical traditions and encompasses the period 1850s to the present. Strengths of the collection include published sheet music, folk and ethnic music, scores by contemporary Wisconsin composers, and recordings of state performers or issued by Wisconsin labels. Recordings in the Cuca, Paramount, and Wisconsin Folksong collections.

References

I. Interviews

Excerpts from interviews with the people listed below were used in "Down Home Dairyland" programs and the *Listener's Guide.* All tape-recorded interviews were conducted by James P. Leary (JPL) or Richard March (RM) in Wisconsin except where another interviewer or state is named. Copies of the interview tapes and indexes, unless otherwise indicated, form part of the archive of the Wisconsin Folk Museum. Cedarburg is Cedarburg Cultural Center, and McDowell is McDowell Archives, Northland College.

Ackley, Joe. Interview by JPL, Lac du Flambeau Ojibwa reservation, Nov. 7,1989. Cedarburg.
———. Interview by RM, Mole Lake Ojibwa reservation, Oct. 10, 1992.

Albrecht, Lois Rindlisbacher. Interview by JPL, Cameron, Jan. 23, 1990.

Altenburg, Art. Interview by JPL and RM, Milwaukee, May 17, 1988.

Baldoni, Ivo. Interview by JPL, Milwaukee, Oct. 12,1989. Cedarburg.

Barnak, Bernice. Interview by JPL, Ashland, Feb. 19, 1981. McDowell.

Bashell, Louie. Interview by RM, New Glarus, May 14, 1988.

Bellin, Cletus. Interview by RM, Kewaunee, Jan. 2, 1989.

Berg, Lenore. Interview by JPL, Barron, May 27, 1989.

Beringer, Anton "Speedy." Interview by JPL, Poy Sippi, March 29, 1985.

Bernet, Martha. Interview by JPL, Mount Horeb, Oct. 7, 1989.

Bollerud, Bruce. Interview by JPL, Madison, June 1987 and July 16,1990.

Brevak, Vivian Eckholm, and Netty Day Harvey. Interview by JPL, Barksdale, June 22, 1981. McDowell.

Brueggen, Brian, Madonna, and Phil. Interview by JPL and RM, Evansville, Apr. 30, 1988.

Brueggen, Phil. Interview by JPL, Cashton, July 24, 1991.

Brueggen, Willard, Harry, Gary, and Judy. Interview by JPL and RM, Evansville, Aug. 25, 1990.

Burkhalter, Rudy. Interview by JPL, Madison, Feb. 19 and Apr. 16, 1987.

Cabrera, Orlando. Interview by RM, Madison, Feb. 25, 1990.

Calkins, Ray. Interview by JPL, Chetek, May 25, 1988.

Chaudoir, Harry. Interview by JPL, Rosiere, May 3,1988.

Cleveland, Jerry. Interview by RM, Waukesha, Aug. 19, 1989.

Coopman, Ernie. Interview by JPL, Mankato, Minn., Feb. 6, 1990. Minnesota Historical Society.

Cruz, Miguel. Interview by JPL and Cecil Negron, Milwaukee, Dec. 19,1989. Cedarburg.

Daniels, Agnes. Telephone interview by RM, San Pedro, Calif., Oct. 18, 1991.

DeWitz, Irving. Interview by JPL, Hustisford, Feb. 15, 1985.

Dombrowski, Norm. Interview by JPL, Stevens Point, Apr. 26, 1988.

Dorschner, Ray and Randy. Interview by JPL and RM, Evansville, May 1, 1988.

Dowling, Martin. Interview by RM, Madison, Mar. 25, 1992.

Drea, Larry. Interview by JPL, Loretto, Mar. 9, 1991.

Ebner, Jim. Interview by RM, Milwaukee, 1983.

Finseth, Leonard. Interview by JPL, Mondovi, May 23,1988.

Flanum-Lane, Barbara. Interview by RM, Milwaukee, Oct. 28, 1989.

Gattin, Mrs. Jesse. Interview by Robert Andresen, Danbury, 1973 and 1974. Andresen Collection, Duluth, Minn.

Gilbertsen, George. Interview by JPL, Madison, June 27,1990.

Gornick, Joe. Interview by RM, Mukwanago, July 13,1991.

Groeschl, Syl. Interview by JPL, Calumetville, Aug. 13, 1985.
———. Interview by Becky Miller, Calumetville, Sept. 6, 1990.

Groeschl, Valeria. Interview by Becky Miller, Calumetville, Sept. 7,1990.

Guibord, Ernest "Pea Soup." Interview by Philip Martin, Lac du Flambeau Ojibwa reservation, summer 1979.

Gunderson, Carl. Interview by Katherine Leary Antenne and Minda Hugdahl, Rice Lake, Aug. 9, 1973. Barron County Historical Society.

Hartmann, Gordon. Interview by RM, Madison, June 13,1991.

Hartwich, Karl. Interview by JPL, Appleton, May 4,1988.

Haugh, Loren. Interview by JPL, Hillsboro, Mar. 9, 1991.

Hendrickson, William. Interview by JPL, Herbster, Jan. 13, 1981. McDowell.

Hilgendorf, Earl. Interview by JPL, Friestadt, Apr. 16, 1985.

Hlinak, Larry. Interview by JPL, Appleton, May 4, 1988.

Hodkiewicz, Richie. Interview by JPL, Pulaski, July 29, 1989.

Horner, Darlene. Interview by JPL, DeForest, Feb. 4,1989.

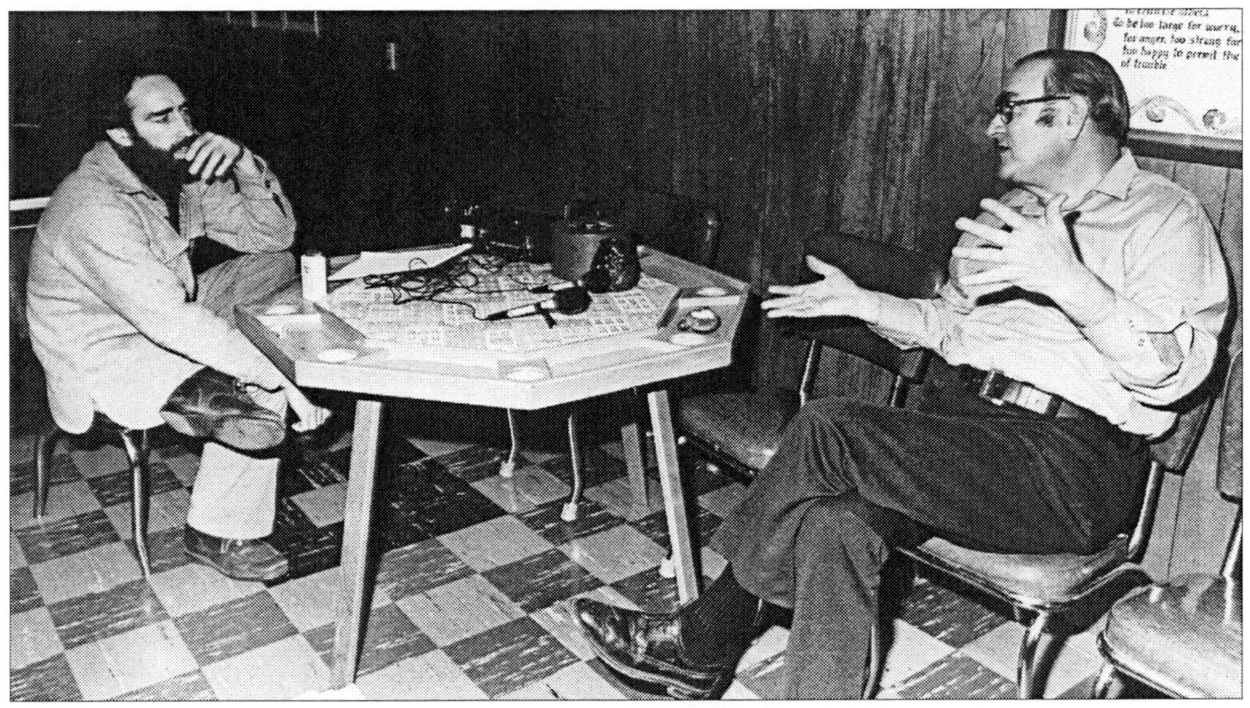

Jim Leary interviewing concertina player Bob Mathiowetz, Ashland, 1980
Photo: Larry Dunlap. Wisconsin Folk Museum Collection

Jerabek, "Tuba Dan." Interview by JPL, Appleton, May 4,1988.

Johanik, Joe. Interview by JPL, Moquah, Mar. 18, 1981. McDowell.

Johnson, Ailie and Walter. Interview by JPL, Oulu, May 23, 1988.

Johnson, Bernard. Interview by JPL, Blue Mounds, July 1, 1989.

Jones, Richard. Interview by JPL, DeForest, Feb. 4,1989.

Justmann, Andrae. Interview by JPL, Appleton, May 4,1988.

Kahle, Ivan. Interview by JPL, Norwood, Minn., Feb. 12,1990. Minnesota Historical Society.

Kaminski, "Concertina Millie." Interview by JPL, Muskego, Oct. 12, 1989.

Kanetzke, Howard. Interview by RM, Madison, Apr. 24, 1990.

Kangas, William. Interview by JPL, Oulu, May 23,1988.

Kania, Ed. Interview by JPL, Metz, Mich., Aug. 24, 1989.

Karpek, Grace. Interview by JPL, Milwaukee, Oct. 12, 1989. Cedarburg.

Karye, Charles. Interview by JPL, Marengo, Dec. 23, 1980.

Kirchstein, Jim. Interview by JPL, Mount Horeb, Mar. 27, 1992.

Kole, Art. Interview by JPL, Metz, Mich., Aug. 24, 1989.

Krevs, Joe. Interview by RM, Middleton, Apr. 11, 1991.

Kuchera, Victor. Interview by JPL, Phillips, June 15,1991.

Kumpula, Richard. Interview by JPL, Iron River, Jan. 1981. McDowell.

Lahti, Rodney. Interview by JPL, Oulu, May 23,1988.

Lashua, Famous. Interview by Robert Andresen, Mountain Iron, Minn., 1983. Andresen Collection, Duluth.

Liska, Ray. Interview by JPL, Hillsboro, Mar. 9, 1991.

Lucas, Patsy Yurkovich. Interview by RM, Hartford, Dec. 14,1988.

Magayne, Hank. Interview by RM, Middleton, Apr. 11, 1991.

Maroszek, Brenda. Interview by RM, Pulaski, July 29, 1989.

Maroszek, John. Interview by RM, Poaaski, July 29,1989.

Maroszek, Mike. Interview by JPL, Poaaski, July 29, 1989.

Martin, Philip. Interview by JPL, Mount Horeb, Apr. 1990.

Mathiowetz, Robert. Interview by JPL, Ashland, Dec. 2, 1980. McDowell.

McDermott, Tommy. Interview by RM, Madison, Mar. 18, 1992.

McHenry, Leah Bensman. Interview by JPL, Mequon, Jan. 8, 1991.

McMahon, Francis. Interview by JPL and RM, Madison, May 9, 1988.

Meisner, Steve. Interview by RM, Whitewater, June 11, 1991.

Menard, Rosemary Korger. Interview by JPL, Rice Lake, May 11, 1985.

Meuret, George. Interview by JPL, Haugen, May 27,1989.

Montano, Frank. Interview by RM, Danbury, Dec. 3, 1988.

Morgan, Lee. Interview by JPL, Cambria, Oct. 8, 1989.

Mouth, Sophea. Interview by RM, Madison, Feb. 9, 1990.

Novak, Jerry. Interview by JPL, Moquah, Aug. 2, 1979. McDowell.

Ostrowiecki, Richie. Interview by JPL and RM, Cudahy, May 17, 1988.

Pakiz, Frank and Rose. Interview by JPL, Greenwood, Nov. 16,1989.

Peters, Max. Interview by Andy Rolls, St. Louis, Mo., fall 1981.

Poast, Ron. Interview by JPL, Black Earth, Oct. 13, 1989. Cedarburg.

Podboy, Ray. Interview by RM, Willard, July 18, 1985.

Polarski, Ray. Interview by JPL, Three Lakes, Jan. 7, 1989. Cedarburg.

Radicevich, Mike. Interview by RM, Milwaukee, Nov. 2,1990.

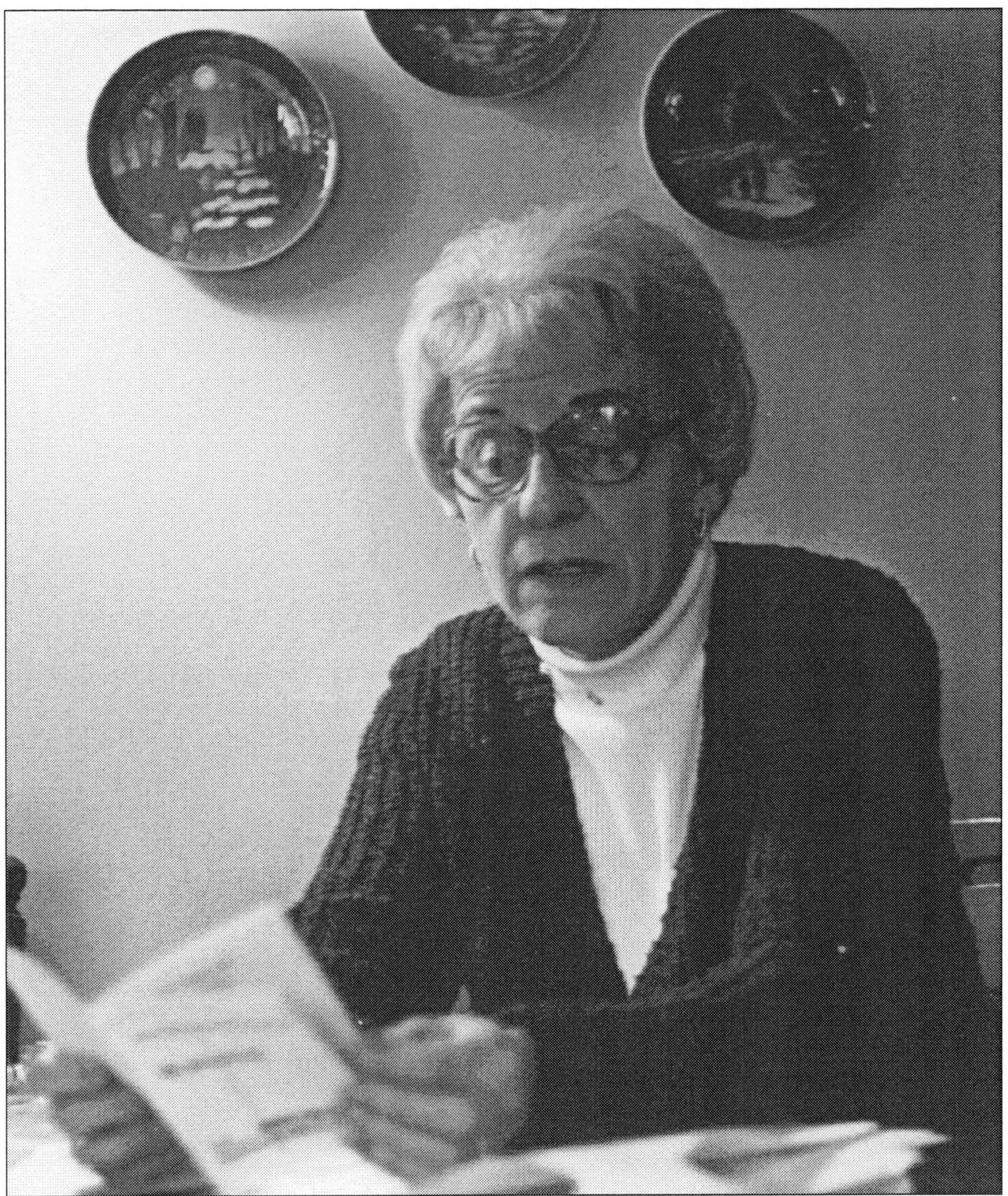

Vera Dvorak Schultz consulting a Czech songbook, Washburn, 1980 **Photo: Jim Leary**

Razer, Jim. Interview by JPL, Tony, Nov. 11, 1989. Cedarburg.

Renard, Arthur. Interview by JPL, Duval, May 4,1988.

Rice, Lorraine and Mary. Interview by RM, Oregon, June 21, 1991.

Rodgers, Dick Interview by JPL and RM, Pulaski, July 29, 1989.

Romel, Bill and Sylvester. Interview by JPL, Posen, Mich., Aug. 24, 1989.

Schwartz, William. Interview by JPL, Sheboygan, Nov. 2, 1989.

Shulfer, Gene, and Jim Weisbrod. Interview by JPL and RM, Evansville, May 1, 1988.

Siedlecki, Alexei. Interview by JPL, Ashland, Jan. 9,1981. McDowell.

Slusarski, Dominic. Interview by JPL, Stevens Point, July 7, 1983.

Splettstoesser, Wally. Interview by RM, Madison, Nov. 18, 1988.

Stangle, Stanley. Interview by JPL, Ashland, Nov. 6, 1980. McDowell.

Stelmach, Mary. Interview by JPL, Ashland, Feb. 19,1981. McDowell.

St. Germaine, Jeff. Interview by JPL, Lac Court Oreilles Ojibwa reservation, May 24, 1989.
———. Interview by RM, Lac Court Oreilles, Jan. 1991.

St. Germaine, Robert ("Bobby Bullett"). Interview by JPL, Madison, Sept. 30,1990.

Streiff, Clayton. Interview by JPL, Mount Horeb, Oct. 7, 1989.

Strzelecki, Joseph. Interview by JPL, Posen, Mich., Mar. 30, 1989.

Suess, Erwin. Interview by JPL, North Mankato, Minn., Feb. 6, 1990. Minnesota Historical Society.

Sundell, Steve. Interview by JPL, Madison, Apr. 1990.

Timm, Agnes Thomas. Interview by JPL, Cambria, Oct. 8, 1989.

Tomesh, Joe and John. Interview by JPL, Haugen, July 31, 1990.

Trudeau, Coleman. Interview by Michael Loukinen, Macmillan, Mich., Mar. 1984. UP North Films.

Vandertie, Alfred. Interview by RM, Algoma, June 12, 1989.

Vang, Wang Chou. Interview by JPL, Menomonie, Nov. 8, 1989. Cedarburg.

Vetterli, Betty. Interview by JPL, Mount Horeb, Oct. 7, 1989.

Waupoose, Everett "Butch." Interview by JPL, Neopit, Menominee reservation, May 13,1989.

Waupoose, Sarah. Interview by Michael Loukinen, Neopit, Menominee reservation, May 13, 1989. UP North Films.

Webster, Louis. Interview by JPL, Keshena, Menominee reservation, Jan. 6, 1989. Cedarburg.

Weisbrod, Jim, and Gene Shulfer. Interview by JPL and RM, Evansville, May 1, 1988.

Welk, Olwen Morgan. Interview by JPL, Cambria, Oct. 8, 1989.

Whitford, K. Wendell. Interview by JPL, Cottage Grove, July 12, 1990.

Wilfahrt, Fritz. Interview by JPL and RM, Pulaski, July 29, 1989.

Williams, Dorothy and Will. Interview by JPL, DeForest, Feb. 4,1989.

Wojta, Jerome. Interview by JPL, Two Creeks, May 3, 1988.

Wolf, Betty. Interview by JPL, St. Joseph, Minn., Feb. 8, 1990. Minnesota Historical Society.

Wolfe, Anton. Interview by JPL, Stevens Point, Apr. 19, 1985.

Xiong, Mai Soua. Interview by RM, Appleton, Mar. 1, 1990.

Yang, Vue. Interview by RM, Sheboygan, Mar. 1, 1990.

Yurkovich, Richie. Interview by JPL, Willard, Apr. 25, 1988, and Nov. 16, 1990.

Zellmer, Blanche Havel. Interview by JPL, Montgomery, Minn., Feb. 13, 1990. Minnesota Historical Society.

Zurawski, Greg. Interview by JPL, Custer, Feb. 26, 1988.

II. Printed Sources

Andresen, Robert. 1978. "Traditional Music, the Real Story of Ethnic Music and How It Evolved in Minnesota and Wisconsin." *Minnesota Monthly,* October, 9–13.

Atterbury, Louis. 1979. "The Fiddle Tune: An American Artifact." In *Readings in American Folklore,* ed. Jan Harold Brunvand, 324-333. New York: W. W. Norton. First published in *Northwest Folklore* 2 (1967):2.

Barden, Thomas. 1982. "The Yuba, Wisconsin, *Masopust* Festival." *Midwestern Journal of Language and Folklore* 8, no. 1: 48-51.

Barfuss, Gerald. 1983. *David Stone in Sunset Valley: The Story of the KSTP Barn Dance.* Minneapolis: James D. Thueson, Publisher.

Bayard, Samuel P. 1944. Hill Country Tunes. Philadelphia: American Folklore Society.

Bercovici, Konrad. 1925. *On New Shores.* New York: Century Co.

Bohlman, Philip V. 1980. "The Folk Songs of Charles Bannen: The Interaction of Music and History in Southwestern Wisconsin." *Wisconsin Academy of Sciences, Arts and Letters* 68:167–87

———. 1979. Music in the Culture of German-Americans in North-Central Wisconsin. M.A. thesis, Department of Ethnomusicology, University of Illinois, Champaign-Urbana.

Brink, Carol Ryrie. 1935. *Caddie Woodlawn.* New York: Macmillan.

Bronner, Simon J. 1987. *Old-Time Music Makers of New York State.* Syracuse, N.Y.: Syracuse University Press.
———. 1978. "The Country Music Tradition in Western New York State." *Journal of Country Music* 6, no. 4: 30–59.

Broughton, Viv. 1985. *Black Gospel.* Dorset: Blandford Press.

Bruce, Dix. 1991. "On Wisconsin." *Fretted Instrument Guild of America* 35, no. 5: 37–39.

Buchen, Gustave W. 1944. *Historic Sheboygan County.* Sheboygan, Wis.: Sheboygan County Historical Society.

Calt, Stephen. 1988. "Paramount: The Anatomy of a 'Race' Label." *78 Quarterly* 1, no. 3: 9-23.

Corenthal, Michael G., ed. 1991. *The Illustrated History of Wisconsin Music,* 1840-1990. Milwaukee: Yesterday's Memories, MGC Publications.

Crystal, Eric. 1983. "Hmong Traditions in the Crucible of Change." In *Michigan Hmong Arts: Textiles in Transition,* ed. C. Kurt Dewhurst and Marsha MacDowell, 5-13. East Lansing: Michigan State University Museum.

Densmore, Frances. 1932. *Menominee Music.* Bureau of American Ethnology Bulletin no. 102. Washington, D.C.: Smithsonian Institution.
———. 1929. *Chippewa Customs.* Bureau of American Ethnology Bulletin no. 86. Washington, D.C.: Smithsonian Institution.
———. 1910-13. *Chippewa Music. 2* vols. Bureau of American Ethnology. Washington, D.C.: Smithsonian Institution.

Ericson, Uno Myggan. 1978. *Fran scen och cabaret.* Stockholm: Stegelands.

Evans, James F. 1969. *Prairie Farmer and WLS.* Urbana: University of Illinois Press.

Federal Writers' Project. 1941. *Michigan: A Guide to the Wolverine State.* New York: Oxford University Press.

Fletcher, Alice C. 1893. *A Study of Omaha Indian Music.* Cambridge, Mass.: Peabody Museum of American Achaeology and Ethnology.

Folstad, Ardis. ca. 1987. *Vi hadde def godt her* (We had it good here). n.p. [possibly Dunn County, Wis.]

Greene, Daniel W. 1968. "'Fiddle and I': The Story of Franz Rickaby." *Journal of American Folklore* 81:316-36.

Greene, Victor. 1992. *A Passion for Polka.* Berkeley: University of California Press.

Gronow, Pekka. 1982. "Ethnic Recordings: An Introduction." In *Ethnic Recordings in America,* ed. Judith McCulloh, 1-49. Washington, D.C.: American Folklife Center.
———. 1977. *Studies in Scandinavian-American Discography.* 2 vols. Helsinki: Finnish Institute of Recorded Sound.

Hale, Frederick. 1984. *The Swiss in Wisconsin.* Madison: State Historical Society of Wisconsin.

Harvey, Anne-Charlotte Hanes. 1983. "Swedish-American Theatre." In *Ethnic Theatre in the United States,* ed. Maxine S. Seller, 491-524. Westport, Conn.: Greenwood Press.

Harvey, Anne-Charlotte, and Richard Hulan. 1982. *Teater, visafton och bal: A National Tour of Theatre, Music and Dance Traditions of Swedish America.* Washington, D.C.: National Council for the Traditional Arts.

Haugen, Einar. 1969. *The Norwegian Language in America: A Study in Bilingual Behavior*. Bloomington: Indiana University Press.

Heilbut, Anthony. 1985. *The Gospel Sound.* New York: Doubleday.

Hendrix, Glenn. 1988. "An Island of Fiddlers." *Journal of Beaver Island History* 3:51-57.

Hickerson, Joseph. 1982. "Early Field Recordings of Ethnic Music." In *Ethnic Recordings in America,* ed. Judith McCulloh, 67-83. Washington, D.C.: American Folklife Center.

Holmes, Fred L. 1944. Old World Wisconsin: Around Europe in the Badger State. Madison, Wis.

Janda, Robert. 1976. *Entertainment Tonight: An Account of Bands in Manitowoc County since 1910.* Manitowoc County Historical Society Monograph Series, no. 28. Manitowoc, Wis.

Johnson, James Weldon. 1929. "The Origins of the 'Barber Chord.'" *Mentor,* February.

Kallio, Sandra. 1987. "In Yuba, It's Masopust." *Wisconsin State Journal,* sec. 3, Feb. 18.

Kearney, Luke Sylvester "Lakeshore." 1928. *The Hodag*. Wausau, Wis.: Democrat Printing Co.

Kolar, Walter W. 1975. *A History of the Tambura.* Vol. 2. Tamburitzan Institute of Folk Arts. Pittsburgh: Duquesne University.

Kolehmainen, John I., and George W. Hill. 1951. *Haven in the Woods: The Story of the Finns in Wisconsin.* Madison: State Historical Society of Wisconsin.

Leary, James P. 1992. "Sawdust and Devils: Indian Fiddling in the Western Great Lakes Region." In *Medicine Fiddle,* ed. J. P. Leary. Bismarck: North Dakota Humanities Council.

———. 1991a. Folk Arts of Eastern Europeans in the Chippewa Valley. Research report. Eau Claire, Wis.: Chippewa Valley Museum.

———. 1991b. *Polka Music, Ethnic Music.* Wisconsin Folk Museum Bulletin no. 1. Mount Horeb.

———. 1991c. *Yodeling in Dairyland: A History of Swiss Music in Wisconsin.* Mount Horeb: Wisconsin Folk Museum.

———. 1990a. Minnesota Polka: Dance Music from Four Traditions. St. Paul: Minnesota Historical Society.

———. 1990b. "The Legacy of Viola Turpeinen." *Finnish Americana* 8:6-11.

———. 1990c. "Wisconsin Folk Musical Instruments: Objects, Sounds and Symbols." In *In Tune with Tradition,* ed. Robert T. Teske and James P. Leary,13-28. Cedarburg, Wis.: Cedarburg Cultural Center.

———. 1987a. "Czech Polka Styles in the United States: From America's Dairyland to the Lone Star State." In *Czech Music from Texas: A Sesquicentennial Symposium,* ed. Clinton Machann, 79-95. College Station, Tex.: Komensky Press.

———. 1987b. The Wisconsin Patchwork: Recordings from the Helene Stratman-Thomas Collection of Wisconsin Folk Music. Madison: Department of Continuing Education in the Arts, University of Wisconsin.

———. 1983[1984]. "Ethnic Country Music along Superior's South Shore." *John Edwards Memorial Foundation Quarterly* 19, no. 72: 219-230.

Leary, James P., and Richard March. 1991. "Dutchman Bands: Genre, Ethnicity and Pluralism in the Upper

Midwest." In *Creative Ethnicity: Symbols and Strategies of Contemporary Ethnic Life,* ed. Stephen Stern and John Allen Cicala, 21–43. Logan: Utah State University Press.

Lederman, Anne. 1988. "Old Native and Métis Fiddling in Manitoba: Origins, Structure and the Question of Syncretism." *Canadian Journal of Native Studies* 8:2.

Levy, Marcella. 1987. "Richland Ramblings." *Richland County Observer,* sec. 1, Feb. 19.

Lomax, Alan. 1960. *Folk Songs of North America.* New York: Doubleday.
———. 1938. Field notes on Joe Cloud. Archive of Folk Song, Library of Congress, Washington, D.C.

Lornell, Kip. 1985[1989]. "The Early Career of Whoopee John Wilfahrt." *John Edwards Memorial Foundation Quarterly* 21, nos. 75-76: 51-53.

Luchsinger, John. 1884. "The Swiss Colony of New Glarus." In *History of Green County,* ed. C. W. Butterfield. Springfield, Ill.: Union Publishing Co.

Malone, Bill C. 1974. *Country Music USA.* Austin: University of Texas Press.

Mao, Chhuk Meng, and Ho Tong Ho. 1969. "Importance de la musique dans la vie cambodgienne." In *Musique khmere,* ed. Hang Thun Hak et al. Phnom Penh.

March, Richard. 1991. "Polkas in Wisconsin Music." In *The Illustrated History of Wisconsin Music,* 1840-1990, ed. Michael G. Corenthal, 385-97. Milwaukee: Yesterday's Memories, MGC Publications.
———. 1985[1989]. "Slovenian Polka Music: Tradition and Transition." *John Edwards Memorial Foundation Quarterly* 21, nos. 75-76: 47-50.
———. 1983. The Tamburitza Tradition. Ph.D. diss., Department of Folklore, Indiana University, Bloomington.

Martin, Philip. ca. 1980. Tom Croal, Wisconsin Fiddler. Field notes. Wisconsin Folk Museum Archives, Mount Horeb.

Meade, Guthrie. 1987. Fiddle contests in Minnesota and Wisconsin in 1926. Survey of newspaper articles. James P. Leary, photocopy.

Miller, Mike. 1991. "It's the Law of the State: Lutefisk Won't Hurt You." *Capital Times* (Madison) November.

Miller, Terry. 1985. *Traditional Music of the Lao.* New York: Greenwood Press.

Mishler, Craig. 1987. "Athabaskan Indian Fiddling: A Musical History." *Alaska Magazine,* November, 47–51.

Moloney, Mick. 1982. "Irish Recordings and the Irish-American Imagination." In *Ethnic Recordings in America,* ed. Judith McCulloh, 84-101. Washington, D.C.: American Folklife Center.

Monroe County Pictorial History. 1976. Tomah, Wis.: Tomah Printing Co.

Palmer, Robert. 1981. *Deep Blues.* New York: Penguin Books.

Peters, Harry. 1977. *Folksongs out of Wisconsin.* Madison: State Historical Society.

Pine, Howard. 1980. "The Swede from North Dakota." Liner notes for the LP *Slim Jim,* Hep Records 00228.

Polso, Sylvia. n.d. The musical careers of Sylvia Polso and Viola Turpeinen. Scrapbook of newspaper clippings. James P. Leary, photocopy.

Posen Centennial. 1970. Posen, Mich.

Rickaby, Franz. 1926. *Ballads and Songs of the Shanty-Boy.* Cambridge: Harvard University Press.

Rindlisbacher, Otto. 1938. "The Hardanger Violin." *Etude,* June.
———. 1937. Letter to Sarah Gertrude Knott. Helene Stratman-Thomas Papers. Wisconsin Music Archives, Mills Music Library, University of Wisconsin-Madison.
———. *1931. Twenty Original Reels, Jigs, and Hornpipes.* Rice Lake, Wis.: Rice Lake Chronotype.
———. 1929. "The Alphorn: The Story of a Unique Swiss Instrument Now Rarely Seen." *Etude,* February.

Rippley, LaVern J.1992. *The Whoopee John Wilfahrt Dance Band.* Northfield, Minn.: St. Olaf College.
———. 1985. *The Immigrant Experience in Wisconsin.* Boston: Twayne Publishers.

Roberts, Roderick J. 1978. "An Introduction to the Study of Northern Country Music." *Journal of Country Music* 7:22–28.

Rosholt, Malcolm. 1959. *Our County, Our Story.* Stevens Point: Portage County Board of Supervisors.

Silberhorn, Henry. 1928. *Fifteen Children's Songs and Games with Words.* Chicago.
———. 1910-13. *German Song Album.* 3 vols. Chicago.
———. 1910. *Henry Silberhorn's Instructor for the Concertina.* Chicago.

Spencer, Jon Michael. 1990. *Protest and Praise: Sacred Music of Black Religion.* Minneapolis: Fortress Press.

Spottswood, Richard K. 1990. *Ethnic Music on Records: A Discography of Commercial Ethnic Recordings Produced in the United States 1894-1942.* 7 vols. Urbana: University of Illinois Press.
———. 1982. "The Sajewski Story: Eighty Years of Polish Music in Chicago." In *Ethnic Recordings in America,* ed. Judith McCulloh, 132-173. Washington, D.C.: American Folklife Center.

Springer, George T. 1932. *Yumpin' Yiminy: Scandinavian Dialect Selections.* Long Prairie, Minn.: Hart Publications.

Stangland, Red. 1979. *Norwegian Jokes.* Sioux Falls, S.D.: Norse Press.

Stokes, Bill. n.d. [1960s]. "'Buckhorn' Features Lighter Side of Life." *Milwaukee Journal.* Lois Rindlisbacher Albrecht, Cameron, Wis., scrapbook clipping. Rindlisbacher file, Wisconsin Folk Museum, Mount Horeb, photocopy.

Suelflow, Roy A. ca. 1954. *History of the Trinity Lutheran Congregation, 1839-1954.* Friestadt, Wis.

Swanson, Kenneth. 1970. "Music of Two Finnish-Apostolic Lutheran Groups in Minnesota: The Heidemanians and the Pollarites." *Student Musicologists at Minnesota* 14:1-36.

Taft, Michael. 1975. *A Regional Discography of Newfoundland and Labrador.* Bibliographic and Special Series, no. 1. St. Johns: Memorial University of Newfoundland Folklore and Language Archive.

Taylor, Rose Schuster. 1944-46. "Peter Schuster, Dane County Farmer." *Wisconsin Magazine of History. Vols.* 28–29.

Tlahac, Math S. 1974. *The History of the Belgian Settlements in Door, Kewaunee and Brown Counties.* Brussels, Wis.: Belgian-American Club.

28th Swiss-American Songfest. 1976. Pamphlet. Monroe, Wis.: Green County Herald.

Uskovaisten Lauluja. 1948. Ironwood, Mich.: National Publishing Co.

Uskovaisten Virsia. 1953. Ironwood, Mich.: National Publishing Co.

Vachon, Jingo. 1973. *Tall Timber Tales.* L'Anse, Mich.: L'Anse Sentinel.

Vennum, Thomas, Jr. 1989. *Ojibway Music from Minnesota.* Companion booklet to a sound recording of the same name. St. Paul: Minnesota Historical Society.
———. 1982. *The Ojibwa Dance Drum, Its History and Construction.* Washington, D.C.: Smithsonian Institution Press.

Vrooman, Nicholas Curchin Peterson. *1992.* "Tale of the Medicine Fiddle: How a Tune Was Played and the Metchif Came to Be." In *Medicine Fiddle,* ed. J. P. Leary. Bismarck: North Dakota Humanities Council.

Wilgus, D.K. 1975. "Bradley Kincaid." In *Stars of Country Music,* ed. Bill C. Malone and Judith McCulloh, *86-94.* Urbana: University of Illinois Press.

Winton, Ward. 1976. *Washburn County Historical Collections.* Washburn, Wis.: Washburn County Historical Society.

Wood, Dave. 1990. "The King of Scandinavian One-Liners." *Lutheran Brotherhood Bond,* Winter, 20-21.

Yankovic, Frankie, and Robert Dolgan. 1977. *The Polka King: The Life of Frankie Yankovic.* Cleveland: Dillon/Liederbach.

Zurawik, Dave. 1975. "Old Time Good Time." *Milwaukee Sentinel,* Mar. *7.*

III. Recorded Performances

All field recordings by James P. Leary (JPL) and Richard March (RM) were made in Wisconsin and are deposited at the Wisconsin Folk Museum, unless otherwise indicated. Field recordings by Helene Stratman-Thomas, Ivan Walton, and Alan Lomax are kept in the Archive of American Folk Culture of the Library of Congress.

"Home" recordings are made by the musicians themselves. "Privately produced" recordings are produced for sale but lack label information. Label information is given only the first time a recording is listed for a performer. Recordings cited by title only are as follows:

Accordions in the Cutover
Accordions in the Cutover: Field Recordings from Lake Superior's South Shore. Double LP, booklet. Wisconsin Folklife Center (now Wisconsin Folk Museum).

Ach Ya!
Ach Ya! Traditional German-American Music from Wisconsin. Double LP, notes. Wisconsin Folklife Center (now Wisconsin Folk Museum) FVF 301.

Across the Fields
Across the Fields: Traditional Norwegian-American Music from Wisconsin. LP, notes. Wisconsin Folklife Center (now Wisconsin Folk Museum) FVF 201.

Folk Music from Wisconsin
Folk Music from Wisconsin. LP, notes. Library of Congress AFS L 55.

Minnesota Polka
Minnesota Polka: Dance Music from Four Traditions. LP, booklet. Minnesota Historical Society.

Swissconsin My Homeland
Swissconsin My Homeland: Swiss Folk Music in Wisconsin. Cassette, notes. Wisconsin Folk Museum 8801.

Wallons d'Amérique
Les Wallons d'Amérique (Wisconsin). LP, notes. Centre d'action culturelle de la communauté d'expression française (Belgium) FM 33010.

Al and the Family. "Polka." Field recording by the Wisconsin Folk Museum, Family Music Festival, Milwaukee, June 30, 1984.

Alder, Louis, and His Swiss Yodelers. "Mountaineer Song." 78 rpm. Gennett 20351-A. Reissued on *Swissconsin My Homeland.*

Allery, Fred, and Mike Keplin. "Red River Jig." *Turtle Mountain Music.* Double LP, booklet. Folkways Records FES 4140.
———. "Soldier's Joy." *Turtle Mountain Music.*

Alphorn Trio. "Alphorn Melody." See *Swissconsin My Homeland.*

Altenburg, Art. "Wedding Dance." Field recording by JPL and RM, Art's Concertina Bar, Milwaukee, May 17, 1988.

American Croatian Silver Strings Tamburitzans. "Mariner mars (Sailor march)." *Silver Anniversary Album.* LP. Dave Kennedy Studio 408038.

Andando Solo. "En la vida todo es ir." *Music of the World in Milwaukee.* Cassette. Milwaukee Public Museum, 1989.

Anonymous. "Money for the Church." Field recording by JPL, Fall Fest, Mount Horeb, Oct. 6, 1990.

Aro, Bobby. "Highway Number 7." *Kapakka in the kaupunki* (Tavern in the town). LP. Quality Records (Finland) QRS 1002.

Ashlaw, Ted. "Driving Saw Logs on the Plover." *Adirondack Woods Singer.* LP, notes. Philo 1022.

Aunt Sharlene and Cousin Eleanor. "Dick's Polka." 45 rpm. KL Recording KS-65.

Badger Singers. "Flag Song." *Badger Singers.* Cassette. WOJB Radio, Reserve, ca. 1988.

Baldoni, Alfonso. "Spring Polka." Field recording by JPL, Milwaukee, Oct. 12,1989. Cedarburg Cultural Center.

Balkan Serenaders. "Domovina zovi nas (The homeland calls us)." 78 rpm. Privately produced, ca. 1945.

Bannen, Charles. "Pat Malone." Field recording by Philip V. Bohlman, Crawford County, 1981. Bohlman Collection, Chicago.

Barbara and the Karousels. "El Rio Drive." *Mmm Mmm Good.* LP. Rainbow Records NR 1746.
———. "Growling Mickey's Polka." *On Call.* LP. Rainbow Records NR 17389.

Barich Brothers. "Pod mojim okincem (Under my little window)." *How Bout This One?* Cassette. RY Recording RY C-3567.

Barnak, Bernice, and Mary Stelmach. "Pojdzmy wszysy do stojenki (Let's all go to the stable)." See *Accordions in the Cutover.*

Bashell, Louie. "Dad's Polka." Field recording by RM, Milwaukee, summer 1984.
———. "Silk Umbrella Polka." *Beer Barrel Polka Party.* LP. RCA Camden CL50033.
———. "South." *The Music That Made Milwaukee Famous.* LP. King 842.
———. "Won't You All Come Dance with Me?" *Music That Made Milwaukee Famous.*

Bayon Dontre. Wedding music. Cassette. Home recording, 1990.

Bayon Dontre with Chanda Ra. "Memories of Lost Love in Michigan." Cassette. Home recording, 1990.

Bechtel, Fritz, and.the Jolly Ramblers. "When the Sun Comes over the Brewery." 78 rpm. Polkaland 93.

Bellin, Cletus. "La vieux gris caval (The old gray mare)." Cassette. WAUN Radio, ca. 1988.

Benjamin, Fred. "Moccasin Game Song." *Ojibway Music from Minnesota.* LP, booklet. Minnesota Historical Society.

Bentetu. "Bomba Medley." Field recording by RM, Madison, Dec. 8, 1989.
———. "Plena Bentetu." Field recording by RM, Madison, Dec. 8,1989.

Berg, Eric. "Chillicothe Schottische." Reel tape. Home recording by Lenore Berg of a broadcast over WJMC radio, Rice Lake, 1957.

Berg, Lenore, and the Rhythm Badgers. "Finska Waltz." *Beautiful Wisconsin.* LP. Cuca KS-2117.
———. "Oskar Carlson's Waltz." Field recording by JPL, Barron, May 27,1989.

Berquist, John. "Hilda, O Hilda. *"Ya Sure, You Bet You."* Cassette. Half Moon Records HM 1005.
———. "Three Uncles." *Ya Sure, You Bet You.*

Bethany Swedish Baptist String Band. "Lofven Gud (Praise the Lord)." See *Accordions in the Cutover.*

Blihovde, Otto. "Gamel'ost (Old Cheese) Song." *Otto Blihovde Plays and Sings.* LP. Polka City 8000.

Bollerud, Bruce. "No Norwegians in Dickeyville." Field recording by JPL and RM, Madison, June 1987.
———. "Stegen vals (Stepladder waltz)." See *Across the Fields.*

Bonner, Patrick. "The Maid of Kildare." Field recording by Ivan Walton and Alan Lomax, Beaver Island, Mich., 1938. AFS 4483B.

Boreson, Stan. "Chickens in a Sack." *Stan Boreson Tells Diamond Jim's Favorite Yokes.* LP. Golden Crest CR-31028.
———. "The Yanitor's Tale." *Stan Boreson Tells.*

Bowe, Howie. "Little German Ball." 78 rpm. Polkaland 190.

Boxty. "Hammy Hamilton's Jigs." Cassette. Privately produced, ca. 1988.

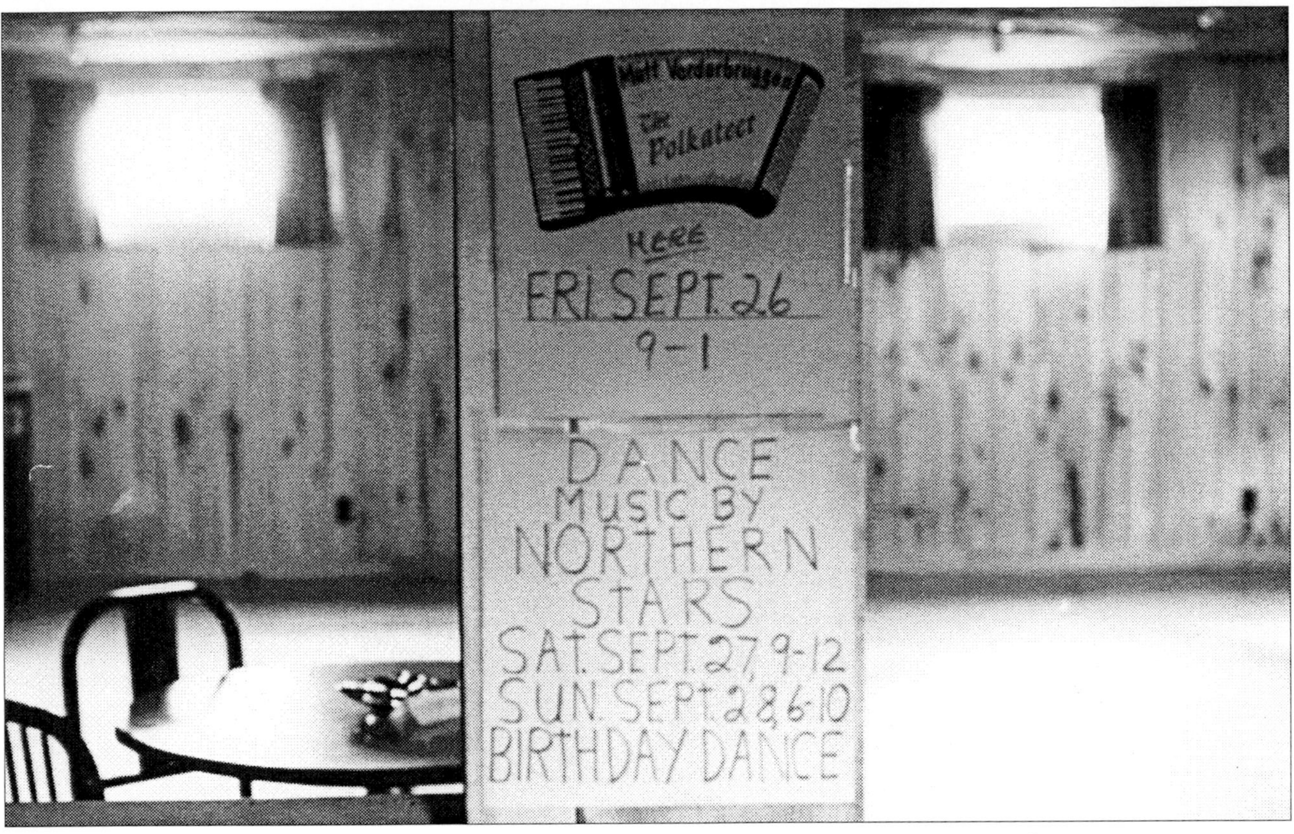

Upcoming dances listed at the Silver Star Tavern, Wentworth, 1980 **Photo: Jim Leary**

Brevak, Vivian. "Swedish Waltz." See *Accordions in the Cutover.*

Brian and the Mississippi Valley Dutchmen. "At the Mill Polka." Music from Mississippi. LP. B&B 12-13-89.
———. "Cherry Polka." *Music from Mississippi.*
———. "Koster's Waltz." *Music from Mississippi.*
———. "Pine Hollow Schottische." *Volume Two.* LP. B&B 1987.
———. "Reh braune Augen (Doe eyes)." *Music from Mississippi.*

Brouchoud, Marvin. "Raise the Window Down." 78 rpm. Polkaland 223.

Brown, Sunny. "Spanish Two-Step." Radio transcription. WIBU Radio, Poynette, Feb. 22, 1948.

Bullett, Bobby. *See* St. Germaine, Robert ("Bobby Bullett").

Burkhalter, Rudy. "My Swiss Girl." See *Swissconsin My Homeland.*

Burton, Jannie Lee. "Will You Pay a Price?" 45 rpm. New Beginning NB 7469.

Calkins, Ray. "The River in the Pines." Field recording by JPL, Chetek, May 25,1988.

Carroll, Liz and Kevin. "Hare's Paw"/ "Castle Kelly." *Fathers and Daughters: Irish Traditional Music in America.* LP, booklet. Shanachie 79054.

Cavaliers, The. "Chubby Mama's Oberek." *Twirl Your Girl. LP.* Cuca K-2072.

Cedar Swamp Boys. "Hupaj siupaj (Whoopee, whoopee)." Field recording by JPL, Larks Lake, Mich., Apr. 2,1989. Michigan Traditional Arts Program.

Chicago Button Box Club. "Na mostu (On the bridge)." *Remember Slovenia.* LP. Bud Presner BP 3517.

Cleveland Junior Tamburitzans. "U Dalmaciji (In Dalmatia)." *Nova Domovina: Balkan Slavic Music from the Industrial Midwest.* LP, notes. Ohio Arts Council OAC 601,1987.

Cloud, Joe. "Devil's Dream." Field recording by Alan Lomax, Odanah, Aug. 1938. AFS 2469A1.
———. "Squaw Dance." Field recording by Alan Lomax, Odanah, Aug. 1938. AFS 2469A3.

Concertina Millie. *See* Kaminski, "Concertina Millie."

Continentals, The. "Oj djevojko mala (Oh little girl)." *Croatia Americana.* LP. Balkan BLP 5004.

Coopman, Ernie, and the Stagemen. "Cuckoo Waltz." *I Am Yours.* Cassette. JBM Productions. Reissued on *Minnesota Polka.*

Corinth Missionary Baptist Church. "You Don't Have to Move a Mountain." Self-titled LP. Privately produced.

Cousin Fuzzy. "Hillbilly Leprechaun." *Cousin Fuzzy and His Cousins.* LP. Polkaland LP-4.
———. "Why Don't You Squeeze Me." 78 rpm. Polkaland 541.

Cox, Harv. "Mule's Dream." 45 rpm. Cuca J-6491.

Cunneen, Oljanna Venden. "Ole Meets Lena," "Ole Goes to Church." Field recording by JPL and Reid Miller, Madison, Mar. 19, 1987. (Published with notes in J. P. Leary, 1991, *Midwestern Folk Humor,* Little Rock, Ark.: August House.)

Dachauer Bauern Kapelle (Dachau peasant band). "An der Moldau." 78 rpm. Puritan 70012.

Dahill, Tom. "The Newry Highwayman." *The Ragged Hank of Yarn.* Cassette. Flying Fish FF90490.

Detroit Croatian Radio Program. "Lijepa nasa domovina (Our homeland is beautiful)." 78 rpm. Home recording by Agnes Daniels, 1945.

Deutschmeisters, The. "Du, du liegst mir im Herzen (You lie in my heart)." *Peanuts.* LP. Pleasant Peasant PPS-142. Reissued on Minnesota Polka.

DeWitz, Irving. "Ländler." See *Accordions in the Cutover.*

Dombrowski, Norm, and the Happy Notes. "Great Musicians Polka." *Waltzes and Polkas That Turn You On.* LP. Gold Records GS 1004.
———. "Swiss Boy." *Dance and Sing in 76.* LP. Gold Records GS-1005.
———. "Wonderful Life Polka." *Waltzes and Polkas That Turn You On.*

Dorschner, Ray, and the Rainbow Valley Dutchmen. "Kermiss Waltz." *On Stage Live.* Cassette. Privately produced.
———. "Putzig Polka." 78 rpm. Polkaland 103.
———. "Village Blacksmith Waltz." *Clean and Clear.* LP. Lodestar LP 10132.

Doser, Mayme, and Mrs. Frank Stevens. "Kdyr jsem sel cestickou surkou (As I walked that narrow path)." Field recording by Helene Stratman-Thomas, Prairie du Chien, Wis., Aug. 19,1941. AFS 5021.

Duchow, Lawrence. "Red Raven Polka." *Old Time Polka Time.* LP. Vocalion VL 73739.
———. "Our Mike Polka." Cassette. Provided by Duchow accordionist Wally Splettstoesser.

Dybedol, George. "Den store hvite flok vie se (Behold a host arrayed in white)." See *Accordions in the Cutover.*

Ebner, James. "Blue Chips Polkas." Cassette. Home recording of a broadcast over WYMS radio, Milwaukee, 1985.

Edlebeck, Whoopee Norm, and His Dairyland Dutchmen. "More Beer Polka." *Polka Jamboree.* LP. NR13070.

Een, Andrea. "Bruremarj etter Ola Mosafinn (Bridal march from Ola Mosafinn)." *NorwegianAmerican Music from Minnesota.* LP, booklet. Minnesota Historical Society.

Eggum, Sammy, with John Schermerhom. "San Antonio Rose"/ "Hoop-De-Do." *Dairyland Jubilee.* LP. Cuca.

Elias Serenaders. "Na selo (In the village)." Field recording by Helene Stratman-Thomas, Madison, Wis., Nov. 15,1940. AFS 4949.

Emerald Isle Ceili Band. "Kesh Jig." Field recording by RM, Madison, Mar. 1988.

Fendermen, The. "Heartbreak Special." *Muleskinner Blues.* LP. Soma MG 1240.
———. "Muleskinner Blues." *Muleskinner Blues.*

Feron, Gladys Etienne. "Mi feye, mi feye elle (av)ot frwed ses pids (My daughter was cold in the feet)." See *Wallons d'Amérique.*

Finseth, Leonard. "Indian War Whoop." *Scandinavian Old Time.* LP, notes. Banjar Records BR1834.
———. "Randi Severson's Waltz." See *Across the Fields.*
———. "Rindlisbacher's Mazurka." *Scandinavian Old Time.*
———. "Swamper's Revenge on the Windfall." *Scandinavian-American Folk Dance Music.* Vol. 2. LP, notes. Banjar Records BR 1830.

Flaker, Ruth Zemke. "Liebster Jesu, wir sind hier (Dear Jesus, we are here)." See *Ach Ya!*

Flett, Lawrence. "The Devil's Reel." *Old Native and Métis Fiddling.* Vol. 1. Double LP, booklet. Falcon Productions (Canada) FP-187.

Foley, Red, with the Dixie Dons. "Chocolate Ice Cream Cone." 78 rpm. Decca 46234.

Fontaine, Alvina. "Le jardin de Martin Plicotin (The garden of Martin Plicotin)." See *Wallons d'Amérique.*

Ford, Marge, and the Alaska Polka Chips. "Two Sisters Polka." *Old Time, Good Time, Anytime.* LP. Alaska Folk Music AFM 1179.

Ford, Warde. "Keith and Hiles Line." *Wolf River Songs.* LP, notes. Folkways FE 4001.

Gary and the Ridgeland Dutchmen. "Musette Polka." *Music for Young and Old.* Cassette. RY 8811.
———. "Old Stylers Polka." *Polka Music for the Nineties.* Cassette. RY C-4216.
———. "Seven Beers with the Wrong Woman." *Polka Music for the Nineties.*

Gary and the Ridgeland Dutchmen with the Polka Mass Trio. "Christ Is Knocking." Self-titled cassette. RY 8710.

Gill Singers. "All the Way with God." Cassette. Privately produced.

Goose Island Ramblers. "Auction pa Strømmen's." *Midwest Ramblin'.* Cassette, notes. Wisconsin Folk Museum 9001.
———. "Barney McCoy." *Doin' the Hurley Hop.* LP. Cuca KS-1112. Reissued on cassette, Polkaland 826.
———. "Break Song." *Midwest Ramblin'.*
———. "Brother." *Midwest Ramblin'.*
———. "Francuszka Polka." *From Blue Grass to Russian Gypsy.* LP. Cuca K-1110.
———. "Going Back to the Hills." *From Blue Grass to Russian Gypsy.*
———. "Hurley Hop." *Doin' the Hurley Hop.*
———. "I Worked for a Farmer." *Midwest Ramblin'.*
———. "Milwaukee Fire." *Midwest Ramblin'.*
———. "Milwaukee Waltz." *From Blue Grass to Russian Gypsy.*
———. "Mountain Dew." *From Blue Grass to Russian Gypsy.*
———. "Mrs. Johnson, Turn Me Loose." *From Blue Grass to Russian Gypsy.*
———. "My Blue Eyes Are Gone." *A Session with the Goose Island Ramblers.* LP. Cuca K-1111.
———. "Norwegian War Chant." *From Blue Grass to Russian Gypsy.*
———. "Ole Olson the Hobo from Norway." *Sounds of Syttende Mai.* LP. Cuca K-2010.
———. "On the Beach at Waunakee." *Doin' the Hurley Hop.*
———. "Oscar's Cannonball." *From Blue Grass to Russian Gypsy.*
———. "Paul pa haugen (Paul on the hill)." *Sounds of Syttende Mai.*
———. "Reierson's Two Step." *Midwest Ramblin'.*
———. "Ryerson's [sic] Waltz." *Sounds of Syttende Mai.*
———. "Swiss Yodel Waltz." *Midwest Ramblin'.*
———. "Wendy's Schottische." *Midwest Ramblin'.*

Gosz, Romy. "Ja mam kocoura (Tom cat polka)." 78 rpm. Columbia 257-F. Reissued on *Roman Gosz and His Orchestra.* Polkaland LP-33.
———. "Svestkova alej (The prune song)." 78 rpm. Vocalion 15981. Reissued on *Roman Gosz and His Orchestra.*

Gralak, Don. "Lori Lynn Ländler." *The Happy Polkateer.* LP. GNP Crescendo GNPS 2143.

Gravelle, Dick. "French Tune." Field recording by Michael Loukinen, Sault St. Marie, Mich., summer 1989. Northern Michigan University. Performed in the film *Medicine Fiddle,* UP North Films, 1991.

Green, J. W. "Skibbereen." Field recording by Alan Lomax, Beaver Island, Mich., Aug. 27, 1938. AFS 2292A.

Groeschl, Syl. "Alexander's Ragtime Band." *Syl Groeschl's Old Time Dance Album.* LP. Cuca KS2149.
———. "Brass 'n' Sax Polka." *Tony Groeschl Memorial Album.* LP. Cuca K-2031.
———. "Herman, Take Me Home." *More Old German Songs.* LP. Cuca K-2021.
———. "Hooter Waltz." *Tony Groeschl Memorial Album.*
———. "Immer noch ein Tropfen (Just another little drop)." Syl *Groeschl Sings Old German Songs.* LP. Cuca K-2015.
———. "Jolly Coppersmith." *Syl Groeschl Sings Old German Songs.*
———. "One Beer for One." *Syl Groeschl Sings Old German Songs.*
———. "Two-Step Medley." *More Old German Songs.*
———. "Ve Get So Soon Oldt." *Ve Get So Soon Oldt.* LP. Cuca KS-2076.
———. "We Left Our Wives at Home." *Syl Groeschl Sings Old German Songs.*

Gymanfa Ganu Choir. "Crug y bar (Yonder in glory)." Field recording by Judy Rose and Tom Martin-Erickson, Peniel, 1980s. Wisconsin Public Radio.

Happy Harmonizers. "Happy with Jesus." *Thank You Lord.* LP. Four Winds FW-LP 3669.

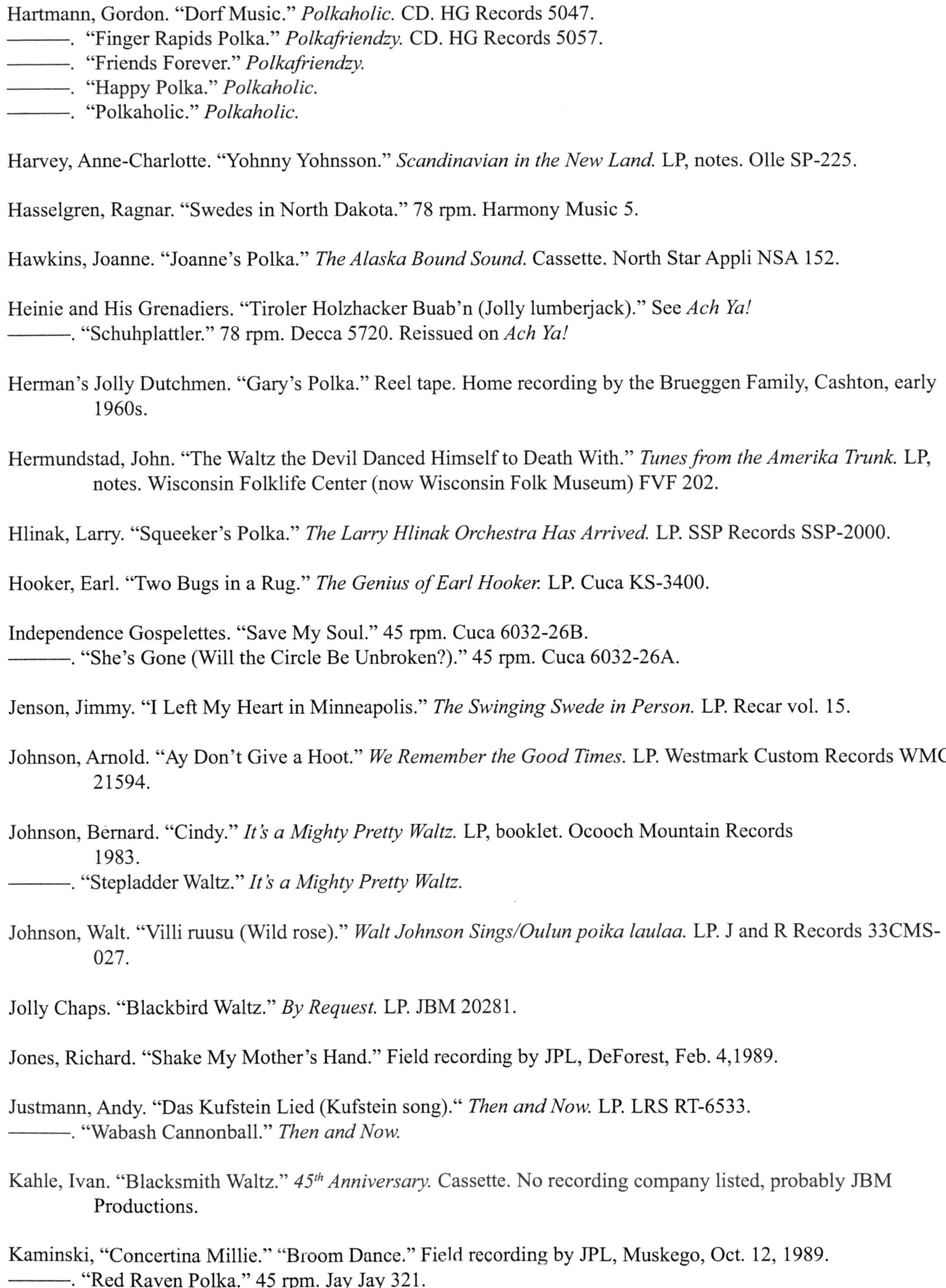

Hartmann, Gordon. "Dorf Music." *Polkaholic.* CD. HG Records 5047.

———. "Finger Rapids Polka." *Polkafriendzy.* CD. HG Records 5057.

———. "Friends Forever." *Polkafriendzy.*

———. "Happy Polka." *Polkaholic.*

———. "Polkaholic." *Polkaholic.*

Harvey, Anne-Charlotte. "Yohnny Yohnsson." *Scandinavian in the New Land.* LP, notes. Olle SP-225.

Hasselgren, Ragnar. "Swedes in North Dakota." 78 rpm. Harmony Music 5.

Hawkins, Joanne. "Joanne's Polka." *The Alaska Bound Sound.* Cassette. North Star Appli NSA 152.

Heinie and His Grenadiers. "Tiroler Holzhacker Buab'n (Jolly lumberjack)." See *Ach Ya!*

———. "Schuhplattler." 78 rpm. Decca 5720. Reissued on *Ach Ya!*

Herman's Jolly Dutchmen. "Gary's Polka." Reel tape. Home recording by the Brueggen Family, Cashton, early 1960s.

Hermundstad, John. "The Waltz the Devil Danced Himself to Death With." *Tunes from the Amerika Trunk.* LP, notes. Wisconsin Folklife Center (now Wisconsin Folk Museum) FVF 202.

Hlinak, Larry. "Squeeker's Polka." *The Larry Hlinak Orchestra Has Arrived.* LP. SSP Records SSP-2000.

Hooker, Earl. "Two Bugs in a Rug." *The Genius of Earl Hooker.* LP. Cuca KS-3400.

Independence Gospelettes. "Save My Soul." 45 rpm. Cuca 6032-26B.

———. "She's Gone (Will the Circle Be Unbroken?)." 45 rpm. Cuca 6032-26A.

Jenson, Jimmy. "I Left My Heart in Minneapolis." *The Swinging Swede in Person.* LP. Recar vol. 15.

Johnson, Arnold. "Ay Don't Give a Hoot." *We Remember the Good Times.* LP. Westmark Custom Records WMC-21594.

Johnson, Bernard. "Cindy." *It's a Mighty Pretty Waltz.* LP, booklet. Ocooch Mountain Records 1983.

———. "Stepladder Waltz." *It's a Mighty Pretty Waltz.*

Johnson, Walt. "Villi ruusu (Wild rose)." *Walt Johnson Sings/Oulun poika laulaa.* LP. J and R Records 33CMS-027.

Jolly Chaps. "Blackbird Waltz." *By Request.* LP. JBM 20281.

Jones, Richard. "Shake My Mother's Hand." Field recording by JPL, DeForest, Feb. 4,1989.

Justmann, Andy. "Das Kufstein Lied (Kufstein song)." *Then and Now.* LP. LRS RT-6533.

———. "Wabash Cannonball." *Then and Now.*

Kahle, Ivan. "Blacksmith Waltz." *45th Anniversary.* Cassette. No recording company listed, probably JBM Productions.

Kaminski, "Concertina Millie." "Broom Dance." Field recording by JPL, Muskego, Oct. 12, 1989.

———. "Red Raven Polka." 45 rpm. Jay Jay 321.

Kania, Ed. “Wedding March.” Field recording by JPL, Metz, Mich., Mar. 29, 1989. Michigan Traditional Arts Program.

Kania, Felix. “Wedding March.” Field recording by Alan Lomax, Metz, Mich., Sept. 1938. AFS 2311A1

Karl and the Country Dutchmen. “Chopsticks.” *Hooked on Old Time.* LP. JBM Sound Productions 35785.
———. “Mississippi Valley/Chicken Polka.” *Down on the Farm.* Vol. 1. LP. JBM KH-1983.

Karl [Hartwich] and Brian [Brueggen]. “Green Is Green.” *I Must Be Dreaming.* Cassette. Karl and Brian 1779.

Karye, Charles, and Lempi Luoma. Finnish Apostolic Lutheran hymn. Field recording by JPL, Highbridge, Dec. 1, 1980. McDowell Archives, Northland College.

Kaszuba Aces. “Tam pod Krakowem (Here under Krakow).” *Naturally.* LP. North Star Appli NSA 101.

Kaulitz, Fred. “Herr Schmidt (Mr. Schmidt).” See *Ach Ya!*

Kauppi, Leo. “Villi ruusu (Wild rose).” 78 rpm. Columbia 3135-F.

Kezele, John. “Radujte se narodi (Rejoice you nations).” See *Accordions in the Cutover.*

King, Pee Wee. “Tennessee Polka.” *Country Music Polkas.* LP. Cuca K-2024.

Klass, Joey. “Peppy’s Polka.” *First Klass. LP.* Bright 1014.

Kolberg, Al. “Lauterbach.” See *Ach Ya!*

Kole, Art, and Walter Bartolmiej. Unnamed tune. Home recording by Art Kole, Alpena, Mich., 1950s.

Konkol, Ray. “Varsuvienne (Dance of Warsaw).” *One More Time.* LP. JBM 10385B.

Kosek, Harry, and the Red River Boys. “By the Rivers of Babylon.” *Ein Lied für dich* (A song for you). LP. Dave Kennedy Recording Studios 908011-1810.

Kuchera, Victor, and Dolly Petruzalek. “Do lesticka na cekanou (Into the shady forest).” Field recording by JPL, Phillips, June 15, 1991.

Lashua, Famous. “Chocolate Ice Cream Cone.” 78 rpm. FM 544 486.
———. “Wont You Share Your Love with Me?” 78 rpm. FM 521L 474.

LeBotte, Gene. “Black Gypsy Waltz.” *The Gene LeBotte Orchestra.* LP. Polkaland LP-51.

Liebl, Syl, and the Jolly Swiss Boys. “Baby Waltz.” *Syl Liebl’s Originals: Music from God’s Country.* Cassette. Reissue of Cuca recordings and radio transcriptions, JBM Productions SL-1989.
———. “Heinie Polka.” *Best Polka Band in the Land.* LP. KS7601.

Long House Singers [women’s ensemble]. “Alligator Dance.” *Social Dance Songs.* Cassette. Privately produced. 1988.

Madison Gospelaires. “Guide Me.” Field recording by JPL, DeForest, Feb. 4, 1989.
———. “I Know I Am a Child of God.” Field recording by JPL, DeForest, Feb. 4,1989.

Madison Maennerchor with Lawrence Duchow’s Red Ravens. “O Tannenbaum (O Christmas tree).” 78 rpm. Potter PR 1007.

Magayne, Hank. "Barking Dog Polka." 45 rpm. MLAY M325.

Magayne, Hank, with Richard March. "Slovenian Waltz Medley." Field recording by RM, Hartford, July 1986.

Maki, Einard. "Orpo pojan valssi (Orphan boy's waltz)." See *Accordions in the Cutover.*

Maki, Hugo. "Itin Tiltu (Tiltu's Iti)." See *Accordions in the Cutover.*

Marincel, Tom. "Croatian Kolo." See *Accordions in the Cutover.*
———. "Na levoj strani kraj srca (On the left side by the heart)." See *Accordions in the Cutover.*

Maroszek Brothers. "Kujawiak." *Polka Enjoyment.* LP. SSP-4000.

Mathiowetz, Bob. "Concertina Gallop." See *Accordions in the Cutover.*

McDermott, Tommy. "The Walsh Dancers" /"Tom's Polka." Field recording by RM, Madison, Mar. 10, 1992.

Meckawigabau. "Gi daga wadan (You desire vainly that I seek you)." *Songs of the Chippewa.* LP, booklet. Library of Congress AAFS L 22.

Meisner, Steve. "Blue Island." *Jammin' Polkas.* LP. HG Records HG 5045.
———. "Burgettstown Polka." *Jammin' Polkas.*
———. "Jammin' Polkas." *Jammin' Polkas.*

Meisner, Verne and Steve. "Bohemian Laendler." *Meisner Magic. LP.* HG Records HG 5029.
———. "Meisner Magic." *Meisner Magic.*

Meuret, George. "Barbara Polka." Field recording by JPL, Haugen, May 27, 1989.
———. "Cripple Creek." Field recording by JPL, Haugen, May 27,1989.

Michaels, Mad Man. "Czarnina Kid"/ "Lincoln Avenue." 78 rpm. Michaels F80B-1194.

Michalski, Richie. "No Beer Today." 45 rpm. KL Recording KS.

Minar, Jerry, and Friends. "Bev's Polka." *Jerry Minar and Friends*. LP. JBM Productions JBM 9785.

Montano, Frank. Woodland flute music. Field recording by RM, Danbury, Dec. 3, 1988.
———. "My Spirit Friend." *Reservation Reflections.* Cassette. 1988. Sunshine Studios.

Moquah Slovak Singers. "Bodaj by vas (Doggone you)." See *Accordions in the Cutover.*

Morgan, Lee. "Uncle Joe." Field recording by JPL, Cambria, Oct. 8, 1989.

Morgan, Moses. "Uncle Joe." Field recording by Helene Stratman-Thomas, Pickett, Wis., Aug. 27, 1940. AFS 4184.

Moser Brothers. "Jodler Ländler." 78 rpm. Victor 78502.

Mouth, Sophea. *Tro* solo. Cassette. Home recording.

North Country Band. "No Count Blues." *North Country Band.* LP. NCB Records NCB 1001.

Novak, Jerry. "Sli panenki (The girls went down the road)." See *Accordions in the Cutover.*

O'Brien, Paddy. "The Lament for Eoin Rhua." *Stranger at the Gate: Irish Accordion Music.* LP, notes. Green Linnet Records SIF 1091.

Oja, Niilo. "Minnesota, We Love You." *Northland Hoedown.* Cassette. Inland Sea Recording.

Old Town Strollers. "Donesi vino, Krcmarice (Bring wine, Barmaid)." Cassette. Home recording.
———. "Jovano Jovance (Johnny, oh Johnny)." Home recording.

Olson Sisters, The. "The Ladies' Aid." 78 rpm. Victor 7517.

Oneida Singers. "Hymn #18 (What a Friend We Have in Jesus)." *Hymns in the Oneida Language.* Cassette. Privately produced, 1988.

Ostrowiecki, Richie, and the Polka Pals. "Don't Cry, Anna." 45 rpm. KL Recording KS-115.

Oulu Hotshots, The. "Maailman Matti (Matti, man of the world)." *Bringin' It Back: Old Time Finnish Music.* LP. Inland Sea Recording ISR 83033.
———. "Raatikko." *Northern Nights.* Cassette. Inland Sea Recording.
———. "Sakki jarven polkka (Gunny sack polka)." *Bringin' It Back.*

Pakiz, Frank. "The Clap Dance." Field recording by JPL, Greenwood, Nov. 16,1990.

Patton, Charlie. "Pony Blues." 78 rpm. Paramount. Reissued on *Charley Patton: Founder of the Delta Blues.* LP, notes. Yazoo L-1020.

Pearson, Edwin. "Comparative Banking." Field recording by JPL, Maple, July 29, 1987. (Published with notes in J. P. Leary,1991, *Midwestern Folk Humor,* Little Rock, Ark.: August House.)

Perkovich, Father Frank. "We Offer Bread and Wine." *Songs and Hymns from the Polka Mass.* LP. Sound 80 S80-665.

Peters Brothers, The. "Alte Deutsche Melodien (Old-time German airs)." 78 rpm. Okeh 10415.

Phillips Czech Singers. "Cocovicka." Field recording by JPL, Phillips, June 15, 1991.

Polarski, Ray. "Schottische." Field recording by JPL, Three Lakes, Oct. 31, 1989.

Polish Pride. "Sat on a Cow Polka." *Polkas with Pride.* LP. North Star Appli NSA 129.

Polka Dimensions. "Merka, Merka." Field recording by JPL, Poaaski, July 29, 1989.

Polka Stars. "Pytala sie panie (A lady asked)." *Follow the Stars.* LP. PB 1360.
———. "Stevens Point Polka." *Follow the Stars.*

Polkatown Sound. "I've Just Seen a Face." *Polkatown Sound.* Cassette. Sunshine Records SN 107.

Popovich Brothers. "Mene majka jednog ima (My mother has only me)." LP. Privately produced, ca. 1976.

Prairie Ramblers. "Shady Grove." 78 rpm. Reissued on *Kentucky Country 1927-1937.* LP, notes. Rounder RNR 1037.

Preservation Singers. "Da ge na zaya nel." *Favorite Hymns in the Oneida Language.* Cassette. Privately produced.

Prohut, Lou. “The Boomba Polka.” *Polka Party.* LP. TeleHouse CD 2034.

Radicevich, Mike. “Cacacko kolo (Kolo from Cacak).” Cassette. Home recording.

Radosevich, Matt. “Mladi kapetani (Young captain).” See *Accordions in the Cutover.*

Renard, Arthur “Zeke.” “A la fête (At the fair).” See *Wallons d’Amérique.*
———. “Dji m’fou d’ça (I don’t care a rap about it).” See *Wallons d’Amérique.*

Renata and Girls, Girls, Girls. “Honky Time Medley.” *Tickled Pink.* LP. Aleatoric A-4013.

Rhythm Kings, The (Don Ring). “One Has My Name, the Other Has My Heart.” *Waltz across Texas.* LP. Bright Productions BP-102.

Rice, Bobby and Lorraine. “Tippy-Toein.” *The Rice Family Album.* LP. Cuca KS-5540.

Rice, Lorraine. “Shoes.” *Rice Family Album.*

Ridgeland Dutchmen. “Heidelberg Polka.” *Present to You.* Vol. 2. LP. Ridgeland Dutchmen *001-01.*
———. “Jolly Coppersmith.” *Present to You.*
———. “While You’re Away.” *Present to You.*

Rindlisbacher, Iva Kundert. “The Pinery Boy.” See *Folk Music from Wisconsin.*

Rindlisbacher, Otto. “Couderay Jig.” See *Folk Music from Wisconsin.*
———. “Halling.” Field recording by Helene Stratman-Thomas, Rice Lake, Wis., Aug. 15, 1941. AFS 5016.
———. “Hounds in the Woods.” See *Folk Music from Wisconsin.*
———. “Pig Schottische.” See *Folk Music from Wisconsin.*
———. “Swiss Polka.” Field recording by Helene Stratman-Thomas, Rice Lake, Wis., Aug. 15, 1941. AFS 5017.

Rindlisbacher, Otto, and Karl Hoppe. “Auf dem schoenen Zurichsee (By beautiful Lake Zurich).” 78 rpm. Helvetia 500.

Ristow, Rodney, and the Swiss Girls. “Out behind the Barn.” *Let’s Go “Out behind the Barn” with the Swiss Girls.* LP. Triple Crown Records RR 2026.

Robbie’s Yodel Club. “Teach Me How to Yodel.” *Come to the Mountain.* LP. Cuca K-2400.

Roberts, Bernie. “Flying Saucer Polka.” 78 rpm. Pfau 4-50-3A.

Rodgers, Dick. “Chocolate Soda Polka.” *Wisconsin’s Greatest.* LP. Polka City 393.
———. “Dan’s Dizzy Hop.” 78 rpm. Polkaland 101.

Rodgers, Steve, and Friends. “Down on the Corner.” *Let There Be Music.* LP. Bel-Aire LP 4051.

Romel Brothers. “Factory Song.” Field recording by Alan Lomax, Posen, Mich., Sept. 1938. AFS 2320A3.

Royal Lancers, The. “Badger.” 45 rpm. Reissued on *The Cuca Rock Story.* Vol. 3. LP, notes. White Label WLP 8849.

Rubenzer’s, Ray, Guys and Gals. “Yoo-Hoo Valley Waltz.” *Guys and Gals.* Vol. 2. Cassette. WR IRR-580.

Ryba, Mike. “Evening on the Lehigh.” *Variety Time.* LP. Fab Records 300.

Rydeski, Mike, and the Polka Jacks. "Treba ne (Don't flirt with my girl)." *More Happiness.* Cassette. RY Recording RY 90013.

Sabor. "Consencias." Cassette. Privately produced as theme for Milwaukee cable television program.

Salomaa, Hiski. "Launen lokkari (Logger of the West)." 78 rpm. Columbia 3158-F. Reissued on *Hiski Salomaa.* Cassette. CBS (Finland) 40-25197.

Sarajevo. "Daj mi casu rakije (Give me a glass of rakije)." Cassette. Privately produced, 1985.
———. "Stara vlahina (The old shepherdess)." Cassette. Privately produced, 1985.

Scheid, Elmer. "Hoolerie Waltz." *Hoolerie Holiday. LP.* Pleasant Peasant 99-63.

Schneider, Jerry. "Emil's Polka." *Music from Winnebagoland.* LP. JV-0050.
———. "Tante Anna (Aunt Anna)." *Music from Winnebagoland.*

Schultz, Harold. "Louka zelena (Green meadow)." *Bohemian Memories.* LP. North Star Appli NSA-133.

Schultz, Vera Dvorak. "Ivanek nas (Our little Ivan)." See *Accordions in the Cutover.*

She and He Haugh Band. "City of Yuba Polka." *The She and He Haughs.* Vol. 1. Cassette. RY Records RY-89033.

Singing Souls, The. "When I'm Gone." 45 rpm. Cuca JS 5042.

Sinovi. "Dedin poklon (Grampa's gift)." Cassette. Privately produced, 1990.
———. "Pjesma Zumberka (Song of the Zumberak mountains)." Cassette. Privately produced, 1990.

Six Fat Dutchmen. "Bohemian Polka." *Polka's Number 1 Band Plays Your Favorites.* LP. Polka City 402.

Skarning, Thorstein. "Maj ball (May dance)." 78 rpm. Brunswick 477.

Skowiak Brothers. "Oberek." Field recording by Paul Gifford, Tecumseh, Mich., ca. 1974.

Slak, Lojze. "Veseli kletar (The merry winemaker)." *Glas njegov v spomin* (His voice remembered). LP. Heudon FLP 04-035.

Slim Jim and the Vagabond Kid. "Nikolina." *Slim Jim Sings.* LP. Soma MG 1225.

Sosnowski Trio. "Wesoly goral mazur (Jolly mountaineers mazurka)." 78 rpm. Columbia 18119-F.

Stangland, E. C. "Red." "The Escaped Kangaroo." Field recording by JPL and RM, Mount Horeb, Oct. 6, 1990.
———. "Telling Jokes to Scandinavians." Field recording by JPL and RM, Mount Horeb, Oct. 6, 1990.

Stangland, Red, and Uncle Torvald. "O Lutefisk." *Uncle Torvald's Norwegian Memories.* Cassette. Norse Press (Nordisk Records).

Starlights, The. "Iron Foundry Polka." 45 rpm. Ampol records 507.

Steiner, Sax. "Flying Dutchman." 78 rpm. Polka Dot 1001.

St. Germaine, Robert ("Bobby Bullett"). "The Devil's Mouth." *Red Man Blues.* Cassette. Privately produced.
———. "Lac du Flambeau Reservation." 45 rpm. USA 002.

———. "Reservation Auto." *Red Man Blues.*

Straight and Fuzzy Band. "Kramer's." *Six Pack.* LP. HG Records HG-5013.

Straight Eight Bohemian Band, Chorus (Charles Pelnar, John Pelnar, Bill Slatky, Louis Kasal). "Svestkova alej (Prune song)." Field recording by Helene Stratman-Thomas, Kewaunee, Wis., Aug. 23, 1940. AFS 4164.

———. "V zahrade (In the garden)." Field recording by Helene Stratman-Thomas, Kewaunee, Wis., Aug. 23, 1940. AFS 4164.

Streiff, Clayton. "Talerschwingen (Coin swinging)." Field recording by JPL, Mount Horeb, Oct. 7, 1989.

Strzelecki, Jake. "Leaves Falling Down." Field recording by JPL, Hawks, Mich., Mar. 30, 1989. Michigan Traditional Arts Program.

Strzelecki, Joe. "Wedding March." Field recording by JPL, Posen, Mich., Mar. 30, 1989. Michigan Traditional Arts Program.

Strzelecki, Tony, and Tony Woczynski. "The Lice That Ate the Pants." Field recording by Alan Lomax, Posen, Mich., Sept. 1938. AFS 2313A1

———. "Turkey in the Straw." Field recording by Alan Lomax, Posen, Mich., Sept. 1938. AFS 2313B2.

Styczynski, Alvin. "Hup sadyna." 45 rpm. Cuca JS-1515.

———. "Krakowiak." *The Midwest Sound of Alvin Styczynski.* LP. Cuca KS-2135.

———. "Pojdzmy wszysy do stojenki (Let's all go to the stable)." *Alvin's Christmas Album.* LP. Cuca KS-2145.

———. "Pulaski Is a Polka Town." *Pulaski Is a Polka Town* LP. Cuca KS-2040.

Suess, Erwin, and the Hoolerie Dutchmen. "Stillwater Landler." *Erwin Suess and the Hoolerie Dutchmen.* Vol. 7. LP. JBM Productions ES-120383.

Sullivan, Agnes. "The Queen of England." *Songs of the Menominee, Mandan and Hidatsa.* LP, booklet. Library of Congress AAFS L33.

Syrjaniemi, Antti. "Viola Turpeinen tanssit Kiipillä (Viola Turpeinen's dance on Cape Ann)." 78 rpm. Victor V-4040.

Tantillo, Joey. "Accordion Polka." 78 rpm. Pfau 10-51-1C.

Three Sharps, The. "Elle est byin trop crausse por mi (She's too fat for me)." See *Wallons d'Amérique.*

Tikkanen, Oren, and Al Reko. "Viola Turpeinen tanssit Kiipillä (Viola Turpeinen's dance on Cape Ann)." *Life in the Finnish-American Woods.* Cassette. Thimbleberry House Recordings THC 1986.

Tomesh, Joe and John. "Louka zelena (Green meadow)." Field recording by JPL, Haugen, July 31, 1990.

Toyras, Helmer. "Finnish Medley." See *Accordions in the Cutover.*

TRAILS Drum. "Intertribal." Field recording by JPL, Lac du Flambeau Ojibwa reservation, Nov. 17, 1989. Cedarburg Cultural Center.

Trudeau, Coleman. "Tahquamenon River Breakdown." Field recording by Michael Loukinen, MacMillan, Mich., Mar. 27, 1984. UP North Films.

Trulla Navidena. "Cortando cana (Cutting cane)." Field recording by RM, Milwaukee, Jan. 7, 1990.
———. "Danza." Field recording by RM, Milwaukee, Jan. 7, 1990.
———. "La banta negrita (The black rooster)." Field recording by RM, Milwaukee, Jan. 7, 1990.

Tuba Dan and the Polkalanders. "Flutaphone Polka." *Czech Souvenirs. LP.* North Star Appli NSA 136.
———. "Narrow Path." *Polkatively Yours.* LP. North Star Appli NSA 123.

Turpeinen, Viola, and John Rosendahl. "Viulu polkka." 78 rpm. Victor V-4051. Reissued on *Viola Turpeinen: The Early Days, 1928–1938.* Cassette, notes. Thimbleberry Recordings THC 1006.

Uncle Julius and His Boys. "Helena Polka." 78 rpm. Tell 5004.

Vandertie, Alfred. "C'est l'cafe,l'cafe (It's coffee)." See *Wallons d'Amérique.*
———. "Estiz lä, quand (Were you there when they crucified my Lord?)." See *Wallons d'Amérique.*
———. "I Went to the Market with a *pania volant* [loose shirt]." See *Wallons d'Amérique.*
———. "Nos-estans quites po l'Amérique (We are going to America)"/ "Au ciel i n 'a pon.y bire (In heaven there is no beer)." See *Wallons d'Amérique.*

Vang, Wang Chou. *Tan blai* [flute] solo. Field recording by JPL, Menomonie, Nov. 1, 1989. Cedarburg Cultural Center.

Vetterli, Betty, and Martha Bernet. "I Want to Be a Cowboy's Sweetheart." *Swiss Echoes from Wisconsin's Switzerland.* LP. Bright Productions BP 1011
———. "Yodel Polka." *Anniversary Album by the Edelweiss and Betty.* LP. Bright Productions BP 1015.

Vila. "Ti Marička peglaj (Marie is ironing)." Live performance recorded by Frank Sepic Jr., Milwaukee, early 1960s.

Vocalaires, The. "Be Careful with Your Soul." *Master's Hand.* LP. Shur Fine Gospel SFG-55022.

Voices of Hmong [Hmoob zas suab]. "Hmoob zha." Cassette. Telstar Records, 1988.

Wachuta, Albert. "Koline, Koline." Field recording by Helene Stratman-Thomas, Prairie du Chien, Aug. 19, 1941. AFS 5025.

Walker, Robert. "Milwaukee Fire." See *Folk Music from Wisconsin.*

Wanta Dance Band. "Dutch Festival Waltz." Cassette. Privately produced.

Waupoose Brothers. "Potawatomi Jig." Field recording by JPL, Keshena, May 13, 1989. UP North Films.
———. Fiddle tune. Field recording by JPL, Keshena, May 13, 1989. UP North Films.
———. "Wedding Chant." Field recording by JPL, Keshena, May 13, 1989. UP North Films.

Webster, Louis. "Growling Old Man, Grumbling Old Woman." Field recording by JPL, Keshena, Nov. 6, 1989. Cedarburg Cultural Center.
———. Medley (loon song, Oneida song, western song). Field recording by JPL, Keshena, Nov. 6, 1989. Cedarburg Cultural Center.

Wenger, Gottfried, and Burnette Kubly. "Wenger's Delight." *The New Glarus Yodel Club.* LP. Bright Productions BP 1026.

Widden, Charles. "Lutfisk (Yule fish)." 78 rpm. Victor 73519.

Wilfahrt, Hans ("Whoopee John"). "Kinder (Children's) Polka." 78 rpm. Okeh 10465.
———. "Country Road Schottische." *Polka Hall of Fame.* LP. Polka City 373.

Wisconsin Dells Singers. "My Friend, That Grizzly Bear Said So." *Traditional Winnebago Songs.* Cassette, notes. Walks on Snow.

Wisconsin Lumberjacks, The (recitation by Earl Schwartztrauber). "The Passing Away of the Lumberjack." Field recording by Mary Agnes Starr, n.p., n.d. (probably Wisconsin, ca. 1960). Recorded Sound Archive, State Historical Society of Wisconsin UC 489A.

Wojta, Jerome, and the Two Creeks Farmhands. "Tinker Polka." *Music from Two Creeks.* LP. North Star Appli NSA 118.

Yang, Nao Chay. *Qeej* solo. Home recording, Sheboygan, 1985.

Yankovic, Frankie. "Dance, Dance, Dance." *Polka Party.* CD. Telehouse CD 2034.

Yuba Bohemian Band. "Wedding Tune." Field recording by Helene Stratman-Thomas, Yuba, Sept. 25, 1946. AFS 8437.

Yurkovich, Richie. "Maricka pegla (Marie is ironing)." *Nuttin' But Button.* Cassette. RY Records RY-8909.
———. "Top of the Hill." *Nuttin' But Button.*

Zagreb. "Popefke sem slagal (I made up songs)." *Zagreb.* LP. Dave Kennedy 90408-135.
———. "Tamburitza Airs." Zagreb.

Zakons, The. "Wasted." 45 rpm. Reissued on *Rock from the Midwest: The Cuca Records Rock Story.* Vol. 2. White Label WLP 8848.

Zingsheim, Joey. "We Love Our Wives (But Oh You Gals)." 78 rpm. Polkaland 221.

About the Authors

Jim Leary and Rick March with some tools of their trade, in the studio at Wisconsin Public Radio **Photo: Rick Kirkpatrick**

James P. Leary is professor of Folklore and Scandinavian Studies at the University of Wisconsin, where he also directs the Folklore Program and co-directs the Center for the Study of Upper Midwestern Cultures. Born in 1950 in Rice Lake, Wisconsin—a rural, ethnically diverse former logging community—Leary holds a Ph.D. in folklore and American Studies from Indiana University. He has worked as a researcher, producer, and writer for numerous media productions, exhibits, and publications concerning the folklore of the Upper Midwest's diverse peoples. Among them: *The Wisconsin Patchwork: A Commentary on Recordings from the Helene Stratman-Thomas Collection of Wisconsin Folk Music* (1987); *Minnesota Polka* (1990); *In Tune with Tradition: Wisconsin Folk Musical Instruments*, with Robert Teske (1990); *Yodeling in Dairyland: A History of Swiss Music in Wisconsin* (1991); *Medicine Fiddle* (1992); *Wisconsin Folklore* (1998); and *So Ole Says to Lena: Folk Humor of the Upper Midwest* (2001).

Richard March is the traditional and ethnic arts coordinator for the Wisconsin Arts Board. Born in 1946 in a Chicago community of Croatian ethnics and packing house union activists, March received a Ph.D. in folklore, with a concentration in Eastern European studies, from Indiana University. In addition to his activities as a scholar and presenter of traditional music, March is an avid player of the tamburitza and the button accordion.

Both Leary and March have served as regular consultants on traditional music for the American Folklife Center at the Library of Congress, the Folk Arts Program at the National Endowment for the Arts, the Office of Folklife and Cultural Studies at the Smithsonian Institution, and the National Council for the Traditional Arts.

Index